servants
of the
goddess

servants
of the
goddess

the modern-day devadasis

Catherine Rubin Kermorgant

Dear Sally and Zoo,
All best wishes.
Wish we were all
still at the Votsalah.
Enjoy!
Catherine

RANDOM HOUSE INDIA

Published by Random House India in 2014
1

Random House Publishers India Private Limited
Windsor IT Park, 7th Floor
Tower-B, A-1, Sector-125
Noida 201301, UP

Random House Group Limited
20 Vauxhall Bridge Road
London SW1V 2SA
United Kingdom

978 81 8400 462 5

Typeset in Sabon by R. Ajith Kumar

Printed and bound in India by Replika Press Private Limited

For sale in the Indian Subcontinent only

for T.K., mon amour

CONTENTS

PART ONE

ONE

The courtesans or dancing-girls attached to each temple are called *deva-dasis* (servants or slaves of the gods), but the public calls them by the more vulgar name of prostitutes. And in fact they are bound by their profession to grant their favours, if such they be, to anybody demanding them in return for ready money . . . Every temple of any importance has in its service a band of eight, twelve or more.[1]

—Abbé Jean-Antoine Dubois, popularly called Dodda
Swamiyoru, moved to India in 1792

AS I MADE MY way across the vacant lot, the mud sucked at the soles of my sandals, threatening to pull them off. It was August 2002, monsoon season. I had arrived in Bangalore three days earlier to find that the New Victoria Hotel, an elegant Raj Era resthouse just off Bangalore's main drag, was being razed to make way for a giant neon mall. Bangalore was in the midst of its IT revolution. The city seemed to be one huge construction site, and the traffic had doubled since my last visit three years earlier.

In a new high-rise hotel, I began setting up appointments with interpreters in the hope of finding someone who spoke Kannada to accompany me to the northern districts.

The educated, urban women my friends arranged for me to meet invariably became skittish when I brought up devadasis; they feared contamination, or worse. I realized I needed a social worker, not a mainstream interpreter, so I took a taxi to Bangalore University, a large, sprawling campus on the outskirts of the city.

The footpath leading to the social sciences department, a grim concrete building, was submerged in mud. The halls were empty. I called out to no one in particular and a woman wearing a white linen sari with red borders and checks appeared at the end of the hallway. 'May I help you?' she asked in perfect English. The bindi on her brow, larger than the store-bought variety, was a perfect circle of red powder. Her hair was tied in a bun and a line of red covered her middle parting. Her only adornments were a mangalsutra, two bangles and a pair of earrings.

'Where might I find Jogan Shankar?' I asked. Jogan Shankar was a sociologist who wrote the only book I had been able to find about modern-day devadasis.

'He's in Mysore. It's an hour from here by car. Would you like his telephone number? My name is Vani Dee,' she said, leading me down the hall to her office. She seated me across from her at the desk and put on a pair of reading glasses. 'What is your interest in devadasis?' she asked, surmising my purpose. I sensed she was a strong and exacting woman.

'I read Shankar's book,' I said. 'And I want to know more. I want to meet devadasis and make a documentary film about their traditions. The BBC is interested in financing a film, if the on-site research looks promising.

I'm looking for an interpreter to take into the field.'

Flipping through the university directory, Vani eyed me suspiciously over the rim of her reading glasses. 'Where are you from?' she asked.

'I was born in Paris, and live there now, but I grew up in New York.' Vani wrote Shankar's number on a piece of paper and pushed it towards me. 'What is your field?' I asked.

'I was trained in education, but now work on poverty alleviation in rural districts, mostly through programmes that empower women,' she said. We studied each other in silence. Vani displayed none of the coy timidity that many women make a show of. She smiled only when she had good reason to, and made a point of looking me in the eye. Our rapport was immediate. 'I came across devadasis as a student,' Vani said. 'We were doing a literacy campaign in the northern part of the state. Compared to other women, devadasis are very independent. They have to be.'

'Would you be interested in coming with me?' I asked.

'How many weeks are you thinking about?'

'Three, maybe four, depending on how it goes,' I said.

'My students are away on summer vacation right now . . .' Vani said cautiously. 'Three weeks is a long time. I'll have to think about it, and discuss it with my husband. Call me tomorrow morning.'

I considered Vani as she wrote down her number. I didn't want to pressure her, but I didn't want to miss this opportunity. I had a hunch she'd be perfect for the job. 'I've budgeted fifty dollars a day for an interpreter,' I said quietly, hoping for the best.

When I called Vani the next morning, she said she'd be ready to leave in three days. Looking back, I marvel at my luck. Vani proved to be an invaluable guide. She didn't merely translate; she interpreted the culture for me. She helped me understand customs and attitudes that would have otherwise remained impenetrable.

*

Devadasis have graced the halls of Indian temples for over a thousand years. Although commonly called 'temple prostitutes', they played a far more important role in society than this label admits. Dedicated to the service of a deity before the age of nine, girls received rigorous training in a wide variety of arts. Devadasis were, in a sense, India's professional dancers and singers. Their devotional dances, performed before the inner sanctum of the temple, served to keep the gods happy; their dance-dramas, performed at celebrations and festivals, enacted the gods' legendary exploits. Devadasis were also noted for their satirical and erotic or 'lascivious' dance rituals. Devotional dance-worship, like the sacrifices of Brahmin priests, helped the community remain in the deity's favour. While devadasis enjoyed a sacred status, marriage was forbidden. Their duties included providing sexual services to male visitors of the temple.

A young devadasi's *arungetram*, her début dance performance before the deity, took place after her first menses and signalled her availability for a sexual liaison.

Deflowering a devadasi was a matter of great prestige. Sexual desire was seen as a manifestation of divine presence; a devadasi's dance was believed to stimulate the cosmic energy within man. As the erotic sculptural relief on temples around India show, the joy of sexual union was seen as a paradigm for religious ecstasy. Men believed that having intercourse with a devadasi, an act of purification, would lead to celestial bliss; devadasis were taught that it was their *dharma*, their sacred duty, to provide sexual services to male devotees, and that by doing so they would improve their lot in the next life, or even better, be liberated from the cycle of eternal returns. But these religious and philosophical concerns veiled more material interests: fees for devadasis' services provided an income to temples and to the king's treasury.

While the system, an outgrowth of the Bhakti movement, dates to the sixth century, its ideological roots stretch back, not only to the Sangam poetry of the Tamil bardic tradition, but to the 3000-year-old Vedas, ancient and sacred texts, hymns used in conjunction with rites to invoke the gods. In the Vedas, fertility, dance and prostitution are closely intertwined—conversation hymns, designed to bring the rains, entailed special ritual performances by dancers and prostitutes. The 'Mahavrata' fertility rite calls for ritual intercourse with a prostitute; the more unrestrained the sex, the greater the influence in the realm of nature. Prostitutes, like the devadasis today, were considered auspicious and associated with the fertility of the land.

In the Vedas, Apsaras, heavenly prostitutes in the court of Indra known not only for their grace and beauty, but also for 'bearing their lovers to the highest heaven,'[2] were used to evoke religious feelings in men. Both intercourse and religious activity lead to the ecstasy of mystical oneness, union with the divine. Ejaculation during sexual union was likened to a form of sacrifice. Woman was the 'ground of sacrifice', and her loins the press that produced Soma, the intoxicating ambrosia of the gods. According to the Upanishads, a body of literature that grew around the Vedas, 'Her vulva is the sacrificial ground; her pubic hair is the sacred grass; her labia majora are the Soma-press; and her labia minora are the fire blazing at the centre. A man who engages in sexual intercourse with this knowledge obtains as great a world as a man who performs a Soma sacrifice.'[3] Sexual union is not only a metaphor for cosmic creation, but also a means to religious ecstasy: 'As man embraced by the woman he loves is oblivious to everything within or without, so this person is embraced by *atman* [the Supreme, Spiritual Self] consisting of knowledge . . . Here a father is not a father, a mother is not a mother, worlds are not worlds, gods are not gods and Vedas are not Vedas . . . Neither the good nor the bad follow him, for he has passed beyond all sorrows of the heart . . . He becomes one ocean, he becomes the sole seer! This is the world of brahman . . . This is the highest goal! This is the highest attainment! This is the highest world! This is the highest bliss!'[4]

✳

While many government officials claim that the devadasi system no longer exists, in the rural villages of south India's poverty belt, it is still alive. Much has changed since medieval times, and classical dance is no longer within the devadasis' purview, but the economic pressures and the mechanisms of exploitation that keep the women in place still prevail.

Dilip Patil, whom I befriended because of our shared interest in documentary films, was the first to mention devadasis to me. Dilip had grown up in a remote village in the northern state of Bihar. After finishing university, he worked on commercials in Mumbai, and then made his way to Paris to attend the summer programme of a French film school. He decided to stay on, but he spoke little French and didn't have a work permit. He showed his documentary projects to producers, but was advised to find a writer to help him shape them for a European audience. At the time I was working as a development manager for Gaumont TV, a French film studio.

Dilip pressed me to work with him, but the subjects he proposed, mostly about mystical phenomena, didn't interest me. India didn't appeal to me either. My cousin had recently spent a year in Varanasi, and was under its spell, but I retained only the images engraved in me by the press: the slums, the poverty, the filth. I listened to her stories with a mixture of fascination and disgust, and secretly swore to myself that I would never travel there. But Dilip made me question my simplistic preconceptions. He told riveting tales about every aspect of life, and had the ability to transform the most banal occurrence into a thrilling adventure. His stories were a blend of fact and fiction, but they were so amusing, I readily overlooked inconsistencies. He painted a picture of a vibrant and wondrous country where ancient and modern worlds mingled in the most unexpected and serendipitous ways.

When Dilip first mentioned devadasis to me, I was incredulous. 'Women dedicated to temples and taught to sing and dance for the gods? Was it some sort of fertility cult, like in Ancient Greece?' I asked. As a Classics major, I had been fascinated by Greek fertility cults and oracles, and began to read in anthropology. What began as a superficial interest soon became a passion, and I found myself spending school vacations in the New York Public Library devouring the works of Emile Durkheim, Claude Lévi-Strauss, Friedrich Nietzsche and Iaon Lewis. Listening to Dilip, I realized that India, where ancient ecstatic cults thrived alongside vibrant artistic and intellectual communities, was a place where all my interests collided head-on.

At that time, it so happened that Gaumont owed me four weeks of vacation. Three months later, in November, I boarded a plane to Delhi with a travelling companion. Dilip drew up an itinerary and arranged for us to stay with his friends. I quickly discovered that the subject of devadasis was taboo; few people even knew of their existence. But I had a wonderful time. Many of Dilip's friends were graduates of the prestigious NID, the National Institute of Design, and had been steeped for five years in both Western and Indian philosophical and artistic traditions. I discovered India through their families, their hopes and their frustrations. Indian history and philosophy intrigued me. Over the next few years, this group of newfound friends invited me along on road trips to the Himalayas, to weddings, and to ancient archeological sites in remote parts of India. We travelled together by train or by jeep for days on end—staying up late, smoking cigarettes, and reimagining the world. I felt privileged to have access to a network of such extraordinary people. Although my research trip to Karnataka in search of devadasis was still three years away, I began to travel to India whenever I had free time, and plunged headfirst into India's seminal texts, the Vedas, the Upanishads, the Mahabharata, the Puranas.

It was after my first trip that I sat down to write a proposal, based on library research, for a historical documentary about devadasis. It quickly became apparent to me that Dilip and I had rather different views on the system. After sending Dilip a copy of the proposal, I went to meet him at his partner's house in the north of Paris. In the opening paragraph of the project I had used the words 'brutal exploitation' to describe the system. After exchanging a few polite phrases, we had a face-off over coffee at the kitchen table.

'The devadasi system was once a great tradition,' he began. 'For over one thousand years, devadasis danced in temples across India. In medieval times, the most beautiful and talented women were devadasis. Temples were centres of artistic creation. In 1004 AD, King Raja Raja I ordered the transfer of some four hundred dancing girls from temples throughout his kingdom—from as far away as Ceylon—to his newly consecrated royal temple.

Have you seen it? Thanjavur—it's magnificent! The names of the girls and the villages they came from are etched in stone inside the temple. Each dancer was allotted a house and a stipend. Girls were trained in the sixty-four arts from the age of seven. One girl from each family was chosen to follow in her mother's footsteps—to be a devadasi was considered an honour. The men became dance teachers, musicians, songsters, playwrights and set decorators! It was the British with their reforms who degraded the system.'

I had read about Raja Raja and the Thanjavur temple. Its consecration in 1004 AD marked the institutionalization of the devadasi system, which flourished in the subsequent centuries. 'Hmmm . . .' I mumbled. We were on such different wavelengths that I didn't know where to begin. Lesser kings paid tribute to their superiors by handing over their best dancing girls . . . *along with horses and elephants,* I thought to myself. 'Look, it's true that some devadasis rose to positions of power; they were, after all, the only women allowed to learn to read and write, some became great poets and artists, but these were the lucky few. The vast majority lived at subsistence-level poverty. Devadasis were dedicated as children—before the age of nine! They were branded in case they ran away. Temple records show that devadasis were bought and sold . . . The system was a form of sexual slavery. They were locked into it. If a woman refused to dedicate a daughter, her property and her jewellery were confiscated.'

'Devadasis were highly regarded in medieval times! They were powerful and free. Before the British arrived, they had high status and came from royal families,' countered Dilip.

'Royal families? I don't know where you got that from. The king's agents sometimes bought devadasis in the market and gave them to the temple; it allowed him to curry favour with the gods and, as temples were taxed, it was a significant source of income for the state. But there is no evidence that devadasis in any significant number came from royal families—unless they happened to be war captives. Temples often recorded women's purchase agreements. Records show that after hereditary service, poverty was the most common reason for dedication. Women dedicated themselves or their daughters in times of drought—to feed their families. If you found any evidence that devadasis came from royal families, I'd be interested in knowing your source.' I prided myself on being an excellent researcher.

'You don't understand,' said Dilip, exasperated. 'India was once a rich country; there was no poverty, and no exploitation. Everything was fine until foreign rulers emptied the coffers. It was only with the British, and their Victorian values, that devadasis came to be looked down upon. A devadasi's first performance was an important event in the community. Men travelled for days by bullock cart to attend!'

'Yeah, so that they could bid on the virginity of a twelve-year-old!' I snapped, and quickly regretted it. This was not the best way to bring Dilip over to my side. 'Look, I agree with you. Some devadasis rose to become the consorts of kings. And there was an interesting philosophical system behind the devadasi tradition; it enabled the emergence and the preservation of a great art. But that doesn't mean we have to look at it through rose-coloured glasses. It was an economic system, too. Temples competed with each other to bring in worshippers—and having beautiful devadasis was one of the ways they did so. Devadasis were exploited for the benefit of the ruling classes. Prostitution was part of it. Let's not forget that. Women didn't choose to become devadasis of their own will, that would be different. And wasn't it the Mughals, when they took aim at the power of the temple, who delivered the first major blow to the devadasi system?'

Dilip stared into his cup. 'I don't think you can use the word prostitution,' he said.

'What do you mean?' I asked, confused.

'I don't think you can equate the devadasi system with prostitution.'

'I'm not equating the system with prostitution, I'm saying that prostitution is an element of it, that is, if we define prostitution as the exchange of sexual services for cash,' I said, nearing the end of my patience. 'Can we agree that in the devadasi system money is exchanged for sex?'

Dilip now stared into the middle distance, avoiding eye contact. 'Yeah. Maybe you're right,' he said, stone-faced.

I left Dilip's house that day expecting never to hear from him again, but he called a few weeks later to ask me to make changes to the proposal. I told him I thought modern-day devadasis should hold centre-stage in the documentary, but he insisted that they were a mere perversion of the medieval system and wanted to exclude them. Although I was just a hired pen, I was not interested in putting to paper a representation of the system I could not endorse. My frustration resulted in inertia. I kept postponing Dilip's 'brainstorming' sessions and often forgot to return his calls. A year went by; the project foundered.

When I had all but forgotten about it, Dilip called to say that he thought including a section on contemporary devadasis was a good idea. Two weeks later, I had a proposal ready for the BBC. At its centre was the question: is the devadasi system a great Hindu tradition or the brutal exploitation of women? Viewers, Dilip and I agreed, should be allowed to decide for themselves. This was my first mistake; the signs that spelled disaster were firmly in place, but I refused to see them.

TWO

Devotees who wash the floors at the lord's temples
will gain ten times more merit
than those who sweep them clean.
For those who weave fresh flower garlands
for his worship,
pure heaven is the reward.
The ineffable knowledge of the true faith
will be theirs, who light lamps at his shrines.
And singing hymns for the Lord
is the sure path to his boundless grace.[5]

—Appar, seventh-century Bhakti saint

A FEW DAYS INTO our research, Vani and I decided to replace our Ambassador with a Sumo, a kind of hard-topped jeep, which was better suited to the dirt roads we had to navigate. Our new driver, Sanjay, was talkative. As soon as we got into the car, he told us he was twenty-five years old, from a Jain family, and the fifth of eight brothers. He had pockmarked cheeks, a mop of curly hair, and annoyed Vani by asking a lot of intrusive questions. 'Where is the lady from? Is she married? What is your job? How did you meet?' We were on our way to a village our Ambassador hadn't been able to reach. Since he was bound to find out anyway, Vani told him that we were researching the devadasi system.

'There are lots of villages I can take you to. Tell me what you need and I will find it for you.' It occurred to me that as a young, unmarried taxi driver, he probably frequented villages where devadasis lived. We plowed slowly through the ravine that our Ambassador hadn't been able to cross. Farther along was the bulwark of an ancient fortification. A large village with several two-storey houses with fancy wooden latticework spread before us. Four hundred feet beyond the village was the *holakeri*, the untouchable hamlet. Sanjay sped straight into the holakeri's main square, nearly grazing a group of toddlers near a tree stump. He jammed on his brakes near the well, where women were filling earthenware jars. We got out of the car. A few men approached and started questioning Sanjay, who told them we were government agents.

Vani cut him off. 'Excuse me. We are *not* government agents. I'm a researcher at Banglore University. We're here for research purposes. If you have any questions, please address them to me. This is our driver . . . he's only been with us since this morning, so he's not well acquainted with our project.' By now a group of women had gathered behind the men. 'Where can we hold a meeting?' Vani asked. An old woman with a child on her hip suggested the Yellamma temple, on the other side of the hamlet. Yellamma was one of the goddesses to whom many modern-day devadasis were dedicated.

Vani took her by the arm and started walking. Turning

back to the crowd, she said, 'Please ask the devadasi women to meet us there.' Speaking confidentially to the old lady, she asked, 'What is your name?' Sanjay locked the car and caught up to Vani.

'I can't believe it,' Vani muttered to me under her breath. She took him aside and told him that we would not need his services at the temple. He was shocked.

'But you need protection,' he said for everyone to hear. 'You don't know these women; they're devious!' Devadasi women were known for working the crowds at open-air markets, but I doubted they would steal from a guest. Vani shook her head in disbelief and walked away. 'You better hold on to your purses,' he called after us. He sauntered back to the Sumo and turned the radio on full blast.

As we walked through the village, it began to rain. Thatched, mud-brick houses seemed to huddle together under the leaden clouds. Smoke from the hearths seeped through the roofs, then lay stagnant, unable to rise any higher. The drab huts were brightened only by the saris of women squatting under their eaves, rinsing off breakfast plates. A bucket of used water came flying from inside a house, narrowly missing a boy hopping barefoot from stone to stone. Above the sound of dishwashing and morning gossip was the occasional trill of a woman calling to a neighbour to come look—strangers had arrived.

While Vani chatted with the women walking near her, others, straining to overhear the conversation, were sullen and nervous. I caught more than a few furtive, questioning glances. They were suspicious of us. I sympathized with them. What would I think if some foreigner showed up on my doorstep and started asking strange questions? But the importance of hospitality was deeply ingrained in India. One never knew in what shape or form a god would come; this tradition is what made our research possible.

On the temple platform, I rejoined the conversation. Vani was talking to a tall, square-shouldered woman in her late forties. 'This is Gowri,' Vani said. 'She's a devadasi, but has lived with a member of her own community for the past ten years. She and her partner both work in the fields.' Gowri had olive eyes and a shock of white hair.

'How does caste work in this village?' I said to Vani. 'Maybe she can explain it to me.'

Vani turned to the women and spoke at length. When she finished, Gowri took my hand and, pausing regularly to allow Vani to translate, said, 'You see, God gave land to the rich, highborn people, and to the poor, outcaste people, he gave the chore of working that land. We work long hours in the blazing sun, hoeing the fields, planting and then harvesting the crops. High-caste women in the *ooru* [the high-caste part of town], they don't have to work. They stay inside and eat fruit all day long. When we were young we were beautiful too, but working in the fields in the hot sun, we ruined our looks and our health. You see that sugarcane over there—beyond the temple—soon we will have to cut it down. Those thick stalks aren't easy to get through. After a lifetime in the fields, we are permanently bent in two. It is backbreaking work . . . we bring rotis to the field, and the landlords give us a ladle of thin stew.

They feed us because otherwise we wouldn't have enough strength to do the job. Our main preoccupation is having enough food to feed our children, so that they don't get hunger pains. I don't mind going to sleep on an empty stomach, but I can't bear to see my children go hungry. Do you understand me?' asked Gowri, placing her hand on my forearm and locking my gaze into hers. 'I can't bear to see my children go hungry.'

'Two women from the Karnataka State Women's Development Committee came here two years ago,' said the woman sitting next to Gowri, breaking the silence.

'Two women, like you,' said Gowri, perking up. 'They told us to form a cooperative and said that we would get assistance. They said that loans would be available. We heard some cooperatives received sewing machines. Well, we formed our cooperative and we're waiting. Can you call them for us and tell them to come back?'

There was a stir in the crowd. A high-caste landlord, recognizable by his starched white cap and ankle-length dhoti, stood 15 feet from the temple, legs apart and both hands firmly on the head of his walking stick. 'Don't talk to those people!' he shouted to the women. 'They're troublemakers.'

'Excuse me,' Vani called out, rising to speak with him, but he turned on his heels and strode away. Gowri sighed in despair and the other women, grumbling under their breath, gradually dispersed.

Vani and I climbed back into the Sumo and continued down the road to the next village. I stared out the window, seething with indignation. Vani looked over at me and chuckled. 'When I see you reacting to the women, I see myself as a student fifteen years ago, in the field for the first time.'

THREE

Why does she act like this?
Is it because our lord with the lotus eyes
has taken her over?
How can I explain our girl,
her lips as red as a fruit,
her body lithe as a doe's?[6]

—Nammalvar, eighth-century Bhakti saint

THE SUMO SPED DOWN a narrow dirt road. At the fork ahead, I spotted a crowd. A girl was lying by the roadside. A grey-haired man in Western clothes waved us down. 'Stop,' I said to Sanjay. He hurtled past the crowd. A boy ran after our car, waving his arms. 'Rok, rok, stop!' I said again, wondering if Sanjay had understood me. Vani leaned over the front seat and scolded him in Kannada. We hit a pothole and flew off the backseat, grazing our heads on the roof of the car. The Sumo ground to a halt fifty yards beyond the crowd. I stepped out. The man in Western clothes caught up with us. He explained that a spirit had possessed the girl. The family was looking to hire a vehicle to take her to the temple. 'I am a priest,' he said. 'I have been hired to exorcize her.'

We walked towards the girl as she struggled to her knees. Her hair was loose and tangled. Two young men, her brothers, I found out later, held her wrists. She moaned and tried to pull free. When she saw me with my fair skin and hair, she twitched, then lowered her eyes and quieted down. Her brother gently swept back the strands of hair hanging in her face.

'Look at her necklace,' Vani said. Near the clasp was a series of eight or so red and white beads. 'Those beads symbolize bondage to the goddess. They are tied around a girl's neck at her dedication ceremony. To remove them is to risk being struck down by the goddess.' Vani and I exchanged looks.

I had considered bringing a mini digital video camera with me, but decided against it for several reasons. First, the image quality would not have been compatible with 16 mm film, which was the medium that Dilip was insisting upon using. And second, cameras alter relationships. Researching other projects, I had noticed that as soon as I brought out a camera, video or still, the conversation lost its intimacy. I had learned to bring out my camera only once a strong bond had been established. Nevertheless, as I watched this drama unfold, I regretted not having something with me.

'I am the mother,' said a tough, pear-shaped, white-haired lady in a pink pastel sari as she waddled over to Vani and me. Tears were now rolling down her daughter's cheeks, and she was trembling. Her brother knelt beside her. Clasping her hand, he wiped away her tears and adjusted her sari. I wondered what demon had possessed her. To me, it looked like she was having some sort of breakdown. I remembered a woman I once saw on Fifth Avenue in New York. She was kneeling on the pavement and screaming at the top of her lungs, pounding the air with her fists. I tried to talk to her, but she ignored me and just kept screaming. The morning crowds walked past without a glance or a word. I don't know what shocked me more—the screams of the woman or the indifference of the passers-by. It occurred to me that both of these women were probably reacting in a primal way to unbearable situations.

The girl didn't look directly at me, but kept me in her peripheral vision. I sensed her alarm. *Could this girl's 'possession' be a desperate reaction?* I wondered. *A rebellion—the only type available to her—against the life she is compelled to lead?* As a student of anthropology, I had read quite a bit about possession, but this was the first time I had ever seen a possessed person. She started to pant heavily; my stare was making her uncomfortable. I thought she might hyperventilate and turned to Vani, who summarized her conversation with the mother for me.

'The girl is sixteen years old. She stopped eating about two months ago and came down with a fever. Then she started having convulsions and speaking in tongues. The priest diagnosed her with spirit possession. A young woman in the village died in childbirth recently, and the family thinks she is haunting their daughter. They want to have her exorcized at the temple, but the spirit refuses to cooperate. It's twisting the girl's body with fits of rage. They want us to take them there in our Sumo.'

'Let's take them!' I said.

'I said we would—if they allow us to witness the ceremony,' replied Vani, one step ahead of me. 'The priest agreed, but warned me that it may last well into the night . . . this is a rare opportunity. I've never seen an exorcism before.'

As the girl, flanked by her brothers, approached the Sumo, our driver shook his head and stood in their path. Vani reprimanded him, and he stepped out of the way. The priest sat in front with Sanjay, and the mother and aunt shared the backseat with Vani and me. The girl and her two brothers crammed into the back. The priest, turning to Vani, filled her in on the details of the case. 'The girl has recently matured and is having trouble adjusting to adult life,' he said. For a young devadasi, this was not hard to imagine. 'Spirits prey upon women when they are ill or unhappy. This is a serious case. The spirit may well be a demon. At first we thought the goddess Yellamma had come into her, but when we questioned her, there was nothing but insults for the goddess.'

The Sumo barrelled down the road. Sweat streamed from Sanjay's face. He was clamped to the steering wheel as if holding on for dear life. Vani observed him for a moment, and then leaned forward to ask if he was okay. It was almost midday. The sun had poked through the clouds enough to make the damp earth steam. 'I'm cold,' he said. Now that he had our attention, he started trembling like a leaf.

Vani placed her shawl around his shoulders. I didn't share her compassion. 'It's a ploy to try to force us to get rid of the girl,' I said. We tried to ignore him, but he started feigning convulsions. He arched his back and banged his head hard against the steering wheel as if he had been struck from behind. This was more than I could take, but Vani insisted there was nothing we could do. Afraid he would cause an accident, she asked him to pull over. The family got out. They understood. 'The spirit is bothering your driver,' the mother said.

Vani wrote down the name of the family's village and promised to come see them in a few days' time. As we pulled away, one of the girl's brothers sprinted after our car. Sanjay screeched to a halt and I opened the door. Staring up at me with black saucer eyes, he pressed his hands together and touched them to his forehead in a formal salutation. 'Namaskar,' he said, 'I salute the god within you.' Staring back at him, feeling his anguish, I returned the salutation.

'Thank you,' he said in barely comprehensible English. Letting out a sob, bursting into tears, and dropping to his knees, he added, 'God bless you.' Sanjay suddenly floored the pedal, leaving the boy in the dust, and me dangling from the door of the Sumo.

Back in control, Sanjay put on a cassette tape of Hindi film songs and started singing along at the top of his lungs. He removed Vani's shawl and used it to wipe the sweat dripping down his face and neck.

*

At the nearest STD booth, Vani called the Sanman Hotel, where we had stayed in Belgaum. She asked the concierge to send an Ambassador with their most trustworthy driver.

Having an Ambassador rather than a Sumo would limit our fieldwork, but Sanjay was not going to work for us and the few other Sumo drivers in town categorically refused to take women 'travelling alone', that is, unaccompanied by male members of the family. The implication, Vani told me, was that we were prostitutes. 'A girl, a young woman, or even an old woman should not do anything independently, even in her own house,' said Vani, smirking as she quoted the *Dharma Shastra*, a text dating to the Common Era, but codifying ideas that had been around for centuries. 'In childhood a woman should be under her father's control, in youth under her husband's, and when her husband is dead, under her son's . . . a woman is not fit for independence.'

*

At seven the next morning, a driver with a cream-coloured Ambassador was waiting for us in the parking lot, burning clumps of incense on his dashboard. Ambassadors, their design unchanged since the 1940s, look like bowler hats on wheels, but their heaviness makes them comfortable on rugged roads.

'Will you please confirm your rate?' Vani asked the driver. In his fifties, he was small and slight. He wore brown pants and a beige shirt, and kept a pen tucked into his breast pocket, even though, I later found out, he did not know how to read or write.

'Six hundred rupees [$15] per day or per 250 kilometres,' he replied in Kannada. He kept his eyes averted in deference.

'And what is your name?' asked Vani.

'Iqbal,' he said, opening the back door. As Vani climbed in, Iqbal bowed to me and said, 'Sir.' Over the coming weeks, this was an appellation I would have to get used to. Although I had long hair and wore a kurta, I was frequently called 'sir.' It was meant as a term of respect; 'sir' was of a higher rank than 'madam'.

Dazed mosquitoes, chased out of hiding by the squeaky springs of the backseat collapsing under our weight, glided along the windows. The engine sputtered, and we were off. Iqbal was used to chauffeuring government agents on tours of duty and knew the region well. The rich fields and wooded foothills of the Western Ghats, dotted with mesmerizing scarecrows, terrifying witches that looked like crosses between Picasso's *Demoiselles d'Avignon* and punk rockers, gave way to long undulating plains. We drove south-east across Bagalkot, towards Talcot district.

The plains, where sugarcane and sunflower fields alternated with scruffy patches of forest, were dotted with small stone temples and massive ruins of hilltop forts, bearing witness to the powerful kingdoms that once vied for control of the valley. Between the sixth and twelfth centuries, the area would have been under the control of the kings of the ancient city of Badami, and later, between the thirteenth and sixteenth centuries, under the control of the kings of Vijayanagara, present-day Hampi, a World Heritage Site.

The rock-cut cave temples of Badami were sculpted at a time when women were first incorporated into temple service, at the beginning of the Bhakti movement. Bhakti has been called the 'Tamil renaissance' and a 'bloodless revolution', but it is perhaps best described as a religious movement which ultimately transformed the social, political and religious landscape of India. The migration of considerable numbers of learned Brahmins to south India in the third century set the stage for the Bhakti movement. Although the details of their infiltration of power structures remain vague, Brahmins soon became the custodians of Tamil shrines and traditions, and brought with them the spread of settled agriculture. Brahmin dominance combined with new agricultural techniques led to gradual changes in the structure and organization of society. Forests were cut and tribesmen were subdued and taught to work the land. The blending of Brahmin and Tamil Sangam traditions gave birth to the cult of the god-kings, Shiva and Vishnu. These new gods quickly spread out from Tamil country to neighbouring territories in modern Karnataka, and up through the rest of India. The dominant versions of Hindu mythology were set down in the Puranas. The new gods and their families, friends and enemies became as real as human dynasties; the first icons were sculpted in stone and massive temples were constructed to house them.

Often, radical anti-Brahmin rebels, the mystic poet-saints of Bhakti rejected Brahminic traditions that only offered spiritual liberation to high-caste men, and proclaimed that the path to liberation was open to all regardless of caste, creed and gender. By following the path of Bhakti, women, Shudras and even untouchables could aspire to spiritual release. Elite Brahmanical Sanskrit, the language of the few, was rejected in favour of vernacular languages. Borrowing, reworking and transforming Vedic as well as indigenous Tamil concepts, Bhakti saints danced, wept and worshipped their way through south India. Accompanied by bands of 'mad devotees', they travelled from shrine to shrine exchanging their sacred hymns for payment. They forged pilgrimage routes across the countryside and converted kings, Brahmins and peasants along the way. Song and dance became important elements of worship and, eventually, female slaves were incorporated into temple ritual to chant and enact the hymns that the saints left behind. These female slaves were the predecessors of the women that would one day come to be called devadasis.

Bhakti devotionalism drew large crowds and, by incorporating it into daily worship, Brahmins popularized the temple and extended its power among the lower castes. One of the *Agamas* (manuals for temple rituals), the *Kumaratantra*, comments, 'The morning rites represent the spiritual bend of the minds of the Brahmins, the brilliant noon puja portrays the splendour of the king and the evening worship brings out the gross, sensuous leanings of the Shudras.' Coming to terms with Bhakti was a matter of survival for the Brahmins, and the alliance with its poet-saints was not always a comfortable one. Brahmins bewailed having to allow untouchable poets and Shudras into their temples and Bhakti saints ridiculed Brahmins, their rituals and rules of conduct. The Bhakti movement, however, can hardly be called a revolution. The first step towards achieving union with the divine is total submission and subservience to God. According to

Bhakti, to be a slave or a 'servant in irrevocable bondage' or even a servant of a servant is a great honour. Bhakti was an expression of dissent against the Brahmin elite, but by promoting an ideology of servitude and carving out a niche for spiritual fulfillment for the lower castes within the existing system, Bhakti sustained rather than challenged the social hierarchy.

*

In Talcot district, a mere 200 miles from medieval Tamil territories, the birthplace of Bhakti, the land was irrigated and the peasants were reasonably well off. Half a mile beyond a market town called Halamid, a 300-yard strip of stores, stalls and eateries, our Ambassador turned off onto a dirt road and then into a walled compound with an overgrown garden. It was a Raj Era inspection bungalow, a government-maintained resthouse for politicians, engineers and healthcare workers. These government lodges were our only option. In small towns, hotels refused to take women travelling alone and those that did were unsafe.

The sloping, triangular roof, held aloft by large wooden beams, came to a peak over a pale blue dining room. Two dilapidated but clean bedrooms gave onto a verandah, overshadowed by an enormous fig tree. Iqbal spoke to the chowkidar, a fellow Muslim. He agreed to let us stay on condition that we leave if government officials needed the rooms.

FOUR

Only a man who has touched the breast of a courtesan can command the army; only a man who has stared her in the face can become king.

—Muddupalani, eighteenth-century
courtesan and poet

I AWOKE WITH A start. Someone was banging at my door. Scanning the dark room, I had to take a moment to remember where I was. Over the past few days Vani and I had visited three or four villages a day, returning often to the same ones. I peeled my journal off the inside of my arm, where it had remained stuck overnight, and breathed a sigh of relief. *We're finally getting somewhere*, I thought to myself. It was already seven-thirty. 'Catherine,' I heard Vani calling through the door.

I stumbled to the door and opened it. 'Sorry,' I mumbled. Through puffy eyelids, I noticed Vani was holding a folded sari. 'Vani . . .' I said, 'we've been through this before.'

'You have to break down all the barriers between you and the women,' Vani said, stepping into my room.

'I can't do it. I'm sorry,' I said, motioning for her to sit in the armchair.

'Anthropologists always wear saris,' she said, declining to sit.

'I guess I'm not a real anthropologist,' I replied cheerfully.

Vani placed the sari on the table. 'I'm not leaving until you put this on,' she said. 'When you're ready, call me and I'll help you put it on.'

I sensed that Vani was not going to give in this time. 'I feel like I would be pretending to be something or someone I'm not,' I said. 'I would be misrepresenting myself.' I was dead set against wearing a sari. Perhaps I feared looking ridiculous.

Vani coaxed me gently. 'Wearing a sari is a way of showing respect. Trust me. It's the right thing to do.' I must have looked anxious, for Vani added, 'Don't worry, if you want we can put in some pins so it doesn't slip. Go on, start getting dressed. I'll get the pins.'

I found the petticoat and blouse in a fold of the sari. Vani had selected a green sari with white embroidered flowers and borders. Green is an auspicious colour for devadasis; Vani knew that the women would be especially pleased to see me in green. I slipped on the petticoat and pulled the string tight around my waist. The end of the skirt fell to my heels. Although blouses are usually made to measure, Vani and I were both petite and it fit well enough.

Vani arrived carrying a small, quilted pouch. 'This time, why don't I tie it for you? Just watch carefully.' Vani tucked one end of the sari into the front of the petticoat and wrapped it counterclockwise around my waist. Measuring out the cloth between her fingers, she made six pleats that ran lengthwise down to my feet. Tucking the top end of the pleats into the front of the petticoat, she let the rest fall to the ground where they spread out like a Chinese fan. She then wrapped the remainder of the sari around my torso and draped the pallu, the loose end of the sari, over my left shoulder. It reached just beneath the back of my knees. 'I'll put a pin here, so that the pallu doesn't slip,' she said, fastening it to the neckline of the blouse. 'You're not too tall; maybe you don't need a pin at the waist,' she said.

'I think I do,' I said, imagining the worst.

As Vani arranged the folds of the pallu across my chest, I felt as if I were crossing into forbidden territory. *I shouldn't be doing this,* I thought. But then, I willed myself to change my thoughts. *Why not? Why shouldn't I? Why is wearing a sari a misrepresentation? Why I can't I wear a sari and still be myself?* I had grown up in a family with a narrow interpretation of life—of what was good and what was bad; what was beautiful and what was not. The only mirror was above the washbasin. As I walked across the room, I admired the way the pleats of the sari bounced off the tops of my feet.

'Wait,' said Vani, unscrewing a small vial filled with kumkum powder. She dipped her finger in, then placed the palm of her hand on my cheekbone for stability and stamped a red circle between my brows.

'I thought bindis were only for married women.'

'They're for anyone. It's just an auspicious mark,' she replied.

In India, where loose hair can sometimes be seen as a sign of sexual licentiousness, I kept my thick, unruly hair in a tight braid that reached down the middle of my back. I now undid my braid and folded my hair into a bun like an Indian woman.

*

Five miles from Halamid, down a rugged dirt road, Kalyana was a knot of narrow lanes hedged in by sugarcane and sunflower fields. Patches of forest covered the rolling hills beyond. The houses were made of stone, brick and unbaked mud. A combination of tile and thatch roofs did their best to keep the rain out. This was our third visit. Sumithra sat in the warm glow of the hearth, pulling a carved wooden comb through her wavy, waist-length hair. She was the guardian of the most important shrine to the goddess Yellamma in Kalyana, and, thus, the head devadasi of the village. Slight of frame with a fine, chiselled face, she couldn't have been more than thirty-two, yet crow's feet bracketed her eyes. Folding her hair in a bun, she motioned for us to sit.

'You're just in time for the ceremony,' she said.

Renuka, her eleven-year-old daughter, stirred a cauldron over the fire. Her limbs were long and slender, and budding breasts were visible beneath her shirt. She still wore a long skirt reserved for girls, but with puberty not far off, she would soon be graduating to a sari. Renuka had inherited her mother's delicate, chiselled face, high cheekbones and graceful carriage, but while Sumithra exuded quiet assurance, Renuka was painfully shy. Every time I caught her eye, she panicked and looked away.

Sumithra had a reputation for being close to the goddess, and was known in the region for the accuracy of her clairvoyance.

'Have some tea,' said Sumithra. 'Renuka—get some jaggery from next door— I just have a few preparations to make.' The entrance door squeaked open and a man stepped in from the rain carrying a bundle of sticks. 'Aha. This is Basappa,' said Sumithra, 'Renuka's father. I've told you about him.' Basappa was a small, wiry man about the same age as Sumithra. He tucked the bundle of sticks into a niche in the wall by the hearth and turned to greet us.

'Namaskar,' he said, pressing his hands together. He looked at me furtively over the tips of his fingers, his thick brows forming a dramatic V. His wide-set eyes betrayed curiosity and confusion. He seemed unsure of what to think of me. Squatting by the hearth, he stoked its flames, which flared and licked the cauldron. Vani whispered to me that he was from the untouchable community; she could tell by the way he wore his dhoti. *As head devadasi, Sumithra earns sufficient money by performing ritual duties*, I thought to myself; *she does not need to rely on an upper-caste landlord or sex work for her livelihood.*

Sumithra lit the end of a twig in the fire and ignited a dozen little oil lamps, placing them one by one on a brass plate. 'Follow me,' she said, leading us to the back of her house. We passed through a small room with two charpais to the third and largest room, where the *jagha* was kept. A jagha is a portable shrine of the goddess Yellamma, which devadasis carry to upper-caste homes and farms for use in the puja. The goddess Yellamma stood almost four feet tall. Adorned with peacock feathers, cowry shells and garlands, her face was fashioned from silver. She had luminous, alabaster eyes. The shrine was fastened with six erect silver cobras to a wicker basket that Sumithra could easily hoist over her head. She spent much of her day carrying the jagha to landlords' houses and fields to perform ceremonies.

'I wonder how many generations the jagha has passed through,' I whispered to Vani.

'I wonder if it'll one day be Renuka's,' she whispered back.

Sumithra placed a clump of burning camphor on the plate with the oil lamps and encircled the goddess with it. The aromatic smoke of camphor filled the room. The goddess's silver face reflected the flames. Sumithra seemed indifferent, as if the acts she was performing were utilitarian actions intended to achieve a particular result. The respectful attitude that, in the West, even non-believers feel obliged to adopt during religious ceremonies was not required. The emphasis was not on 'faith', but on the proper performance of rituals.

Sumithra rang the meditation bell; its strident metallic claps cleared the room of evil spirits. Intoning a mantra, she lit nuggets of incense, and placed them before the shrine. The room filled with smoke and the scent of sandalwood and jasmine. As there were no windows, Sumithra displaced a few of the roof tiles with a long stick to allow the smoke to escape. After wiping the goddess's face clean with a damp cloth, she reapplied fresh haldi to Yellamma's forehead and a dot of kumkum, between her brows. Renuka appeared with balls of rice on a plate and arranged them on a banana leaf before the shrine. Settling into the lotus position, Sumithra began to sing a devotional song when a woman called to her from the lane. Sumithra responded and two women entered. 'These are high-caste women,' Vani whispered to me. 'They want to consult the goddess.' They saluted the goddess without acknowledging Vani or me. Pressing their hands together in prayer, the upper-caste women bowed to the goddess. The older woman, who might have been around thirty-five, continued the movement downward, prostrating herself in a gesture of total submission. I wondered if the intensity with which she paid homage to Yellamma was a gauge of the gravity of her problem. The women now squatted before the jagha, and Sumithra smeared haldi across their foreheads.

'The women are going to ask questions,' whispered Vani. 'The goddess will respond by allowing Sumithra to lift the shrine or by fixing it to the ground.' Sumithra waited indifferently as the women discussed their questions. Her attitude was perfunctory and passive. She was merely the medium through which the goddess made her will known. The movement of the smoke, caught by intermittent shafts of light, accentuated the stillness of the room. Vani was unable to hear all the questions, but they related to the daughter of the older woman. 'Her daughter has some problem with her feet, and is not yet walking,' whispered Vani. The answer to the woman's final question was negative. Sumithra repeatedly tugged at the jagha, and, although it weighed no more than three pounds, she seemed unable to lift it. The women looked at each other, coming to terms with the goddess's response.

After they left, Sumithra asked Vani and me if we had questions for the goddess. I was upset and wanted to get away as quickly as possible. *Sumithra,* I thought, *is hoodwinking her fellow villagers.* It occurred to me that Sumithra, as head devadasi of Kalyana, must dedicate girls. *What a scam,* I thought. Everything that the social workers had said came flooding back: senior devadasis feign possession by the goddess in order to make demands in her name. If villagers don't offer enough, devadasis harass them in the name of the goddess. Poor villagers may have nothing of value to offer except a daughter. Villagers who do not comply with the goddess's requests are brought to the main Yellamma temple in Saundatti, Mecca for devadasis, where priests are secretly informed about the dispute. After the puja, the priest, supposedly possessed by Yellamma, lists the goddess's grievances, taking care to reveal intimate knowledge of the family's life and village. 'I will burn your house down, I will take your son's life, I will make him impotent. I will see to it that you will be outcast from your village,' he threatens them. I could see it all happening so clearly—terrified parents vowing to dedicate their daughters. Wealthy landowners, one social worker had said, collude with senior devadasis to ensure the girls they desire are 'called' into Yellamma's service.

As these thoughts raced through my mind, Vani was asking the goddess questions. I reminded myself to remain detached, but revulsion was getting the better of me. I rose to leave even before Sumithra had finished.

'Catherine . . . you really should ask a question too,' Vani said. 'It's important that you show respect to the goddess. You don't have to ask out loud . . .'

'I don't have any questions.'

'Catherine . . . You must be respectful of her way of life.'

I was unmoved, but then I looked at Sumithra. Standing by the jagha, shifting her weight fretfully, she kept her eyes averted. She sensed my unease. I felt torn. It was all so strange. I had no idea what to do. I hesitated, then sat down again, defeated. After a moment's deliberation, I asked Yellamma if our documentary would get funding. The jagha didn't budge. The answer was no.

'If the goddess is helpful to you, you can bring her a sari next time you come,' said Sumithra. Vani reached down to touch the base of the jagha, presumably the goddess's feet, and placed a ten-rupee note in the basket.

Vani and I walked to edge of the village where the Ambassador was waiting for us. I sank deep into the backseat, brooding over how girls were sacrificed for the benefit of their families, and how families were so poor that they seemed to have little choice. Although I knew that to take issue with Sumithra about the devadasi system was counterproductive, I wondered if, by not saying anything, we were somehow condoning the system. The cultural and material chasms that separated me from devadasis sometimes felt so deep as to be insurmountable, and yet at other times, when the women spoke about their children, their pain, their hopes for the future, I understood them so well.

Once we had put the worst of Kalyana's muddy ruts

behind us, Vani turned to me and said, 'Sumithra is a sincerely religious woman. She's not just "putting one over" on the villagers.'

'But she wasn't even possessed or in a trance. She looked bored!' I protested.

Vani just shook her head. 'I know it's hard to understand, but Sumithra is sincerely religious. She believes in the powers of the goddess. I don't know how to explain it to you.'

We reached an abandoned sugar factory, a jumble of metal tubes and vats, and turned right, onto a dirt road bordered on each side by sunflower fields. 'If she had been in some sort of trance, I'd understand,' I said, half to myself. Dancing and drumming have been used throughout history to induce ecstatic states. Although the visions generated by these experiences are culturally conditioned, the imagery used to describe them is universal. 'Religious ecstasy,' a sense of euphoric communion with the divine or with one's fellow man, is often interpreted by those who experience it as proof that God exists. *But Sumithra had not been in any sort of transcendental state*, I thought to myself.

*

That night after dinner Vani helped me prepare a list of questions for Sumithra. We returned to her house early the next morning. Sumithra and four other devadasis had just finished performing the morning puja. They were preparing to take the jagha to a farm for a ceremony, but stopped their preparations and put on a kettle. Sumithra's neighbour, Ella, joined us.

'Does the goddess ever demand dedications?' I asked.

'Yellamma, Mother of All, demands our daughters and if we don't comply, she will destroy us. She blesses and brings peace to the village. If girls are not dedicated, then Yellamma will be angry and the landlords will scold us. At least one girl must be dedicated every year, or the rains will not come, the crops will fail, and the entire village will be destroyed.'

'But has she ever spoken through you to demand a dedication?'

'No, never,' replied Sumithra, taken aback by the question.

'Have you ever seen her demand a dedication through a devadasi?'

'No. I have never seen such a thing, nor have I heard of it happening.'

'How does Yellamma bring girls into her service?'

'Yellamma calls in different ways. Most often she comes to the parents in a dream, but sometimes she sends a rash that will not go away, or matted hair.'

'Has anyone else ever seen a priest or a devadasi demand a dedication?' asked Vani.

The women shook their heads no. 'The goddess troubles us. That is why we dedicate,' said Ella. Ella was tall with broad shoulders and a strong chin. She earned a living by milking buffalos for high-caste villagers; her husband worked as a bonded labourer. Her son was twelve and her daughters were ten, six and four. She was probably only thirty, but she seemed much older. Walking long distances in the hot sun had taken its toll. 'When my eldest girl was a baby, she was so sick I thought she would die; she had a chronic fever and diarrhoea. I couldn't bear the thought of losing her. We took her for treatment, but still she didn't get better. I prayed and prayed to the goddess for her health . . . she was a beautiful baby and Yellamma, Mother of All, wanted her in her service. Finally, I vowed that if my baby lived, I would dedicate her. Her health improved immediately.'

'Did you take her to the doctor?' Vani asked.

Ella laughed. 'A doctor? We were so poor, we had nothing to eat! My milk dried up when the baby was only four months. How could we afford a doctor? She was treated by the village priest.'

Vani turned to me with a sigh. 'See how it works? She attributes the dedication to "the call of Yellamma", but poverty is the real reason— her baby was sick because her milk had dried up. Her milk dried up because she didn't have enough to eat. She probably was not boiling the baby's water. She's lucky the baby survived . . . Ella, all of you, you must always boil a baby's water, otherwise it'll get sick. Do you understand?' The women nodded in unison.

'Now tell me, Sumithra, when were you dedicated?' asked Vani.

'I don't remember. I was very young. I lost my mother when I was small, and my aunt dedicated me. She made me do *dhanda* [sex work].' Sumithra's delivery was distant and in a monotone, as if she was talking about someone else. 'My aunt didn't care about me; she just wanted me to go to Mumbai. It didn't feel right. I hated dhanda and kept running away. I would hide in the fields and cry . . . a few years later I met Basappa in Halamid. We lived there together. One evening there was a police raid. Hundreds of people were held in jail overnight and the next morning there was a mass wedding. Each couple was promised three thousand rupees in a year's time, if they could show that they stayed together.'

'The forced marriage programme?' asked Vani. 'You were part of that?'

'Yes.'

Vani turned to me. 'Forced marriages. Can you believe it? It was one of the more absurd government programmes aimed at eradicating the system. They raided the brothels, arrested all the couples and then married them the next day. The vast majority of marriages didn't last and, in some cases, the men were already married.'

'So by law you are married,' I said. 'I thought marriage was forbidden for devadasis?'

'Yes, it is. At first, we were terrified. We thought the goddess would slap us down, but when we saw that she did not show anger, we decided to stay together. It wasn't our fault, so how could she get angry? We went to live in Yarwal, Basappa's village. But Basappa is a Madiga [untouchable], and didn't have a penny to his name; my aunt was furious. When she came looking for us, we hid in the fields. We worked for several years as bonded labourers in Basappa's village, that's where Renuka was born. After my aunt died, I inherited the jagha, so we returned to Kalyana and I took over her duties.'

'And what about your daughter, Renuka?' I asked. 'Will she inherit the jagha?'

'Renuka will be married. We are looking for a boy for her,' interjected Basappa, Sumithra's husband, who had been listening quietly by the door.

FIVE

To be born human, endowed with consciousness,
is a rare gift won only by many deeds of merit.
But a woman's birth is beyond price,
for such beings have passion and sexual pleasure
at their most intense.
To reject this gift is a great sin:
is there any evil worse than destroying oneself? [7]

—Venkata Krishnappa Nayakudu, eighteenth-century
Nayaka court playwright

THE RAIN HAD STOPPED, but there was still a chill in the
morning air. Kalyana's lanes had been transformed into
muddy bogs, slowing our progress through the lanes.
The smell of charred wood lingered in the air. A group
of children gathered around me. Their clothes were
threadbare, but for the most part, they had scrubbed faces
and neatly combed hair. I flashed a smile and the children
giggled, revealing perfect rows of white teeth. A tall boy
stepped forward, offering his hand to be shaken, but when
I reached for it, he snatched it back in fright. Nervous
laughter rippled through the crowd. '*Ninna hesaru enu?*'
I asked. 'What is your name?' I repeated myself several

times before they realized I was attempting to speak their language. The children dispersed in peals of laughter.

Over twenty devadasis had joined us by the time Vani and I reached the temple, a whitewashed pavillion with blue trimming and an inner sanctum for the goddess. They hovered around us, a flurry of bright smiles and faded cotton saris, asking questions, laughing, and speculating on the reasons for our visit. With the exception of a few frail, toothless old women, they looked healthy. I had to remind myself that these women were untouchables, at the very bottom of the caste system, that droughts left them hungry on a regular basis, and that some of them were survivors of Mumbai's brothels.

Sumithra, who had called the meeting for us, soon arrived. She installed the jaglia near the inner sanctum and lit clumps of incense. Kassi, a woman with wispy grey hair and full lips, shooed the children away and invited us to sit in a circle. As soon as everyone was settled, the women quieted down. Vani explained to the women that we had come to learn about the devadasi system. She felt it was important for the women to hear my voice even though they didn't understand my words.

'I want to understand your lives so I can bring attention to your struggles, so that the government will do something to help you. People have written about the devadasi system, but I want to hear what you have to say for myself.' Television had not yet made its way to the village, so I was not sure they knew what a documentary was. 'We want to make a film so that people in my country can understand what your lives are like—so they can hear your voices for themselves.' I paused and made a point of making eye contact. 'How do you feel about being devadasis?'

The women studied me carefully as I spoke, and responded by asking me about my family. 'How many brothers and sisters do you have?' 'Are you married?' 'Do you have children?' They commented to each other on my responses, my looks, my clothes. Shoba, a fair-skinned girl, picked up my hand, examined a ring on my finger, and repeated the same question over and over again, ever louder, until Vani came to my rescue. 'Is this solid gold?' Shoba wanted to know. The women were trying to decide whether or not we were worthy of their trust. They had no formal education and with few exceptions did not know how to read or write; intuition was their only guide.

A few adolescent girls cradling small babies in their arms looked so young that I assumed the baby was a brother or sister. Only when a girl named Mariamma pulled out a breast to give suck did it occur to me that, although they hardly looked old enough to be menstruating, they were already mothers.

Vani began to question the women about their lives. 'How many people are in your family? How old were you when you were dedicated? Do you know Yellamma's dances? Who can recount her myth to me?' she asked. Sumithra nodded, and two women rose to get their instruments, a lute and a *chodiki*, a one-sided drum with cymbals and bells. Sumithra sang the lead, and the other women, the refrain. A few words in, Vani whispered to me that she was singing the myth of the goddess Yellamma. Sumithra's voice was clear and strong. Odours of burning wood and cow dung drifted over from the nearby houses. The passion, the pain, the longing in her voice left in its wake an awkward silence.

'Only we old women know how to dance,' said Kassi, an apologetic smile spreading over her face. 'The young generation, they know the songs, but they're not interested in learning the dance. They don't care for tradition.'

'But Rukmini knows how to dance,' Shoba suggested mischievously. The other women burst out laughing. A child was dispatched to fetch her, and presently she was gliding up the steps of the temple, the loose end of her pink sari trailing behind her. She had a high forehead, a narrow, elegant nose, and a swan-like neck. Her poise made her seem older than her fifteen years, but when she smiled, her face was transformed into that of a little girl.

'They are interested in dance; show them how you can dance,' said Kassi. Rukmini laughed and sat down between Vani and me, taking my arm into her lap. Brimming with warmth and curiosity, she examined us as the women explained to her why we had come. She seemed at once amused, perplexed and exhilarated by our presence. Her childlike smile was infectious. A child was sent for Rukmini's cousin, a tabla player.

'Taka-di-nak, taka-di-nak, taka-di-nak,' the young man pummelled the tabla. Rukmini started to move her shoulders to the beat. Shoba pulled her to her feet and pushed her towards the inner sanctum. Rukmini gestured to Vani and me, and, giggling, protested that she could not possibly dance in front of 'important people'. The women laughed and clapped their hands, but Rukmini flopped down onto the floor again, next to her aunt, Ella, grasping her arm for protection. She seemed torn between the desire to dance, and the fear that it was not quite proper to perform this dance that she had undoubtedly learned in a brothel, for ladies from 'God knows where', as she referred to my country. Her friends chided and cajoled her. With embarrassed laughter, she insisted that she could not possibly go through with it. Again, Rukmini was pulled to her feet. Her cousin launched into song, his voice undulating over the beat of the tabla.

Rukmini started to move. Although only a young girl, she was aware of—and at ease with—her charms: that sexy, fresh playfulness unique to adolescent girls. Clapping her hands, she thrust one hip forward and then the other. She tilted her head to the side, letting her hair fall over her shoulder. Drawing her hands to her face, she screened her eyes with her fingers then peeped through them. Placing her hands on her hips, she pursed her lips and nodded in assent. Her hands now moved lightly over the contours of her body. Stamping her right heel into the ground, she turned in a circle. The tempo quickened and her body pulsed; her fingers danced around her eyes. Vani leaned over and whispered to me that the dance was about a woman waiting for her lover.

Suddenly, Rukmini stood straight and still. Her imaginary lover had appeared. She looked at him, then dropped her eyes to the ground, where they remained until, slowly, longingly, she lifted her gaze to his face. Her smile was at once timid and alluring. Quivering in anticipation of his touch, she touched her fingers to her lips.

The dance made me think of the *Gita Govinda*, a mystical poem based on the myth of Krishna's love affair with the cowherdess, Radha. Devadasis had enacted this poem for centuries in temples across south India. But then Vani told me that Rukmini's dance was a number from a Bollywood blockbuster. *The names and places may have changed*, I mused, *but the theme remains the same.*

Ella reached over and pressed my hand. 'Rukmini is talented enough to dance in films,' she said.

*

Rukmini leaned over the crumbling wall of Sumithra's verandah to watch Renuka and me play jacks. Vani and I exchanged looks. Over the past few days, she had been avoiding us. I did my best not to show too much interest for fear of scaring her away. 'Maybe she's decided to come out of hiding,' Vani murmured, as usual, speaking my thoughts. I pretended not to see her and continued with the game. Instead of small iron crosses and a ball, we were using pebbles. I made my way through a full series without a fault. 'Hey, Catherine's good!' Rukmini announced to Sumithra's neighbours.

Vani and I were waiting for Sumithra to return from the river where she had gone to wash clothes. The room where Sumithra kept the jagha provided a degree of privacy rare in Kalyana village, and Vani and I now spent a lot of time there. Conversations about the goddess gave way to conversations about the women's lives: Sumithra was having a hard time finding a match for Renuka. Parents were afraid to marry their son to a girl who, according to custom, was destined to inherit her mother's jagha. Ganga's niece was taking sewing lessons, hoping to become a seamstress. Giddavva's cousin was planning to send her niece to Mumbai. Sagri's sister had died of hepatitis, leaving behind two small children. The women were aware of AIDS, and a few insisted that it was possible to get rid of it by passing it along to someone else.

Rukmini had something special, and I knew she would be strong on camera. Her delicate face and doe-like eyes seemed to betray all her emotions. Although high-spirited and affectionate, when not the focus of attention, she disappeared inside herself with a deep sigh and a blank stare. Beneath her cheerful vivacity lurked the shadow of great sadness. The contrast of her youthful innocence and her spells of melancholy both intrigued me and endeared her to me.

Rukmini lifted her elbows from the wall and came to sit next to Renuka. 'Okay, now it's my turn,' she said, confiscating the jacks from Renuka, and throwing them out on the flagstone. 'Oh, no, that was terrible!' She laughed. 'I haven't done this in years.' She picked them up and threw again. Sending the ball/stone into the air, she nimbly gathered the jacks one by one.

'I can't believe what I'm seeing,' Rukmini's aunt Ella shrieked as she walked by with a dish full of wet clothes on her head. 'Two grown women playing jacks! Don't you have anything better to do?' Sumithra rounded the corner behind her and handed her laundry to Renuka, who spread it out to dry on the stone walls of the terrace.

'Hasn't anybody offered these ladies tea?' Sumithra asked, dispatching a child to get some sugar. She went inside to put a pot of water on the hearth. Vani and I trailed her and sat down inside. Rukmini followed us in. I watched Sumithra stoke the flames. Seven more women entered. Among them were Ranavva, a thin woman in her thirties whom I had seen around, but never spoken to, and a young woman named Shanti. Shanti hesitated, looking for a place to sit—there wasn't much room left— and decided to squeeze into a place next to me. Sumithra motioned for me to move my bag out of the way.

'What do you mean by that?' Shanti exploded in anger. 'I wouldn't steal from her. Who do you think you are? I still have my honour . . .' Although devadasis were infamous pickpockets, I left my bag, with my camera and money in it, unattended all the time. Never had so much as one rupee gone missing. For a devadasi to steal from a guest would have been a stain on the honour of the whole community.

Sumithra sighed and shook her head. 'I just wanted her to make room so you could sit down.' All the women started talking at once, their voices bubbling gently, trying to soothe Shanti. She sat down beside me, grumbling.

Vani noticed that Shanti sprinkled her language with Hindi words. 'How is it that you speak Hindi?' she asked.

'I spent four years in Mumbai,' she replied, her mouth red from chewing betel. Her hair, pulled tightly into a bun, accentuated her round face and almond eyes. She had a café-au-lait complexion and wore a mustard-yellow sari.

'You must have been very young.'

'Her father sent her when she was twelve years old,'

interjected Rukmini, eager to talk. Shanti shot her a look, then leaned forward and sent a wad of red spit flying out the door. She pushed back a curl that had fallen into her face. She had large, masculine hands.

'Why did you come back?' asked Vani.

'I returned for the *rath yathra*, the pilgrimage to Saundatti, and while I was back, I met someone from our village. I returned about a year ago,' she said. Her slow, sensuous movements spoke of great assurance.

'Why did you go to Mumbai?'

'Dhanda, sex work,' she said provocatively, staring at Vani. She was hoping for a reaction, but got none. Most women are not so explicit. They say they worked in Mumbai as *sevakalu*, maidservants. 'I was so young, I didn't know anything,' she continued. 'My parents sent me. It was hard, but after a while, I got used to it. At first, I thought one day I would have a few girls working under me, but it didn't work that way. What my *gharwali* [Madam] did not eat, I sent to my parents. I only saved some nice clothes. At one point I was twenty thousand rupees [$500] in debt . . . I became disgusted with the business, and returned to the village. That's when I met my man. He helped me pay off my debt.'

'What did your parents do with the money you sent?' I asked.

'I have five brothers. They all went to school and three of them are married . . . Each wedding, with the cost of the bride, comes to over thirty thousand rupees.'

'Bride price—not the dowry system—is practised among untouchables in the Dalit community,' Vani explained.

'That means that the boy's family has to pay for the girl. It's better than the dowry system. At least it puts a positive value on women.'

A woman screeched in the lane, 'Shanti, Shanti, the baby is crying . . .'

'The baby,' said Shanti, getting up to go. Vani rose and accompanied her to the door, holding her elbow.

'Where do you live?' she asked. 'We'll come see you.' Shanti nodded and indicated a narrow path between two houses just across the lane from Sumithra's.

Rukmini now filled in for Shanti. 'She is lucky. The son of one of the wealthiest landowners in the village fell in love with her. He takes very good care of her. They have been blessed with a girl-child. Her man is always there at the house. He eats there, he sleeps there, he lives there, even though he's married, even though his wife gave birth a week ago!'

'And what about you, do you have a man?' I asked, smiling.

'Oh, yes. He is as handsome as a god and he loves me very much. If I go one day without seeing his face, I can't eat. We are like Layla and Majnun.'

'Layla and Majnun are the rough equivalent of Romeo and Juliet,' explained Vani.

'What nonsense do I have to listen to?' Ella cut in, getting up to go. 'That man is a scoundrel. He doesn't give her a paisa, not even for his son's medical expenses!'

'He doesn't deserve you, Ruki,' said Sumithra's neighbour. The women chided Rukmini, and shaking their heads in disapproval, got up to go.

SIX

The best pearl of all is the pearl called
Being-Awareness-Bliss
this divine pearl is strung on the thread of
spiritual knowledge
and you can possess it by becoming wise—
even the poorest devotee can easily afford it
once he's become enlightened. [8]

—Purandara Dasa, fifteenth/sixteenth-century
Bhakti saint who was honoured by
Krishna Deva Raya

'HEY, CATHERINE,' VANI CALLED to me from across the temple platform. We were at the Yellamma temple in Kalyana. Night was falling fast. 'Did you bring your recorder? Kassi's going to sing a ballad; why don't we record it?' Vani fluttered about, talking and laughing with the women, cajoling them into singing for us. A fat lady with a mischievous smile plucked at the strings of her lute. Devadasis who knew the words joined in. Sumithra took out her finger bells.

'Tai Yellamma, *udho, udho,*' Vani sang the refrain. An old woman started rocking back and forth. It looked like she had a bad case of hiccups or was hyperventilating. Vani leaned in my direction; she had to shout to make herself heard, 'It is a sign of the goddess. Yellamma has entered her.'

In Kalyana, there are two main locations where worship takes place: at Sumithra's house and at the Yellamma temple, on the edge of the holakeri, with sugarcane fields stretching out beyond. This temple, built two years ago with the help of government subsidies, was an attempt to undermine the tradition of the jagha, which requires that girls be dedicated so that they can carry around the shrine for its worshippers.

A lanky, bucktoothed, high-caste priest named Tamana was in charge of the Yellamma temple. His thinning hair and raggedy beard were salt-and-pepper grey. The door to the inner sanctum was open. The goddess, draped with garlands and cowry shells, was surrounded by latticework laden with burning wicks. Incense burned at her feet. Tamana intoned a mantra as a woman placed balls of rice and sweets on a banana leaf before the shrine. Two dozen women were present.

As soon as he had finished, five devadasis launched into song. Their plaintive lament rang out into the twilight. A woman reached over to turn up a kerosene lamp, and I noticed Rukmini sitting near the open end of the temple. She smiled at me and pointed to her sixteen-month-old son. He was not yet steady on his feet. I scooted over to Rukmini. Her son grabbed my arm and gave me an ear-to-ear smile. Shanti, sitting next to her with a small baby in her arms, eyed me suspiciously, then looked away. I asked Rukmini the name of her son in Hindi. I had picked up a few phrases in Delhi, and devadasis who had been to Mumbai spoke Hindi as well as Kannada. 'Gajanan,' she said, taking no notice of my Hindi, but Shanti whipped her head around and stared me down. Perhaps my Hindi fed the rumour that we had connections to brothels in Mumbai, and were recruiting for them.

'Show me the dances!' Vani insisted to Kassi.

'We know only one dance: the goddess's dance.'

'Teach me,' said Vani, pulling Kassi to her feet.

'I'm too old for this,' Kassi said, laughing. Vani pleaded.

'You go like this,' said Kassi, leaning to the side and tilting her head. Making sweeping motions with her hands, she moved in a circle. 'You see, we dance like this—help me show them, you lazy good-for-nothings!' she said, slapping the backs of some of the older devadasis. Laughing and struggling to their feet, they complained that they were too old for such antics. With a three-step sideways movement accompanied by an undulation of the body and a sweeping movement of the hands, they danced in a circle. The children skipped around gleefully.

Suddenly a warning cry rang out: 'It's Kalyanappa! Kalyanappa is coming . . .'

A hush fell over the crowd. The women dropped into squatting position and scuttled towards the edge of the temple platform. The high-caste villager in his starched white clothes made his way up the steps, walking stick in hand. The older women seemed to cower before him. They pulled their pallus over their heads, covered their mouths and averted their gazes in deference. Rukmini and her friend went through the motions but their attitude was markedly different. Rather than keeping their eyes glued to the ground in fear, they stared, nonplussed, into the middle distance, tingeing the ritual of submission with defiance. Sumithra reached into the inner sanctum of the temple and drew out a stool. Kalyanappa accepted the seat and gestured for the women to stop making a fuss.

'My name is Kalyanappa Mantur; I am the village chief,' he said, turning to Vani and me. With his sculpted, almost feminine face, and twinkling, thoughtful eyes, he seemed young, despite his white hair. 'I have noticed that you have been coming to our village and would like to welcome you . . . are you working for a government agency?'

Vani introduced herself and explained that I had been sent to make a documentary about devadasis. 'There is concern about the devadasi system. Some measures have been taken, but they have not been successful. We are trying to understand why.'

'Yes,' agreed Kalyanappa. 'The ban on dedication has had no effect. Since my youth, there has been no change. The women are poor, their children are hungry, and they do dhanda.' His tone was matter-of-fact. 'Some years ago a women's group came, there was talk of starting an association to help, but they never came back. Women's groups are there at the Gudda, the temple in Saundatti. They try to persuade the women not to dedicate.'

'What is the population of the village?' Vani asked.

'There are five thousand people living in the ooru, the upper-caste village. And over two thousand in the holakeri, the untouchable hamlet.' Although to the uninitiated observer the two villages seem to be one and the same, residents insist that they are separate. In the ooru, most of the houses have windows and are finished with a plaster whitewash and blue trimming. The wealthier homes have intricately carved wooden doorways. Buffaloes, oxen and goats are kept in the large interior courtyards. Most of the households have electricity and running water. In the holakeri, the minuscule houses are rarely finished with whitewash. Only a handful have electricity—a bare bulb dangling from the ceiling—and none have running water. Electricity is provided for only a few hours a day.

'And what about the school?' asked Vani. Vani and I had visited the school, but since the summer vacations were on, the teacher was away.

'The school is our main priority right now. There are only two rooms—it's not enough. We have asked the government for another teacher, and we're raising money for a new building with a classroom for each grade.'

'What is the percentage of children from the holakeri?' asked Vani.

'Education has a price. As soon as the children from poor families are of an age to earn in the fields, they drop out and go to work . . . Change is coming, slowly but surely.'

Kalyanappa then turned his attention to me. He asked if I flew on an airplane to reach Karnataka. Occasionally he sees them flying overhead. We chatted about planes and trains. He had been to Bangalore once. He wished us well with our work and made us promise to come to his house for tea the next day. Before taking leave, he turned to discuss some village matters with Ganga, who played the lute. He spoke to her respectfully; they laughed about something or other. I was astonished. This was a far cry from the other, albeit few, encounters I had had with high-caste landlords in these parts. Landlords had generally been suspicious. Not once had we been welcomed. This was the first agreeable contact we had had with an upper-caste villager. He seemed genuinely concerned about the women and sincere in his welcome. After he left, the women assured us that he was a good man.

'He does not drink,' said Kassi, nodding in appreciation.

'Yes,' said Ganga, the woman with the lute. 'He is the *only* man in Kalyana who does not drink!' The women roared with laughter.

*

After dinner that night, Vani and I sat on the verandah listening to the rainfall through the giant fig tree. I could not get over how the older women cowered before Kalyanappa. They seemed ashamed of their own polluting presence. I was baffled by caste. Why was it not simply rejected as an exploitative sham? It occurred to me that I didn't know Vani's caste.

'My caste is irrelevant,' she said sharply. 'If everyone agreed not to reveal his or her caste, there would be no caste problem. That's why my husband and I use only the first letter of our family name, "D", as a last name—so no one will know our caste. Caste is *the* great obstacle facing Hindu society today. It is *the* tragedy of modern India!' I realized that Vani had been just as disturbed as I was by the scene we had witnessed. After a long silence, she said,

'*Shakti*. These women have so much Shakti. Do you know what that is? Shakti is strength, vitality and wisdom . . . Shakti is divine feminine energy!'

Only years later did Vani confide in me that she came from a tradition-bound upper-caste family and had been raised strictly according to caste rules. While doing her PhD in education, she had participated in a literacy campaign in northern Karnataka and for the first time encountered rural low-caste and untouchable people, among them devadasis. 'My world was turned upside down,' she said. 'I realized that everything I had been taught was nonsense.' Although she finished her degree in education, she decided to commit herself to the battle for social and economic change.

In the past, low-caste people and untouchables did not have access to education. They were officially barred from learning to read and write. They were considered sub-human and were classified as animals. Untouchables were not only untouchable, but also unseeable and unapproachable. Considering these rules, it is not surprising that untouchables—and their problems— have remained largely invisible to upper-caste people. Conveniently, however, when untouchable girls become devadasis, in theory at least, they lose their caste as well as their polluting effect.

Although the Indian government officially abolished caste in 1950, in rural villages such as Kalyana, caste is a visible dimension of everyday life. Untouchables do not approach their superiors, enter their houses, or sit on the same level—they always remain below. In many villages, they still do not have access to the village well. Certain high-caste people, even some educated in England and America, admit, somewhat shamefacedly, to feel nausea in their presence.

The pain and humiliation of the first experiences of 'untouchability' create wounds that run deep. Many untouchables have internalized caste values and see themselves as impure. They accept their lot in the belief that they are paying for misdeeds committed in a previous life, and hope that by fulfilling their dharma they will improve their station in their next life. Increasingly, however, the younger generations are channelling their pain into anger and protest. They have renamed themselves 'Dalits', meaning, 'the Oppressed' or 'the Crushed Ones'. Militant Dalit movements have sprung up throughout India. In the devadasi community, however, men have directed their anger not only at the high castes, but also at their devadasi mothers and sisters, whom they resent for catering to high-caste males. Thus, devadasi women, who have engaged in sex work to feed and educate their children, sometimes find themselves disowned later in life.

SEVEN

'Those born as women see much grief,
but I'll not look at it,'
says the Sun and he hides himself;
our Dark Lord, with red lips and great eyes,
who once measured this earth,
he too will not come . . .
So who will save this long life of mine
that finds no end at all?[9]

—Nammalvar

ON OUR WAY INTO the village the next day, an old man walking along the road hailed us down: tragedy had struck. Arjun, the eldest son of a prominent village elder, had been killed in a scooter accident. The night before, riding home after a bout of drinking in a nearby town, he and two friends had rammed their scooter into the back of a bullock cart. The two passengers escaped with injuries, but Arjun was killed. The village was in mourning.

'I think the best thing would be for you to return home,' said the old man gravely.

'Perhaps we should pay our respects to the family?' asked Vani.

The man considered her suggestion, and agreed. 'Yes,' he said. 'You can go.'

The family lived in a large house down an impressive tree-lined alley half a mile from the village. The men sat outside in the stark light of the whitewashed walls in a shroud of silence. They acknowledged our presence, but did not greet us. An old man gestured for Vani and me to enter the house.

As we pushed open the door, we were overcome by the wailing of twenty women. The dark mud floors and windowless walls absorbed what shafts of light came through the roof. The front room, an enclosed verandah and threshing floor, extended the entire length of the house. It took our eyes a moment to adjust. On the verandah sat a row of old women; off to the left, some younger women sat in a circle around a newborn in a carved wooden crib hanging from a beam. Not knowing local customs, I followed Vani's example. First, she touched the ground before the feet of the older women. They took our hands, spoke to us and gestured. I didn't dare ask Vani to translate for fear of interrupting. Their utterances seemed a sort of ritual chant.

After some time, Vani led me to the circle of younger women. At the centre were Arjun's wife and newborn son. It was difficult not to be affected by the rawness of his widow's grief and anguished lamenting. She gestured angrily as she spoke. Vani whispered to me that she was recounting in detail everything her husband did the last time she saw him: 'He sat just over here. He went to the kitchen and took some biscuits. He promised to take me to town to see a film . . .' Although she was not even eighteen, this woman would never be allowed to marry again. She would be excluded from all joyous occasions in the community. She was fortunate, though, in that Arjun was her cousin. Cross-cousin marriage, a south Indian tradition, meant that she had blood relatives in the village. Widowhood in India can mean social death. The widow usually remains in the in-laws' family but is seen as a burden, an unwanted reminder of the lost and cherished son. If the widow has the misfortune of having borne a girl, her plight is that much more difficult.

After half an hour or so, we emerged into the sunlight, dazed and blinking. Vani suggested we pay a visit to the devadasi women; Iqbal dropped us in the holakeri. We were met by a group of women with anxious, drawn faces. The news of Arjun's death had hit hard. We were escorted to Shanti's house and informed that he had been her '*joolwa* husband', her lover and her keeper. We found her on the patio, swooning against the wall of her house, surrounded by her mother and friends. Sobs welled up from deep inside her, and between gasps for air came torrents of incredulous words.

'How could this happen? What am I going to do now? How am I going to feed my children?' Tears streamed down her cheeks. 'Just yesterday, he was here taking food in my house. He played with his daughter, he sang to her, he held her tight. What am I going to do? How can I go on living? If it were not for the fact that I'm carrying his seed in my stomach, I would take my own life right here and now.'

'You're pregnant?' asked Vani.

'Yes . . . yes, I'm pregnant!' said Shanti, crumpling against the wall of her house. 'Were it not for that, I would have already taken my life.'

Rukmini emerged from the narrow path, sidled up next to Shanti, and took her arm. 'Now, now, you mustn't say things like that,' she said. 'Look at your daughter's face, and have faith in your future.' Vani and I sat against the wall near Shanti. Her sobs and bitter lamenting gradually subsided only to begin again.

'What will happen to her now?' I whispered to Vani.

'She'll probably have to go back to sex work.'

'But she's pregnant!'

'I doubt that she put anything aside. His family won't help her. Maybe her brothers or her parents will, if they can.'

Shanti turned to Vani and said, 'He was a great man. He opposed the caste system. He called it an unjust system, a system by which the lower castes were exploited. And he practised what he preached: he lived with me and ate my food. He drank from the same cup as me! Some say that we offended the gods. I shouldn't have let him do all that . . . after my daughter was born, I was very weak. He fed me, and nursed me back to life . . . how can this have happened? How can I go on living?'

We listened to Shanti, shook our heads and stared at the ground. The extent of the tragedy was difficult to absorb. I couldn't think of anything to say. Words seemed inappropriate. After half an hour, Vani unhooked her arm from Shanti's and said, 'We'll come back tomorrow.'

'You have your car! Please, you must take me to the

site of the accident!' Shanti pleaded. 'I want to lay my eyes on him one last time.'

'Yes,' said Vani. 'Come. We'll take you.'

We came to a stop fifteen miles along a potholed ribbon of blacktop. Flat fields spread out in every direction. A group of mourners stood by the side of the road in silence. Shanti joined them. The indifferent shrubs bore no trace of the tragedy. The body had already been removed.

∗

Vani and I decided to give Shanti four thousand rupees— more than enough for her baby and her for a year. I wrapped the hundred-rupee notes around a one-rupee coin. The extra rupee, Vani explained, transformed the money into a gift, making it more acceptable. 'If you can, put it into the baby's hand,' said Vani. 'She's very proud; I don't want her to take offence.'

We found Shanti sitting with Rukmini on her patio. Several days had gone by and the initial shock had passed. Slouched against the wall, arms limp in her lap, face long and slack, her uncovered legs stretched out before her. She followed us with her gaze, and with great effort, pulled her feet beneath her only after Vani and I had sat down. Nobody said anything. Vani took Shanti's arm in her hands. 'Things will improve,' she said. 'Be strong.' Gently rubbing Shanti's forearm, she said to me, 'I wonder if she has taken something.'

'What do you mean?' I asked.

'Cough syrup or some sort of tonic to deaden the senses.

It's quite common among devadasis. Who could blame her?'

Shanti's house was accessed by a small path and surrounded on three sides by blind walls, affording her patio privacy. Only her parents' house, kitty-corner to Shanti's, looked onto it. All was still and quiet. At length we heard some banging next door. A metal pot clanged and kitchenware crashed to the ground, a man swore loudly and then came stumbling out of the house. It was Shanti's father, his eyes blood-red. He was so drunk he could hardly walk. He staggered across the patio, and then, seeing Vani and me, straightened up, laughed, and pointed a finger at Shanti. 'What good is love if that's what it does to you?' he demanded to know, before stumbling away. It was midday.

Shanti didn't react. Rukmini remarked, 'Shanti's grandmother was a powerful gharwali in Mumbai. Her son is rich, but he pours it all straight down his throat.'

'Shush,' Shanti managed to say.

The baby gurgled inside the house, then started to cry. Rukmini rose to get her, and I reached into my bag for the wad of notes I had prepared. I looked at Vani, and she said, 'Go ahead.' I pressed them into Shanti's hand. Shanti snapped out of her torpor and tucked the wad into her sari blouse. Grabbing my hand, she squeezed it between hers. Her lips quivered, and her eyes brimmed with tears.

'I don't want this to get out. Promise me—not a word to anyone,' said Vani sternly.

Shanti closed her eyes and nodded, forcing the tears back. She leaned forward, bowing her head and pressing the ground before Vani and me with her hands.

EIGHT

Demand cash! If he desires credit, shut him out and
lock the door, oh girls.
The old mother only states our caste tradition;
so it is immaterial whether the customer is Aiyyan or
Appan of even the six-faced Velan.
Demand five gold coins for cosmetics and another five
gold coins for betel leaves and betel nuts.[10]

—Anonymous medieval padam from Tirutani Temple

IT HAD POURED ALL night long and the lanes of the holakeri
were once again transformed into muddy bogs. The
slippery, clay-like mud clung to my thongs as I tried to
glide over the sludge without landing on my bottom.
Twelve-year-old green-eyed Bala, my self-appointed escort,
appeared, offering a shoulder for support.

'This way,' he said.

There was a distant rumble; darkness closed in upon us.
Black shrouds of rain raced across the fields. A big, thick
drop smacked me in the forehead. I slipped my pallu over
my head, gripped Bala's shoulder, and walked as fast as
I dared. The mud sucked off one of my thongs, and as I
leaned over to reclaim it, the rain let loose, thudding into

my bare ribcage, soaking me in a matter of seconds.

Two stout women sitting under the eaves of a house were waiting for Vani and me. The younger woman, Ganga, had requested through a messenger that we pay her a visit. She represented the holakeri in the village assembly. I recognized her mischievous smile. She had played the lute at the puja in the temple and laughed with Kalyanappa, the village elder. In daylight, her skin looked tough and leathery. The other woman seemed to be in her late fifties. She wore a brightly coloured sari, an embroidered shawl, and an abundance of gold jewellery. Her hair and skin had been oiled. Both women had the red and white beads of their dedication ceremonies woven into their necklaces.

'My name is Ganga, I represent the holakeri in the grampanchayat, and this is Ambavva, from Vijapur,' she said. Ambavva tilted her head and smirked, revealing two rows of stubby teeth reddened by betel nut. The rain began to ease.

'Look at Ambavva's shawl and clothes,' Vani said to me. 'She has enough money for perfume and oil. She has more money than most women in these parts. And she's flaunting it. Maybe she's recruiting here for a brothel.'

'So I hear you want to know about our village,' said Ganga. 'Women like you came a few years ago. They said they were going to help us, but never came back. Tell me, what do you want to know?'

'This lady has come from very far away to learn about our ways. Can you tell her, is it better to be a day labourer or a bonded labourer?' Vani asked.

'Families bonded to a landlord have work all year

round, sweeping the yard, cleaning the stable, pounding rice and winnowing lentils,' said Ganga, chewing betel as she spoke and drawing out her words. 'When you are a serf, you will not starve and your landlord will lend you money if there's a wedding or a funeral. But the government says there's to be no more bonded labour—we should all work as day labourers. The wages are higher, but there's no security in it.'

'That's right,' cut in Ambavva, 'when there's a drought, you starve. If you want to help, tell the government to give us land. With even just a small strip of land to cultivate, we could make do. Then we would have enough to feed our children and maybe even buy a goat, but now the high castes are afraid to rent to us because they think we will claim the land for ourselves. They don't want us to improve our condition, sister, because then we might refuse to work their land for twenty-five rupees a day [sixty cents]. It's back-breaking work . . .'

'Tell us, Ambavva, when did you ever work in a field?' asked Ranavva, whom I knew from Sumithra's house, taking a seat next to Ganga.

'As soon as I could walk, I was in the fields,' replied Ambavva, indignant.

'Yeah, on your back!' said Ranavva, making a rhythmic movement with her arms. The women laughed so hard, tears ran down their cheeks.

Ranavva had a glint in her eye. She was warm and talkative, and always seemed to be laughing. 'Look at you,' she said to me, examining my pallu, 'no more pins. You're an Indian woman now!' I had stopped using pins because they were making small tears in Vani's blouses.

'Look,' said Ranavva. 'This is how we working women wear our saris.' She took my pallu, wrapped it around my torso, and tucked it into the front of the sari. 'There, now it won't get in the way.'

'It's comfortable,' I said, smiling, embarrassed by Ranavva's attentions. I pushed a strand of hair out of my face, smearing my bindi.

'Ahhh!' cried Ranavva. '*Thangi*, what are we going to do with you?' She pulled a handkerchief from her blouse and wiped the smeared part away, making the bindi round again.

Vani leaned over and whispered to me, 'She called you "thangi". That means little sister. That's *very* good. You must call her "*akka*" now, older sister. You have been officially adopted.'

'How many devadasis are there in this village?' I asked.

'About a hundred,' said Ganga.

'How many families have devadasis?'

'Every family in the holakeri has at least one devadasi,' said a tall, beautiful woman who had come up behind me. She sounded surprised by the stupidity of the question. 'At least a niece or a cousin. How can we survive otherwise? Landlords give jobs in the fields and loans in times of drought to the families of the devadasis they are involved with. In hard times, having a devadasi in the family is essential. We depend on the upper castes for our survival.'

Ranavva reached out and drew Chandra towards her, making her sit down.

'Devadasis are Madiga [untouchables] but upper-caste

men flock to them? How does that work?' I asked.

'When we are dedicated, we lose our caste,' said Ganga, proudly. 'We are no longer untouchable.'

'Yeah, sure,' Ranavva said, laughing. 'I'll tell you how it works: during the day, if they accidentally brush up against us, they go home and take a bath, but, once night falls, they can't wait to get their hands on us.'

Ganga's stoop was a place of congregation, and Vani and I started to spend more time there. It was a different crowd from the one at Sumithra's. These devadasis had lives akin to those of commercial prostitutes. They did not care much for the goddess and only celebrated her on festival days. In a society obsessed with social hierarchy, they were at the bottom of the ladder. While Sumithra had status as a holy woman, and Ganga and Ranavva as concubines, most devadasis were reviled as 'untouchable prostitutes'. Only during festivals or religious ceremonies were they temporarily resurrected to their status as 'divine vessels' of Yellamma. They snorted at those who judged them, but they were also sensitive to those judgements.

'Of the hundred or so devadasis in Kalyana, only four have longstanding relationships—more than ten years—with high-caste landlords. Some have a series of joolwa husbands, but increasingly, we are obliged to take many men,' said Chandra. 'As we only earn when we are young and beautiful, we have to work hard while we can, and save.'

'By working hard, you mean going to Mumbai?' asked Vani.

'By working hard, I mean juggling many men.'

'But Kalyana is so isolated, where do the men come from?' asked Vani.

'There are men from this village, or from neighbouring villages. We also find clients in the market town: the movie theatre, the bus stop, there are hotels in town where you can rent a room . . . once the men get to know us, they come to the village.'

'What are they like?' I asked.

'Mostly, they are disgusting,' said Chandra. 'They come drunk, they're ugly and smelly. We are not supposed to send men away, but sometimes we do. We tell them to go wash and put on clean clothes and come back. It's all a matter of how desperate you are. If you are earning well, you can afford to send a man away, but if not, well, you're stuck with him.'

'But sometimes women fall for their man, like Rukmini,' I said.

'There will always be one man, there's no doubt about that,' said Ranavva. 'But it's better to make your mind hard. If you let your guard down, you will get taken advantage of. When we are young we are terrified of men, but as time passes, we get used to them, to their different natures, coming and going. We learn to remember the good ones and push the bad ones out of our minds. But still it's better not to fall in love—that always ends badly. It's a fish-eat-fish world.'

'Why were you dedicated, Ganga?' I asked.

'I am the oldest of five children,' said Ganga. 'When my mother was sick—near death—my father promised to dedicate me if the goddess spared her life. My mother lived, and I was dedicated a few months after reaching puberty.'

'Do you remember your dedication ceremony?'

'How could I forget? It is seared into my mind. Three days before the rath yathra [the pilgrimage to the Muthaidu Hunimae festival at Saundatti Temple; the festival during which Yellamma's husband is resurrected and Yellamma regains her married status] they shut me inside the house and stuffed me with sweets. I was scrubbed with turmeric and bathed in neem water. I was given my first sari. When we left for the temple, they took a brass pot and filled it with water from the village well and decorated it with flowers. I led the procession to the temple that year. This was long before dedications were made illegal! I had to walk the whole way, carrying the pot of water on my head. My arms and legs ached. I was terrified. I had no idea what was happening. No one said a thing to me. It was a big mystery.

'After three days we reached the *jogula bhavi*, the bathing ghat at the foot of the Saundatti Temple. I was made to wear a dress made of neem branches. I had to run up the hill with the pot of water on my head, wearing just a few sprigs of neem! We circled the temple three times, then a priest took us before the goddess. They laid down a blanket and put a pot on each corner, decorating them with flowers, bananas, coconut, betel and jaggery. I was told to sit in the middle. Offerings were made and grains were thrown over my head. A thread was wound around me. The priest chanted and then told me about my duties. I was supposed to say yes, but I was so terrified, I couldn't even bring myself to nod. He tied a string of red and white beads around my neck, and blessed my pot of water, telling me to worship it as the goddess.'

'What did he say about your duties?'

'It was so long ago, I don't remember. The usual things, I suppose.'

'What are "the usual things"?' asked Vani.

'The most important is that you cannot claim to be the wife of any one man. On Tuesdays and Fridays you must go begging with a *joga*, a begging bowl, in your hand and visit at least five upper-caste houses . . . what else . . . if you are hungry you shall not tell others, nor shall you ask for food. If you are beaten or abused, you shall not retaliate. You must provide shelter to strangers, and never tell untruths . . . you must never separate a nursing calf from its mother, and if you cross death, you must bathe.'

'Provide shelter to strangers? What does that mean?' I asked.

Vani gave me a sideways glance. 'At what age are girls dedicated?' she continued.

'For the first *pattam* [the tying of the beads before the goddess], the girl is usually between six and thirteen. But the second pattam [the night of the girl virgin] takes place after a girl's first menses,' said Chandra. 'Some landlords consider it a matter of prestige to deflower as many young girls as possible. In Mumbai, virgin devadasis fetch a high price. By deflowering a devadasi, a man can cure himself of disease. He can purify himself.'

'Do you believe that?' I asked.

Chandra shrugged. 'If the goddess wills it, then it is possible.'

'And what about AIDS?'

'It is said you can get rid of it by giving it to a client,' Ganga said. The other women nodded in agreement.

Vani squeezed my arm. 'My goodness. What am I hearing? You mustn't believe that. It's not true. There is no cure. You must protect yourselves.' Vani leaned forward, touching the arms of the women within her reach and looking them in the eye. 'Do you understand me? Protect yourselves—not even the goddess can cure AIDS.' Such a stern warning from Vani had its effect. The women sat silently, looking anxious. I doubted they had the power to oblige their clients to wear condoms.

'Ganga, how do you feel about being a devadasi?' I asked, changing the subject. Ganga looked blank. She didn't understand the question. Vani reframed it, 'Would you rather be a married woman or a devadasi?'

'Given the choice, I would rather be a married woman. There is no question about that. When you are a devadasi, anything can happen to you. One day everything is fine, the next, your life is destroyed. Look at Shanti! There's no security . . . a devadasi's life is full of pain. From the day they tie the beads, it starts. Many women fall to illness; many take their own lives. Devadasis do not live to an old age. Take a look around this village. How many old devadasis do you see? I pray to the gods every day for a child. How am I going to survive when I'm old? But then, I turn it over in my mind, and I think it is better if I have no children. If I had a boy he could look after me in my old age, but if I had a girl, what would happen to her?'

'Who was your first man?' I asked.

'A landlord from a village nearby. He noticed me on the rath yathra and made the arrangements with my parents. For the night of the girl-virgin, there was a big feast in the village . . . He took care of me for about a year, and then dropped me. I had three brothers and they worked in the fields, so I stayed in the village and took men as they came. My family didn't pressure me to take men. It must have been six or seven years later that my current joolwa husband noticed me.'

'Who is your joolwa husband?'

'But you know him, it's Tamana!' interrupted Ranavva. 'I have seen you there many times. The priest at the Yellamma temple. You were taking his picture only yesterday.' *Tamana,* I thought to myself in dismay. *That goofy temple priest.* He looked like a hard-drinking man.

'Ganga has been with Tamana for over twelve years now,' Ranavva informed us. 'He's so in love with her, he can barely stand to let her out of his sight! He used to be a priest at the Shiva temple in the ooru, but transferred here to the Yellamma temple just to be nearer to Ganga. Ganga is his goddess.' Ranavva bowed down before Ganga as if she were a divinity. Spinning around, she added, 'He follows Ganga wherever she goes—that is, as long as he is fit to walk!' The women could hardly contain their laughter.

'Is he married?' I asked.

'Yes,' replied Ranavva. 'But he has forgotten he has a wife! He lives here only!'

'Do you love him?' I asked Ganga.

Ganga laughed, then fell silent. Finally, she said, 'I've

had many men, but until Tamana came along, I trusted no one. He may not be handsome, but he is reliable and he has a good heart. He has good values.'

'Yes, he has good value all right, his family is very rich,' said Ranavva.

'And what about you, Ranavva?' I asked.

'My only love is my field and I must be getting there,' she said, reaching for her hoe.

Although Ranavva had refused to speak to us, many women had begun coming forward. Vani and I were sympathetic listeners, and the women had never had an opportunity to tell their stories before.

*

Beyond the Yellamma temple was a vast expanse of rolling hills, fields separated by thick, overgrown brush and wildflowers, and in the distance, forest. Untainted by telephone poles and roads, the landscape provided a glimpse of pre-modern India. Tamana's solitary whitewashed farmhouse stood at the base of a gently sloping hill. His fields were dotted with fruit trees and traversed by an irrigation canal; a solitary scarecrow provided a perch for some birds. Buffalo grazed on weeds in a fallow patch by the water. He insisted that we visit his house, which his father had built with his own hands. It was a twenty-minute walk from the village. Ganga accompanied us. The house was built in the shape of a cross and had doors on each end, providing it with ample light and ventilation. Tamana led Vani and me inside, but Ganga stopped abruptly at the doorstep—as an untouchable, she was not permitted to enter.

A group of women and a young child, a three-year-old, were sitting on the floor winnowing grains. Tamana pointed at one of the women and, omitting to greet her, said, 'That is my wife.' Although Tamana was at least forty-five, his wife looked twenty-five at most. Small and delicate with large eyes, she was far more attractive than Ganga.

She gaped at us, open-mouthed, then snapped into action, scurrying to the kitchen to prepare tea. Vani and I followed her while Tamana gave instructions to the other women. 'Do you live out here?' Vani asked Tamana's wife.

'No. I stay in the house in the village . . . sometimes during the harvest season we sleep here.' Tamana's wife hesitated, and then abruptly changed the subject, 'Madam, you are educated people. You must use your influence with my husband. He is neglecting his fields and his duties . . .' Tamana now passed through the kitchen, carrying his daughter in his arms, and went outside, looking for Ganga. His wife fell silent, then said, 'Our role as women is to suffer.'

Through the doorway, I saw Tamana place his daughter in Ganga's arms. I followed them outside to photograph them. After dutifully counting to three and smiling, the child called for her mother. Tamana's wife appeared at the door but didn't want to come too close to Ganga. The tension was intolerable; Tamana strode away.

'Why have you called me?' The child's mother asked. 'Where has your father gone?'

Still in Ganga's arms, the girl replied, 'He has gone to the whore's street.'

NINE

The rich will make temples for Shiva.
What shall I, a poor man, do?
My legs are pillars,
the body the shrine,
the head a cupola of gold.
Listen, O Lord Kudal Sangama-deva [Shiva],
Things standing shall fall, but the moving ever shall stay.[11]

—Basavanna, twelfth-century Bhakti saint

IN HALAMID'S BUSTLING DINER, where Vani and I had breakfast every morning, no one ever asked us to move to the curtained-off 'family' booth in the back. We sat by the window, overlooking the main street. It was Tuesday, market day. Thousands of people were in town; the crowds swarmed this way and that, parting for buffalo carts, then coming together again. Devadasis plied the crowds with their begging bowls. An occasional vehicle ploughed through, beeping continuously to no effect.

The waiter placed two plates of steaming *uppittu* on our table. Uppittu looks like cream of wheat, only instead of brown sugar, it is laced with cumin, cardamom and finely chopped coriander. I cracked open the mound with my spoon to cool it, releasing the smell of delicately balanced spices. As Vani and I sipped our coffee and watched the crowds, I noticed Ganga and Ranavva with huge bundles balanced on their heads working their way towards our Ambassador, parked out front. They waited for us next to the car.

Once done with breakfast, we went to meet them. 'We did our shopping early this morning so we could get a ride back with you,' said Ganga, smiling. I opened the door for them, and she and Ranavva slid in.

'How grand,' said Ranavva, leaning back in her seat. 'We have a chauffeur. Where shall we go? To the Gudda [the temple in Saundatti], maybe?' Ganga and Ranavva giggled like schoolgirls; they were thrilled to be in our car. They pleaded with us to ask the driver to take us right up to their houses so everyone could see them. Chandra and the other women in the lane came to their doorsteps to look on. Ranavva leaned out the window and called to her 'mothers'.

Ranavva shared her two-room house with two women in their fifties, both of whom she called 'mother'. She refused to tell me which one had given birth to her. 'They are both my mothers,' she said. They came to the door and insisted we come inside for tea. The women were always inviting us to eat and drink in their houses, and seemed to be fascinated by the ease with which we accepted. By eating their food, Vani and I gave proof of our sincerity and respect.

Vani sat by the hearth. Mother number one served us tea. 'Aaamu,' I repeated after Ranavva for the third time in a row. Ranavva had taken it upon herself to teach me Kannada. I couldn't get the myriad 'a' vowels right. Ranavva laughed. Two of the neighbour's children peeked around the door. Pulling candy out of my bag, I offered it to them with my left hand.

'Thangi! You know better than that!' Ranavva laughed. She took back the candy, pressed it into my right hand and pushed my arm towards them. 'This is the way you give here.'

I had a particular affection for Ranavva. Although Ganga was the elected official, Ranavva often answered questions on her behalf. She was always the first to grasp my more complicated questions. Her irreverent, witty banter kept the conversation interesting. 'You don't want to hear about my life,' she always said in answer to my questions. 'I live quietly. God has not blessed me with children. I don't have little ones to look after, so I work in the fields. You never know what the future brings. It's better to work while you still can and save.'

'You speak Hindi,' said Vani. 'Did you spend time in Mumbai?'

Ranavva paused for a moment. I could see her deliberating. Our questions weighed upon her, but she liked us and wanted to please. Devadasis were not supposed to complain; it was against their ethic. 'Go ahead,' she said. 'You can take out your contraption for catching voices.'

'I was in Pune, near Mumbai, for some years,' she said. 'When I was growing up, we lived in complete and utter poverty. Do you understand what that means? My mother and I worked in the fields and, between the two of us, we brought home one rupee a day. Just one rupee!' Ranavva laughed. 'My mother would buy cornmeal at the shop and make a roti [flat bread] for dinner—we would eat half and keep the rest for the morning. I had only one set of clothing. Washing them was such a problem. Until they dried, I had nothing to wear!' she chuckled, then added on a serious note, 'My mother dedicated me when I was six or seven, and when I was old enough, I was given to a landlord for fifty rupees and a sari. He didn't come back, and after that the business started.'

Ranavva lowered her voice, as if someone might overhear. 'The first year was terrible for me. I cried all the time and kept running away. I couldn't take more than one man a day. I was terrified of men and hated even being touched by them, but I made five, ten and sometimes even twenty rupees. After a while I got used to it. And then I went to Pune.' Ranavva paused and shook her head. 'We don't usually talk about these things. I have never talked about all this before. My life has been so full of sorrow; I can't bear to think about it. My name, Ranavva, means only pain to me. *Dukha*, do you know what that word means? Sorrow. Sorrow, pain, suffering . . . this is what our lives are about . . . I haven't allowed my brother to name any of his children after me; it could only bring hardship. To be born a girl is dukha . . .'

'But things are better now,' interjected Vani.

'I have been with my man for fourteen years now. Since he came into my life, I have everything I need. He gave me a small patch of land. He makes sure I always have food to eat and clothes to wear. He brings me firewood. My brother works hard . . . we are never hungry.' Ranavva's pain was still so raw after all these years. By asking questions about her past, I felt as if I had poured salt in her wounds. Ranavva looked away, and I stared at the floor in shame.

*

Lagoli's holakeri mushroomed out from underneath the ruins of a massive Shiva temple, over seven hundred years old. The vimana, the tower over the inner sanctum, was intact. Although the countryside was littered with ruins of medieval temples, few were this spectacular.

Ranavva had insisted upon taking us to this village, thirty miles north, where her aunt Thimmavva was the head devadasi. We found Thimmavva lounging on a charpai on her patio. According to Ranavva, she and her troupe were famous in the region for their traditional repertoire. They were called far and wide to perform rituals, and a musicologist from Dharwad had recorded their songs. A beautiful woman in her fifties, Thimmavva had a plump moon-like face with silky caramel skin. After sending her daughter-in-law off with two claps to prepare tea, she greeted us warmly. Her two-room house had been whitewashed and decorated with toran door hangings. 'Lagoli was the birthplace of Gopala Dasa [A Bhakti saint],' she announced after hearing about our project. Judging from what I had seen, I believed her.

*

Basavanna, an extraordinary twelfth-century poet-saint and reformer, who founded a community based on egalitarian ideals, was born not far away. His Vachanas, some of which I have used as chapter headings, are poems offered to the gods as worship. They are breathtaking not only for their simple elegance and modernity, but for their profound, passionate humanism. In his poems, I discovered a man whose values, though he lived in India *nine hundred years ago*, were identical to my own. Basavanna fought for human rights. He advocated gender equality, widow-remarriage, abolition of caste, and eradication of the devadasi system. His monotheistic conception of God was as an impersonal and supernatural power, larger than the universe itself, and yet within every living thing. Spirituality, for Basavanna, was to be derived from personal conduct, contributing to society, and generosity of spirit. He saw investment in one's work, whatever that work may be, as a form of worship.

Brahmin by birth, Basavanna reportedly tore off his sacred thread as a young boy. In his poems, he ridiculed Brahmin purity, rituals and temples. Bijala, a twelfth-century king, made Basavanna minister and gave him the title, 'Treasurer of the Lord's Love'. Basavanna founded a 'spiritual parliament' called the Anubhava Mantapa where followers from across south India met for dialogue and communion. Representatives in his parliament, men and women alike, were drawn from all castes. During his lifetime, Basavanna's followers numbered over two hundred thousand. Their ranks swelled in the centuries following his death, and even today Lingayates, as they are known, are numerous. The upper castes in Kalyana, and in Thimmavva's village, claim to be Lingayates, but they have forgotten Basavanna's original creed and live like other caste-abiding Hindus.

'When and why was the Shiva temple abandoned? Does anybody have any memory of it being in use? Did your ancestors dance there?' I asked. Glancing over my shoulder at the looming temple, I was reminded that, in medieval times, devadasis were allocated houses in streets adjacent to the temple, precisely where the devadasis of Lagoli lived today. I wondered if they were descendants of those who had danced in the temple hundreds of years ago. Yellamma had been a popular goddess in the region since the eleventh century. I wondered how many generations of girls had been sacrificed to her.

Thimmavva laughed. 'So many questions we don't have the answers to. All I can say is this: as long as anyone can remember, we have been worshipping at the Yellamma temple in the ooru. 'Come, I see you can't take your eyes off that old temple. Let's go take a look. A flame still burns for Shiva in the inner sanctum.'

As we climbed the steps, Ranavva reminded me to take off my shoes. Although in ruins, it was still considered sacred ground. The vast, elevated platform was made of enormous stone slabs. Facing the god's sanctuary was a hall of worship, known as a *mandapa*, with a circular stone before the inner sanctum where devadasis performed dance-worship. The stone pillars and slabs that once formed the roof now lay pell-mell to the side of the temple, but the thirty-foot vimana still stood tall. Basavanna's followers, devotees of Shiva, and even Basavanna himself, had surely stood here. Seeing us at the temple, children began to gather. Looking at their tattered clothes, I wondered if some women gave themselves to the temple for protection. Any position at all in the temple would have been better than watching one's child starve.

'Do you see that tank over there?' asked Ranavva, pointing to a swimming pool-sized stone-covered reservoir obscured by vines. 'All around the village there are remnants of an irrigation system far more sophisticated than the one we have today. We don't even have the technology to move stones that size anymore. We're pathetic.'

By the time we returned to Thimmavva's house, tea was waiting for us and members of her troupe began to filter in one at a time: a fierce woman in her late twenties with long tangled locks, a pretty young mother with two small children, Thimmavva's sister, who looked just like her, and finally, a timid, toothless old woman who batted her eyelashes at me then lowered her gaze with coy timidity every time I looked at her.

As Vani chatted with the women, I studied the toothless old woman and finally realized that she was not a woman at all, but a man in drag. 'Vani—did you see? She's a man!' I interrupted. Vani laughed. 'You only just noticed? She'll be very happy. She's a *jogappa*, a male devotee of Yellamma!' Jogappas had only been mentioned in passing in the books I had read. They claimed to carry the curse that Yellamma's husband, Jamadagni, threw upon his sons for refusing to behead their mother: to live like women. Jogappas generally wore saris and adopted feminine mannerisms. 'They're not as problematic as devadasis.

There are far fewer jogappas than devadasis, and most enter the cult as consenting adults,' said Vani.

'Did your parents dedicate you?' I asked Ramappa, the jogappa.

Ramappa's voice was breathy and highly affected. He spoke with his hand over his mouth to mask his toothlessness. 'No. I dedicated myself. I come from very far away,' he whispered. 'I heard about the goddess for the first time when I was twelve, and I knew I was destined for her. I decided to run away from home—it was a long way to the Yellamma temple, but the goddess showed me the way . . . even as a small boy, I was different from the others. I never wanted to go outside and play. I stayed inside with my mother and helped her in the kitchen. The other boys teased me mercilessly and beat me up all the time. Even my father beat me. I hated my life and prayed to God for deliverance . . . the first time I heard about Yellamma, I knew what I had to do. I live only to worship her; that is the sole objective of my life.'

'How did you survive, so young and all alone?'

'I lived at the temple as a beggar. There were a lot of pilgrims . . . an old jogappa was doing the puja then—he taught me the dance. I quickly learned the songs. After a few years at the temple, I met Thimmavva and her sister, and became part of their troupe. Then I came here to live in this village. That was many, many years ago.'

'Did you ever return home?'

'Never. I never looked back once. This is my home. I have given my life to Yellamma and want only to worship her. I have no other needs.'

'Can married men become jogappas?' I asked, fascinated.

'Yes, but then you have to live separately from your wife. Once you are a jogappa you must serve Yellamma exclusively.'

'Do all jogappas wear saris?'

'Some do and some do not.'

'Do you consider yourself to be a man or a woman?'

'A woman. Yellamma, mother of all, has the power to change man into woman and woman into man.'

'Woman into man?' I could hardly believe my ears.

'Yes, woman into man,' confirmed Ranavva. 'Haven't you been to the Yellamma temple? Haven't you seen women wearing dhotis?'

'Women wearing dhotis?' I asked.

'Yes. It happens. Yellamma can hound a devadasi or a married woman to wear a dhoti. If she's a devadasi, she can still sing in a troupe, but she is like a man.'

'Is she still obliged to have sexual relationships with men?'

'Sometimes yes, sometimes no. Every case is different. Sometimes even married women are made to wear a dhoti. But if a married woman devotes herself to Yellamma, then she must stop marital relations.'

For the first time, I understood that the Yellamma cult had the potential to be—indeed was—a refuge for men and women who didn't fit the rigid constraints of mainstream Hindu society: homosexuals, transvestites, men and women who found their marriages intolerable. *Perhaps the devadasi cult isn't such a bad thing,* I thought to myself.

But what about girls getting trafficked to Mumbai and who knows where else? If only the cult didn't entail forcing young girls into prostitution—then it could have been an empowering alternative for the margins of Hindu society.

*

A dusty haze blanketed the village. The light was falling fast. We accompanied Thimmavva and her troupe to the temple in the ooru where the priest was waiting for them. The priest motioned for Vani and me to climb the stairs and approach the goddess. The brightness of the inner sanctum—two bare bulbs hung from the ceiling—blinded me. I suddenly felt disoriented. *Is this the desired effect?* I wondered. What looked like garlands of golden laurel leaves on the wall behind the goddess reflected a dappled light over Vani and me. Yellamma, imperious, stared down at us from her pedestal. Thimmavva's voice rang forth. Her first mournful notes filled the temple and wrapped themselves around us. The troupe joined in with the luth and chodiki, strengthening Thimmavva's hold. I was expecting the troupe to approach the goddess, as they did in Kalyana, but they remained outside the temple. This was a high-caste temple; they were not allowed inside. They stayed below, in the dark. A small boy herding five buffaloes passed behind the troupe, covering them in dust.

*

Vani and I returned to the inspection bungalow lodge in the

evening to find that our rooms had been given to a group of civil engineers from Bangalore. Iqbal felt it was too late to drive back to Belgaum—bandits were known to set roadblocks at night and ambush travellers, so we decided to drive back to Lagoli where we had left Ranavva. Thimmavva had pressed us to accept her hospitality for the night and so, with no other option, we decided to take her up on it.

There was no moon that night, and the beams of Iqbal's headlights were so short that we only saw the bullock carts on the road when we were upon them. As we approached Lagoli, our headlights abruptly lit a knot of garishly painted trucks, parked at the edge of the holakeri. They loomed over the village like huge beasts around a waterhole. Their presence seemed ominous and threatening. I could not help but think of the diseases their drivers were carrying.

The Talcot district was only a two-hour detour from the main route between Mumbai and Bangalore, and devadasi villages were an increasingly popular overnight stop for truckers. Not only was the food better and lodgings cleaner, but drivers found a large array of tender young girls at their disposal, who, with a little sweet talk and the slippery promise of a yearly fee, could be persuaded to remain faithful. NGOs had been focusing their AIDS awareness campaigns on truck drivers who, like infected cells in the bloodstream, were moving the disease up and down India's arteries. By forging attachments along their routes, truckers felt safe, but in many cases, they were simply infecting young girls with AIDS and/or hepatitis B.

Iqbal pulled over onto the shoulder of the road just

beyond Thimmavva's house. Repetitive squeaks and rattles betrayed the presence of bicycles, but I couldn't see a thing. Animated conversations and laughter bubbled over the rooftops as distorted voices on the radio brayed in the background. In the lanes, shafts of light from lanterns hanging on the eaves intermittently illuminated men strolling arm in arm. Smoke from hearths drifted off the roofs, carrying the smell of tangy black lentils, cumin and thick, gooey rice. The conviviality and the cover of the night lacquered over the seedy desolation that reigned that day.

Thimmavva's house was locked. We started down a lane that led to the Hanuman temple where her neighbour told us she could be found. A group of drunken men reeled in our direction. A large, beefy man with bloodshot eyes began shouting at us. He raised his clenched fist over his head. Insults and bits of spittle rolled off his lips. He stank of alcohol and dried sweat. Further down the lane, a group of men, passive and indifferent, turned around to look, but no one helped us. Vani and I stood frozen like deer in the beams of a headlight. Then I heard a trill. A group of women materialized out of nowhere. I recognized the young mother from Thimmavva's troupe. They formed a tight, outward-facing circle around us, arms locked at the elbows, like Greek hoplites, our human shield. They herded us to the car, shoved us in and warned us not to come to the village at night. Iqbal sped off before we even had a chance to wave goodbye. This was my first glimpse of the violence that permeated the devadasi system—the violence that devadasis were supposed to endure in silence.

TEN

There is no other God on earth for a woman other than her husband. The most excellent of all good works she can do is to seek to please him by manifesting perfect obedience to him. Therein should lie the sole rule of her life. Be her husband deformed, aged, infirm, offensive in his manners; let him also be choleric, debauched, immoral, a drunkard, a gambler; let him frequent places of ill-repute, live in open sin with other women, have no affection whatever for his home; let him rave like a lunatic; let him live without honour; let him be blind, deaf, dumb or crippled; in a word, let his defects be what they may, let his wickedness be what it may, a wife should always look upon him as her God.[12]

—*Padma Purana*, a popular medieval text prescribing the
proper behaviour of women

AS BHAKTI DEVOTIONALISM WAS first transforming south India, marauding chieftains from the north began forging power-sharing alliances with Brahmins and their temples. Chieftans gave land and money to Brahmins and temples; the latter reciprocated by performing powerful rites that ritually converted them into kings. If an upstart king lacked a genealogy, the priests provided one. By funding Brahmins, kings were perceived to uphold dharma, the cosmic order of the universe, and thereby legitimized their rule. Temples came to represent not only communities of worshippers, but also political constituencies, and soon became the prime locus of authority, dominance and decision-making. They were the medium through which men and resources could be controlled.

While the devotees of Bhakti contested the established order by challenging the caste system, they were ultimately incorporated into a Brahmin-dominated society. King Bijala, under pressure from the Brahmin elite, exiled Basavanna after twelve years of service as minister for condoning the high-profile marriage of a Brahmin woman to an untouchable man. Bijala punished the young inter-caste couple by having their eyes torn out before elephants dragged them to their death. Basavanna's followers, much to his chagrin, rioted in the streets for days, and finally murdered Bijala.

The eleventh and twelfth centuries witnessed a boom in temple construction, and an increase in the number of devadasis. By the twelfth century, most important urban temples had hundreds of devadasis attached to them; their number was in direct proportion to a temple's wealth and prestige. The rapid proliferation of the devadasi system can be seen in light of the competition between temples vying for political power. By sponsoring dance-worship and elaborate festivals, priests drew crowds to the temple and attracted followers, thereby filling the coffers of the temple and the kings. Exceptionally talented and beautiful dancing girls were transferred, through a system of tributes, from the provinces to the more sophisticated city temples, enabling dance-worship to reach high levels of artistic achievement. While women in Bhakti's bands of wandering poet-saints, may have found respite from the rigid constraints of caste and gender, they were an exception to Brahmin dominance and caste, the rule of the day.

*

Less than a hundred miles from Kalyana, lay Vijayanagara, the City of Victory, present/ day Hampi, the largest and wealthiest south Indian empire. Founded in the middle of the fourteenth century, its power extended over most of the southern peninsula until it was sacked in the sixteenth century. Ruins of magnificent, intricately carved palaces, temples, bazaars, bathing ghats, audience halls, gateways and watchtowers leave no doubt of the city's former greatness.

The royal centre, where the king lived, and the sacred centre, where the gods lived, lay at the heart of the city and emanated their protective powers over the kingdom. The citadel was enclosed by seven concentric fortifications, which included many shops and bazaars whose arcades, some 300 yards long, are still standing. Sophisticated waterworks consisting of dams, reservoirs, tanks and aqueducts brought water to the many mango, lime and pomegranate orchards. Abdur Razzak, a fifteenth-century Persian envoy to south India, remarks, 'The City of Bijanagar [Vijayanagara] is such that the eye has not seen nor ear heard of any place resembling it upon the whole earth . . . Between the first, second and third walls [as one approaches the centre] there are cultivated fields, gardens, and houses. From the third to the seventh fortress, shops and bazaars are closely crowded together . . . At the head of each bazaar, there is a lofty arcade and magnificent gallery, but the palace of the king is loftier than all of them.'[13]

Domingo Paes, a Portuguese traveller who visited in Vijayanagara in the early sixteenth century wrote, 'The size of the city was as large as Rome, and very beautiful to the sight . . . The people are countless in number, so much so that I do not wish to write it down for fear it should be thought fabulous.'[14] Vijayanagara's inhabitants numbered five hundred thousand and the city, slightly larger than the island of Manhattan, stretched over 24 square miles. The wealth came primarily from trade with Persia, China, Africa, Southeast Asia and, from the fifteenth century onwards, Europe. Rubies, emeralds, pearls and diamonds were traded in the market as openly as fruit. The imperial diamond mines located to the north of the city were among the richest in the world. Vijayanagara's kings were said to keep chests full of diamonds, some the size of hens' eggs.

According to indigenous accounts, Krishna Deva Raya, Vijayanagara's greatest king, who ruled from 1509 to 1529, spent a portion of his highly ritualized day listening to recitations of verses from ancient texts, including the *Arthashastra*, a political treatise dating to the second century CE. Laying down prescriptions for state-organized prostitution, the text advises kings to organize prostitution under the auspices of a Chief Superintendent whose duties should include hiring and classifying prostitutes according to a ranked hierarchy, paying their salaries and fixing their fees.

In the words of the *Arthashastra*, 'The state shall bear expenditure on training courtesans and prostitutes in the following accomplishments: singing, dancing, playing musical instruments, conversing, writing, painting, mind-reading, acting, preparing garlands, shampooing and making love, etc . . . Their sons shall be trained at state expense to produce plays and dances . . . On appointment, courtesans shall be given a grant of 1000 *panas* [small silver coins] for setting up her establishment. Her deputy will be given a grant of 500 panas . . . If a Madam of an establishment dies, her daughter or sister shall take over. If no such arrangements are made, the establishment shall revert to the king and the Chief Superintendent shall place it under the charge of someone else. . . Courtesans who are no longer beautiful shall be put in charge of the supervision of court attendants and prostitutes shall be given work in the pantry or kitchen.'[15]

The kings of Vijayanagara seem to have heeded the *Arthashastra*'s advice for no foreign traveller fails to remark upon the city's prostitutes. One third of the king's income was said to come from brothels. According to Abdur Razzak, 'Opposite the mint is the office of the Prefect of the City, to which it is said 12,000 policemen are attached. Their pay, which comes to 12,000 *fanams* [small gold coins] per day, is derived from the proceeds of brothels . . . The splendour of those houses, the beauty of the heart ravishers, their blandishments and ogles, are beyond all description. It is best to be brief on the matter.'[16]

The most important annual celebration in Vijayanagara was the nine-day Mahanavami festival, which Razzak and Paes both describe vividly. Religious and political in significance, the festival combined the worship of the fierce goddess Durga, slayer of the buffalo-demons, and the consecration of royal arms. Little kings and chieftains, priests and notables from throughout the realm were required to attend and pay tribute. The king and the gods, adorned with crimson velvet and jewel-encrusted silks, shared the dais. Brahmins occasionally whisked the deity away to a curtained room to perform secret rites. Dancing girls, horses and elephants from throughout the realm passed below for review by the king and the gods. There were athletic contests, dance performances and fireworks displays. The royal horses were honoured and on the tenth day, the king reviewed the troops stationed outside the city.

Dancing girls adorned not only the processions and chariots of gods and notables, but also the courtyards and verandahs of the temples and palaces. According to foreigners' descriptions, dance was a continuous feature of the festival—for nine days straight, one set of dancers followed upon another. Ornamental dances mimed a bee hovering above a flower, a lotus moving in the breeze or a swan gliding on a lake. Erotic dance worship was said to encourage the god to engage in sexual union with his consort.

Of the courtesans, Razzak writes, 'The singers were for the most part young girls with cheeks like the moon, and faces more blooming than the spring, adorned with beautiful garments and displaying figures which ravished the heart like fresh roses . . . The girls moved their feet with such grace, that wisdom lost all senses, and the soul was intoxicated with delight.'

Prostitution organized under the auspices of the king, as it is described in the *Arthashastra*, was also a feature of ancient Indian society, and is described in detail in Buddhist and Jain literature dating back to 500 BCE. In this literature, courtesans, jewels of the king's court, are portrayed as evil temptresses who make sport of seducing rich men, sucking them dry of all their money only to repudiate, insult and publicly humiliate them when they have nothing left. As we shall see later, there may have been some truth to this. While courtesans and prostitutes were regarded as wicked and their establishments referred to as 'houses of ill-fame', they were deemed a necessary evil; they had rights and responsibilities and were protected by the king's courts of law. Men had to be careful in their treatment of them lest they be dragged to court; beating up a prostitute was akin to damaging the king's property.

Like devadasis of a later period, courtesans in ancient literature began their training in music and dance at the age of seven. As auspicious women, they had a role of honour at religious festivals and processions, dancing on the floats, waving the horsetails whisks. Like devadasis, if they were unable to provide an heir, they lost their property. The remarkable similarity of the role of courtesans in the court of the king to the role of devadasis in the palaces of the gods leaves no doubt that the pre-existing structures of prostitution provided a template for the devadasi system when it emerged. In the new conception of the world that gave birth to Shiva and Vishnu, gods were to be treated like kings. 'Koyil', the word for the king's palace also came to mean the god's temple. Just as the king was bathed, dressed and praised in song by courtesans, so were the new gods, Shiva and Vishnu. Devadasis in the god's temple and courtesans in the king's courts were simply the earthly versions of the Apsaras of the Vedas, the prostitutes who sang and danced in the court of Indra, and whose duty it was to tempt and seduce.

*

One of the more intriguing passages in the *Arthashastra* concerns fines. Fines were stipulated for crimes committed against prostitutes, but also for crimes committed by prostitutes. The latter are telling: verbally abusing a client, *24 panas*; causing physical injury to a client, *48 panas*; selling or mortgaging belongings, *50 panas*; disfiguring a client (for example, cutting off an ear), *51 panas*; showing dislike to a client after receiving payment, *double her fee*; refusing to have sex with an overnight client, *8 times her fee*; disobeying the king's command to attend on someone, *1000 strokes* or *5000 panas*; killing a client, *death by burning or drowning*.[17]

If laws were prescribed to prevent them, then it can be assumed that such occurrences were not unheard of. Although in literature prostitutes do not kill and maim their clients or disobey the king, they gave as good as they got. They were clearly not passive victims of male exploitation, as received wisdom would have us believe. In fact, such a view gravely underestimates women in general, their resilience, their ingenuity, and their ability to take control of their lives. While courtesans operated in an oppressive, patriarchal, caste-stratified society, by creating distinctive female sub-cultures, governed by a separate set of values, they found ways to challenge, with the means available to them, dominant society and the constraints imposed upon women. While their tactics may have been underhanded, subversive and limited in terms of improving the overall status of women, courtesans nevertheless succeeded in carving out a space for themselves in which they could gain a significant measure of material and emotional autonomy. Like brutally oppressed slaves, peasants and menial workers the world over, for whom open revolt was not an option, prostitutes resorted to 'weapons of the weak': subversion, sabotage, false compliance, feigned ignorance, pilfering and dissimulation. By adding sexuality to this arsenal, they transformed themselves into lethal weapons.

Just like family women, courtesans had their own dharma. Courtesans were expected to be independent, make money and take any man as long as he could pay her fee. They were not supposed to fall in love and if they did they were nevertheless expected to obey the Madam. The tricks developed by courtesans in order to achieve their aims are found in the mouths of Madams giving advice to their charges in literature throughout the ages. According to these Madams, courtesans can most easily ensnare rich men by pretending to be in love and behaving like a wife. They advise courtesans to feign pleasure and tell her to pretend her client is a wonderful lover. A courtesan should learn to read a man's mind and gauge his moods so that she can mould herself according to his tastes. She must try to estrange men from their families and relatives. She should tell her client that before she met him her life had no meaning and pretend to want to bear him a son. If caught with another man, she must pass her evil deed onto the shoulders of her Madam, as a king passes his evil deeds onto the shoulders of his ministers, pretending to want to commit suicide because her Madam forces her to take other clients. If her client looks at other woman, she should feign jealousy and if he does not come to see her every day, anger. She should pretend to hate his enemies and praise his friends and good qualities, even if he has none. In order to gain his esteem and convince him of her sincerity, she should pretend to want to return the money and ornaments he gave her. If he tries to leave her, she should stage a suicide attempt and make sure he hears about it.

According to these Madams in literature, once a courtesan has taken control of her lover using these methods, she should be able to double her fees by using an assortment of tricks. She can pretend to pawn her jewels and ask her lover to recover them for her; or she can stage a drama whereby a shop owner comes to her house, rants, raves and refuses to leave until her lover settles her debts. She can also extort money under the pretext of making a donation to the temple for his good health or she can send a messenger to his house with the news that she has been robbed. The messenger should pay careful attention to the lover's reaction and judge how much the courtesan can reasonably extract. If all else fails she should empty her house of its contents, set it on fire and claim she lost everything. When a lover has no money left, he must be dumped; however, if he somehow manages to regain his fortune, he must be won back.

While family women are, in theory, chaste, modest, submissive and dependent, courtesans seek economic and social liberation by reversing the constraints imposed upon women's chastity and economic rights. They establish a female lineage in which their wealth is passed to their daughters and not to their sons. While in dominant Hindu society the birth of male children is celebrated, in the world of the courtesan it is girl children who are celebrated; the birth of boys is passed over. Cherished and nurtured, girls are brought up to be confident, bold and take their fate into their own hands. This is nowhere better exemplified than by Muddupalani, a devadasi and a poet who lived in eighteenth-century Thanjavur. Her erotic epic, *The Appeasement of Radhika*, celebrates female desire and sexuality. She describes in detail the life of a devadasi and every aspect of what it means to be a woman. Her heroines demand to be satisfied; they are proud, sensitive, passionate and wilful.

The alternative moral order of the courtesan was passed on with the help of private rituals, tales, songs and dances. Occasionally performed at wedding ceremonies, their satirical farces mocked repressive relationships, male sexuality and the traditional mores of Hindu society. Carefully distilled and transmitted from generation to generation, they formed the core of the courtesan's private consciousness and oral heritage. Like folktales, they served to educate, but were also therapeutic devices that liberated and empowered women by redefining the meaning of womanhood.

ELEVEN

These women [devadasis] are present at marriages and
other solemn family meetings. All the time which they
have to spare in the intervals of the various ceremonies is
devoted to infinitely more shameful practices; and it is not
an uncommon thing to see even sacred temples converted
into mere brothels.[18]

—Abbé Dubois

AFTER A DAY OFF, Vani and I arrived in Kalyana by mid-
afternoon. Rukmini came running to meet us. She was
wearing a brand new cobalt-blue sari with a black border.
Her hair was oiled and neatly tied into a bun, her eyes
lined with kohl. I wondered if she had primped herself for
an important client. She climbed into the car with her six-
year-old cousin. 'Where have you been? Everyone has left
already,' she said. 'Unless we take the car we will miss it.'

'Miss what?'

'The blessing ceremony! At the landlord's new
farmhouse!' Fortunately, I had my tape recorder with
me. This sounded like the perfect opportunity to record
some myths.

The dirt roads behind the village were suitable for

bullock carts, but not cars. We bumped past the fields of sugarcane, green gram and soybean at 5 miles an hour. The house was a rectangular structure made of mud, brick, and stone. A fresh patina of ochre-stained cow dung had been applied to the walls. The doors and windows had been finished with a white trim. The landlord stepped outside to meet us. He was a slender man with white hair and a close-cropped beard.

'Namaskar,' he said, welcoming us inside as if he was expecting us.

Sumithra had not yet arrived. Around thirty devadasis and their children were already squatting in one corner of the threshing floor, an enclosed forecourt extending the length of the house. The forecourt provided an intermediate space between the interior family rooms and the outside world. Freshly harvested crops would be sheltered there from wind and rain. Above the threshing floor, along the front of the house, was a verandah for the family to receive guests. Untouchables were allowed to access the threshing floor, but not the verandah. Five Yellamma shrines, brought by devadasis from their homes, were lined up on the verandah, facing the threshing floor. The landlord invited Vani and me to sit with the family, but out of solidarity with the devadasi women, Vani declined. We sat on a wooden log just below the verandah. The landlord's daughter served us tea and biscuits, while the landlord took up his post by the front door. When he saw Sumithra approaching, he called to his wife, who hurried outside with a brass water jug.

Sumithra wore fetter-like silver anklets covered with

little bells that tinkled as she walked. With the goddess towering above her and the pedestal concealing her head, Sumithra's head appeared decapitated, like Yellamma in the myth. The landlord's wife ritually cleaned Sumithra's feet, then prostrated herself on the ground before her. Sumithra entered the house and installed the jagha on the verandah with the other, smaller images of Yellamma. Encircling the goddess with a camphor flame, she placed incense at her feet. Sumithra and four other devadasis sang a devotional song. The landlord's wife and daughters carried two cauldrons out of the interior rooms and placed them on the verandah. They heaped servings of lentils and rice onto battered tin plates and carried them to the devadasis squatting in the corner. When the women finished eating, the daughters again made the rounds, heaping more rice and pouring buffalo milk onto their plates. The landlord oversaw these operations, barking an occasional command at his wife and daughters, but smiling graciously.

The blessing ceremony of their new house, which they had built with their own hands, was an important event for them. When the meal was over, Sumithra, Kassi, and three other women sang more devotional songs. The devadasis rose and paid their respects to the goddess. I placed a fifty-rupee note in the goddess's sari, then flashed my recorder at Sumithra. She made Kassi, me and several old women sit down near the jagha, and the children and remaining devadasis gathered around us expectantly, happy to see their myths being recorded. After placing a kerosene lamp near Sumithra and Kassi, the landlord's family perched themselves on the edge of the verandah.

'So, tell me,' said Vani, cueing Kassi and Sumithra. 'What happened to Yellamma? Why did her head get cut off?'

Kassi spoke slowly, with a rhythmic, lilting cadence, as if discussing a very important matter. She had the wheeze of a heavy smoker, the result of cooking over an open fire all her life. Leaning forward into the glow of the lamp, she said, 'It was not her fault. No, it was not her fault. Yellamma, you see, was married to the sage Jamadagni, and every morning she went to the river to fetch water for his puja. She would make a jug out of the sand in the riverbank and carry the water home on her head, coiling a snake on her head so that the hardness of the jug did not hurt her.

'One day, deciding to test her chastity, Jamadagni followed her to the river and disguised himself as a *gandharva*, a demigod known for his licentious ways. Yellamma saw the gandharva frolicking with a nymph in the reflection of the water. Holding the jug on her head, she did not look away. She looked and she compared her own chaste life to theirs, full of fun and games. An "impure" thought crossed her mind. The jug she built from the riverbank crumbled; Yellamma became wet. The snake slithered away.'[19] Kassi's hands cascaded around her head like falling water. She mimicked the movement of the snake.

'Yellamma tried to make another jug, but she had lost her powers and had no choice but to return to her husband empty-handed. She fell at his feet, saying, "Let bygones be bygones . . . please forgive me." He said nothing, but gave her a necklace. When she put it on, her whole body became full of red spots. She fled and began roaming the countryside, begging for food and shelter, and worshipping her husband. Finally, one day the twin physicians of the gods spotted her. They told her she was not to blame. They took her under their protection and taught her the cures for smallpox, chickenpox, and leprosy. Yellamma returned to Jamadagni restored to her youth and beauty, but, enraged, he ordered his sons to behead her . . .

'The three elder sons refused, and he cursed them to live like women. But the youngest son, Parasurama, agreed to carry out his wish. Yellamma ran away and was helped by Madiga, an untouchable woman. When Parasurama came for them, they hid inside two large pots, but he found them and cut off their heads. Jamadagni was delighted and granted his son a boon; Parasurama requested that his mother be brought back to life. But when Jamadagni revived the women, he mixed up their heads, putting Madiga's head on Yellamma's body. Thenceforth, Yellamma was part high-caste and part untouchable. Jamadagni fled to the Himalayas to lead a life of meditation . . .'

*

Kassi's version of the myth differed significantly from other versions I had heard. Kassi insisted upon Yellamma's innocence, emphasizing that the gods' physicians said that Yellamma's disgrace was not her fault. Her version implied that Jamadagni had asked his wife to uphold an impossible feminine ideal, and cruelly put her to the test. In Tamana's version, as in other high-caste versions, the question of justice was not raised: Yellamma had an impure thought, and was therefore punished. Kassi, like most devadasi women, considered that Yellamma was part high caste, part low caste. Tamana, on the other hand, omitted this aspect of the myth. But the big difference was the ending. In Kassi's version, Jamadagni fled from Yellamma, taking refuge in the mountains. In Tamana's version of the myth, Jamadagni erased the memory of Yellamma's trials, and the family was happily reunited. While the upper-caste version had a happy ending, Kassi's did not.

Devadasi women frequently referred to Yellamma's myth to explain their duties and actions, drawing parallels between their own life stories and Yellamma's. Indeed, like many devadasis, Yellamma was repudiated by her keeper, reviled as impure, and reduced to begging. Devadasis re-enact the foundation myth not only with their rituals, but also with their own life experience. 'She is like Yellamma,' Rukmini's aunt Ella had said of her. 'Her man curses and abuses her, but still she worships him.' The women perceive such behaviour as foolish, because it is self-destructive, but also as heroic, because they are following in Yellamma's footsteps. By identifying with the goddess, devadasis are able to retain their pride and dignity.

Devadasi women choose to invest in the Yellamma cult because it confers power and responsibility on them. Without the Yellamma cult, devadasis are merely untouchable prostitutes. But by embracing the tradition, they are able to see themselves as divine vessels of the goddess, and are worshipped as such by the community at large. Devadasis are imbued with 'Shakti', divine feminine energy, power and strength. They have the power to appease the gods and call forth the rain. If the rains are sufficient, the harvest will be abundant, the children well be well fed, and the village blessed. Devadasis are thus responsible for the prosperity and wellbeing of the entire community, and the maintenance of the cosmic order. While they are despised as impure because of their sexual activity and their low birth, they are also considered highly auspicious. High-caste women, who generally refer to devadasis with disdain and disgust, bend down and touch their feet during rituals in an extraordinary inversion of caste hierarchy. On one plane, devadasis are reviled by society, and on another, they are revered as mediums of the goddess. By investing in the tradition, devadasis are able to see themselves not as 'untouchable prostitutes', but as living representatives of the goddess with important responsibilities in the community.

The yearly, weekly and daily rituals they perform reinforce this vision; they make it tangible and real. Because rituals communicate not on the level of reason, but through sight, sound, taste, touch and smell—and because they sometimes provoke transcendental states— they have tremendous emotional power. Rituals construct and sustain the women's beliefs in Yellamma. They make the myth seem real.

Devadasis often say that if they submit to Yellamma's will and worship her, they will achieve liberation, or at least improve their station in their next life. But submitting to Yellamma's will means fulfilling their dharma, their duty as devadasis: it means providing sexual services to men. Thus, the Yellamma cult is a double-edged sword: while holding out the promise of redemption, it condemns the women to a life of prostitution.

TWELVE

What can they give, these gods, who live off the charity of people?[20]

—Basavanna

THE ROAD TO THE Saundatti Temple is riddled with potholes, so although only 40 miles from Kalyana, the drive took us almost two hours. We left at six in the morning to be sure we reached the temple in time for the morning puja, but we hadn't counted on Ranavva getting carsick so many times. I sat in the front, while Vani shared the backseat with Rukmini and Ranavva, both of whom turned green and rode with their noses pointed towards the cracked window. The rolling farmland of the Talcot district gave way to barren red mountains topped by ruins of ancient forts. As we descended from a plateau into the river valley of the Malaprabha river, Ranavva pointed to a vast square well, a bathing ghat, with four banks of steps on each side leading down to the water. A single neem tree on the narrow strip of land between the well's corner and the precipitous riverbank spread its branches like a giant bird poised for flight.

'There's the jogula bhavi. That's where we purify

ourselves before climbing the mountain to the temple,' said Ranavva.

'Girls bathe there before their dedication, then run up to the temple,' said Vani. I looked up at the almost vertical, boulder-strewn field leading to the crest of the mountain where the temple loomed, and imagined it swarming with dedication parties led by naked girls.

We crossed the river and began our ascent. The Ambassador's engine whined, and the road, with its hairpin bends, zigzagged up the mountain. Ten minutes later, spires stretching above the massive, 20-foot walls of the temple compound came into view. It looked more like a fortress than a religious centre. On the far side sprawled a town. The road petered out. Parking the car, we took a footpath leading to the temple.

Tuesday, though a special day, was not the busiest. Many of the merchant stalls and teashops along the path to the temple were closed, but the square in front of the entrance gate was alive with vendors hawking their goods—ritual offerings for the goddess—bananas, coconuts, flowers, jasmine, rice balls, sweetmeats. A spice merchant wrapped in a faded green sari sat immobile between similar-sized mounds of haldi and kumkum powder. Ranavva and Rukmini stopped before a stall selling necessities for the puja; I bought a deluxe kit (that is, with coconut and flowers) for each of us. Leaving our shoes at the entrance, we passed through the gate into the temple compound.

The stone walls were over 15 feet thick. In medieval times, peasants would have taken refuge here from the predatory raids of neighbouring chieftains. In the tunnel-like archway, thousands of names were scrawled on slate—these were the names of the temple's donors. Giving to the temple was a way of expiating one's sins. Inside, the atmosphere was still and peaceful. A few people were scattered about. Three devotees circled the temple clockwise. A devadasi waved a horsetail whisk from side to side; another wailed and prostrated herself on the ground every few feet. Perhaps some calamity had befallen her family and she had come to beg Yellamma for mercy. A third devotee wearing a bright orange sari and carrying a pot of water on her head, circled past, flashing a smile and batting her eyelashes at us. She was a he, a jogappa.

In a far corner, a banyan tree—a tree of wisdom—grew from the base of the compound wall. Branches high above sprouted twisted aerial roots that plunged back into the earth and the 'netherworld' beneath. The tree and the temple reservoir—in this case, a small stone tank that looked like a crypt—represented the transformation of the primordial chaos at the earth's centre into a life-giving force.

The temple had been constructed over a period of nine hundred years and was a hodge-podge of medieval, eighteenth-century and modern architecture. The goddess's sanctuary, a rectangular edifice with a terraced, pyramid-like tower, covered with multi-coloured relief stood in the middle of the compound. A bare-breasted priest in a dhoti with a thick gold chain draped over his belly gestured for us to hurry; the puja had begun. I climbed the steps to the sanctuary and followed the priest through a series of concentric pavilions, redolent with the musty odours of oil lamps, camphor and incense. The sickly sweet smell of coconut milk and wilting flowers emanated from the dark, womb-like cave where the goddess presided. Twenty or so devotees bearing offerings stood on the far side of a metal barrier, waiting for the right moment to step forward for benediction. I realized too late that I was in the area closest to the goddess, reserved for the upper castes. Rukmini and Ranavva appeared on the other side of the metal barrier, looking intimidated.

Four priests in dhotis attended the goddess, whose black granite core was hardly visible under the colourful mass of accoutrements that adorned her. Her face and hands were fashioned from silver and gold; her eyes were garnets. She wore a gold-embroidered sari, a silver-spiked crown and necklaces of semi-precious stones. Wreaths of flowers and cowry shells cascaded over her garments. The black granite glistened with the goddess's daily anointing of perfume and oil. I stared at her, transfixed as the priests waved their instruments in and out of my field of vision. It was disturbing to think that a mere stone could be invested with so much power. In south India, even today, gods, said to 'inhabit' their images, are legally allowed to own land, administered by the temple priests.

One after another, devotees stepped forward. Baskets full of offerings, jasmine, marigolds, spices and sweets were passed before the goddess to be blessed by the priests; coconuts were broken open upon her altar. The priest filled Ranavva and Rukmini's cupped hands with holy water. Ranavva drank a little, then spread the rest over the crown of her head. The priests turned towards the goddess with their hands pressed together and chanted a mantra. One of them rang a brass bell and a golden curtain swooshed closed, sealing off the goddess from the gaze of her worshippers while the priest administered the final, secret rites. The puja had ended.

As the crowd dispersed, I looked around the mandapa, the space before the inner sanctum, wondering how many hundreds of thousands of devadasis had danced there over the years. The floor, a relic of medieval times, was a large granite slab with a geometric design.

The priest who had ushered me in now caught up with Vani and me. 'Foreigners are seldom seen in these parts,' he said in Kannada. Upon hearing that I was interested in temple history, he led us outside and pointed to the South Gate, a massive stone archway. 'The South Gate dates to the eleventh century, but this site, a source of water at the crest of a mountain, was sacred long before that. Please come to my house for tea. I will tell you everything you need to know . . .'

Considering everything I had heard about rapacious temple Brahmins for whom no trick was too low when it came to finagling a few coins from even the poorest of the poor, I balked at the idea of accepting his hospitality, but Vani waved off my objections. We followed the priest through a small gate opposite the main entrance. Vani motioned for Ranavva and Rukmini to follow, but they looked terrified, and gestured that they would wait by the temple tank. They probably feared 'polluting' his house.

The priest lived in a two-room hut built against the exterior wall of the temple. 'These houses,' he explained, pointing to the beehive-like row of houses along the temple wall, 'are reserved for the hereditary servants of the temple.' *Once upon a time,* I thought to myself, *devadasis lived here, too.* The priest called out to his neighbours, who looked on as we climbed the stairs to his house. He was proud to be receiving foreigners as guests.

'Welcome to my home,' he said, spreading out a cotton durry for us to sit on, then lighting the flame under a burner for tea. 'So you want to know about the temple. Well, the inner sanctum was carved out of rock several thousands of years ago. The source that bubbles up inside is connected to the Ganges. India's most sacred rivers all run underneath the temple, invisible to the naked eye.'

'The Ganges?' I said. 'That's hundreds of miles away.'

Vani smiled. 'Myth is history,' she said in English, then turned back to the priest. 'How many priests are in service at the temple?'

'Several thousand! There are several different clans that serve the goddess, each with different hereditary functions. My clan descends from Yellamma's younger brother.'

'That might not be an exaggeration,' said Vani. 'If you include the garland-makers, the cooks, the sweepers. Some deities even have servants to brush their teeth and put them to bed.'

'Do devadasis still dance in the temple?' I asked.

'No,' he said. 'Occasionally jogappas, the male servants, perform the dance. Until a few years ago, there were a few old devadasis, but the young ones, they no longer know how.'

Rumour had it that priests performed dedications in their homes for a small fortune. 'I hear dedications are still taking place,' I said, knowing the question would raise his guard.

'No, no, no,' he replied. 'No dedication has taken place here since the ban.'

Shifting in his seat and clearing his throat, he pointed to a portrait of Gandhi on the wall, from which hung a garland of carnations, and embarked upon a monologue. Vani rolled her eyes. Shaking her head, she said, 'Gandhi is worshipped like a god in India, but few know or even care what he had to say.'

Anxious to get back to Ranavva and Rukmini, Vani and I took our leave. We found them waiting patiently by the temple tank and sat down next to them. 'How does it feel to be here?' asked Vani.

Ranavva nodded, wide eyed, and said, 'It feels good. We got good *darshan*. I've never been so close to the goddess. Even though it's not festival time, her power is strong. I can feel it.'

'Darshan,' Vani explained, 'is the act of seeing and being seen by God . . . of bathing in His or Her divine grace.'

Rukmini looked chastened. 'I haven't come in a long time,' she said. 'I have been neglecting the goddess. It is good that I have come.'

*

There were twenty different shrines scattered in and around the Yellamma temple compound; each related to a figure in the goddess's life. They were supposed to be visited in a specific order. The shrines to Madiga, the untouchable woman who protected Yellamma, and Parasurama, Yellamma's son, were side by side. They were built into the west wall of the temple. Their physical placement, under the ramparts of the temple wall, echoed their supporting roles in her life.

Stone steps led down into a dank, dark cave where Madiga presided. It smelled of rotting flowers, coconut milk and stale incense. Madiga was a lump of black granite on a three-foot pedestal, wrapped in a blood-red sari, draped in garlands and anointed with oil. Scattered offerings and flickering oil lamps lay before her. Her forehead was smeared with horizontal lines of haldi and kumkum; she seemed to smirk. I felt uneasy, as if some terrible event had taken place there. The damp walls seemed to sweat. I had heard that buffaloes were sacrificed upon her altar, and, looking down at the mud-packed floor, I imagined it on festival days glistening with the viscous blood of her victims.

Along the path leading to Jamadagni's pavilion was a modern cement shrine containing Yellamma's body parts represented by loaf-sized rocks, splattered with kumkum and oil: her blood-soaked head, her torso, her hands and feet. According to this version of the myth, Yellamma was not just decapitated, but dismembered. Murals on the wall depicted the foundation myth: Yellamma watching the gandharva frolicking with his lover, the pot of water on her head crumbling, Jamadagni cursing Yellamma. By placing the shrine of Yellamma's dismembered body along the path to Jamadagni's hilltop meditation spot, it served as a warning to those who transgressed their wifely duties, a celebration of the sacrificial dismemberment of women on the altar of patriarchy.

The shrine was closed, but the priest, seeing a potential source of great wealth (Vani and me), unlocked the metal gate and invited us in. 'Is this a new shrine?' Vani asked. 'I was here ten years ago, but I don't remember it.'

'Yes,' he replied. 'It was built a few years ago with funds donated by the Saundatti police force.' Since giving to the temple is a way of expiating one's sins, I wondered what sins the police were trying to shake. How logical, I thought, that agents of the law should offer this shrine, essentially a reminder to women of the dire consequences that await those who overstep the rigid constraints society imposes on them.

Ranavva and Rukmini sat on the ground before Yellamma's head. The priest lit a few clumps of incense and performed a perfunctory puja. Ranavva and Rukmini each lifted the stone three times. 'If you are able to lift the head three times,' the priest explained, 'Yellamma will grant your wish.' A troupe of five devadasis with a jagha now approached, plucking their instruments and singing a devotional song. Their tones were flat and their harmonies, if that's what they were intended to be, were off. They placed the jagha before the shrine and prostrated themselves on the ground. They took turns lifting Yellamma's head. 'Rituals such as these give devadasis strength and hope,' said Vani. 'They compare their lives to Yellamma's and find consolation in the fact that she, too, suffered.'

By the time we made our way back to the temple, the vendors along the street leading to the temple had opened for business. The sting of roasting chillies made my eyes water. The aromas of jasmine and incense mingled with those of coriander, tamarind, fried onions and sweat. Rukmini perked up. Stopping before a bangle vendor, she bounced with excitement. 'Oh, Catherine, you must buy some bangles for yourself. How is it possible to wear so little jewellery?' I bought two shoe-sized boxes of bangles as a farewell present for the women of Kalyana. At a tea stall, sitting on benches around a wooden table, Rukmini kneaded and warmed my hand, then slipped on ten glass bangles. 'There, that's much better. Now you have to learn how to make them tinkle nicely when you speak.' She sat back and eyed me thoughtfully. Removing a string of gold-plated beads from her neck, she slipped her life's savings over my head and said, 'Now you look beautiful.'

*

We arrived in Kalyana at four in the afternoon to find Rukmini's aunt Ella sitting at the entrance to the village. I had no doubt that she had been there for hours, staring down the road, waiting for our return. Rukmini laughed and said, 'My uncle must have convinced her that you finally kidnapped me.' Visibly relieved to see us, she insisted we come back to her house for a cup of buffalo milk. Along the way, we spread word that we would be leaving in the morning and wanted to say goodbye to everyone at the temple. It was market day, and many of the women were still in town. Sumithra, we were told, would not be back until late.

Rukmini and her son, Gajanan, shared three rooms with the six members of Ella's family. In the front room a cauldron in which Ella sterilized the milk she earned as a commission for tending to the landlords' buffalo sat above a small fire. Ella listened, rapt, as Rukmini told her in detail about our visit to the temple. When Rukmini recounted how close she came to the goddess, and how the priest had invited us to his house, she pressed her hands together and bent down, touching her head to the ground before Vani and me. By the way she looked at me, I knew that by sundown, this story would have made its way several times around the village.

'Ella, you raised Rukmini, didn't you?' I asked.

'Yes, Rukmini is *my* daughter. My sister has been there in Mumbai since she was young. I married, but for many years I had no children. I raised Rukmini like my own daughter . . . My sister and I lost our parents when we were very young. Our uncle didn't take care of us properly. We lived in complete poverty. We had no clothes to wear. We had no place to sleep! Do you understand? Padmini [Rukmini's mother] was the beautiful one, and as the saying goes, "a beautiful girl equals three acres of land." My uncle dedicated her, and she went to Mumbai. After that we started eating. She came back to the village to deliver Rukmini. When she regained her strength, she went back to Mumbai, taking the baby with her, but Rukmini got very sick and had to go to the hospital. She spent thousands of rupees on doctor's bills. So she brought Rukmini back to the village, and I took over caring for her.'

'Why was Rukmini dedicated?' I asked.

'We had no choice. A landlord noticed Rukmini in the field and took her [raped her]. Besides, Padmini has no other children. Who will take care of her in her old age? Padmini came to the village and had her tied with the beads. Then she took her to Mumbai.'

Rukmini moved her new bangles up and down her arm. 'I hated it there,' she said. 'Wholeheartedly, I hated it. I ran away and came back to the village. My friends are here.'

Ella slipped her arm around Rukmini's shoulders and pulled her close. 'She is not emotionally strong enough for Mumbai. We keep her here with us,' she said.

'My mother is old now, but she is still working,' Rukmini said, her voice wavering. 'I should be the one in Mumbai . . .'

'What is it like there?' I asked.

Rukmini thought about the question for a while. Then, shaking her head, she said, 'In Mumbai, you have to sell your body no matter what. Your life depends on it, even for just a few rupees . . . but we have it easy compared to some of the other girls. Girls from Nepal, they're brought to Mumbai and sold—just like that. If they are supposed to earn one hundred rupees, they are lucky if they get even ten. They have to pay rent, the gharwali, and then the police. After, there is nothing left. We don't have to pay anyone. The police leave us alone. We only pay rent on the room. The gharwalis are like us, they come from here only, from villages like this one.'

'Do you think Rukmini's mother is a gharwali?' I asked.

'Probably,' Vani replied, then turned to Rukmini. 'But now you have a man in the village?'

'I have been with Gajanan's father for three years, but I have known him since we were children. I love him, but he does not care for me. I fight with my family about him every day. They tell me to leave him, but unless I see his face, I cannot eat,' said Rukmini.

'Why doesn't he give you anything?' I asked.

'He says if I truly love him, then I shouldn't ask for money.'

'But then how do you manage?'

Ella cut in, 'She takes other clients, that's how she manages. How else can she pay her son's doctor's bills? He obliges her to take other clients!'

'I think his parents don't give him any money,' Rukmini mumbled. 'They don't want him cavorting with the likes of me.'

'And what about you, Ella?' asked Vani. 'What are you going to do with your other daughter?'

'Why should I give her to Yellamma? I'm not afraid. Yellamma has gone into the hands of the government. She is sitting quietly. She's blindfolded—her hands are tied now!'

*

By the time we finished our buffalo milk, it was almost six o'clock. I heard the tinkle of ankle bells and turned to see Sumithra and her troupe passing through the lanes on their way home. I rose to follow them. 'Vani, I'll go get Sumithra. Let's meet at the temple,' I said.

Covered with dust and visibly exhausted, the troupe

filed into Sumithra's house. I entered behind them, but Sumithra ignored me. The women seemed solemn and serious. Sumithra lit a lantern and hung it on a peg; the jagha was set in its place. They had just returned from their bi-weekly ritual of worshipping in upper-caste households and begging for alms in the market. The women, still standing, began to empty the folds of their saris, gathering into piles what must have been over thirty pounds of millet, rice and lentils. When they were finished, they sat in a circle, and Sumithra, with slow, deliberate movements, measured out the grains with a dented tin cup, dividing it evenly among the five members of the troupe. The women silently followed her every movement. *How many mouths will this bounty feed?* I wondered. The Yellamma cult, I realized, provided old women with a concrete means of subsistence.

By the time Sumithra and I reached the temple, a noisy crowd had gathered. Ranavva, Ganga, Sumithra, Rukmini, Chandra, Renuka, Mahadevi, Durga, Shoba—in all, over thirty women were present. My imminent departure had emboldened many women who now took me in their arms and spoke to me kindly. Vani was too immersed in coversation to translate for me. Only Shanti was absent.

As we walked to the car, the women began to sing a farewell ballad. Kassi, Ranavva, Rukmini and many other women huddled around me, simultaneously pinching my cheeks and clucking their tongues— the local version of a kiss. Vani exuded calm, quiet confidence, and strength; I felt as if I were about to crumble. When we reached the car, Vani turned to the women, took hold of their arms and reassured them, 'In three months, in six months, we'll be back. You can count on us.' This was what I had told Vani, but what if Yellamma was right and we couldn't find financing? I shut my eyes and promised myself that no matter what happened, I would return. 'Mathé Barthivi, we'll be back,' I said.

Shanti and her mother appeared just as we were about to slip into the car. We embraced silently. 'Make sure she's okay,' Vani said to Shanti's mother.

As I slid across the backseat, the women began to sing again. I recognized the cadence of a ritual lament. Vani pulled the car door closed, and we sped off.

THIRTEEN

Life lasts only a couple of days
Nobody knows what it means
Be wise and be kind . . .
Life is only a two-day affair
The meaning of which is never too clear
Enlightened to the way things are
better be generous and give with care.[21]

—Kanaka-dasa, a sixteenth-century Bhakti saint
who worked as a revenue collector for the kings in
Vijayanagara

VANI AND I ARRIVED in Belgaum, a lovely hill town with tree-lined avenues, the next morning and took a room at the Sanman Hotel. Our train was not scheduled to leave until eight in the evening, so we got to work on translations. Vani sat at the desk, rolling back and forth over the tapes, listening and re-listening to the important passages, struggling at times with the local dialect. Ranavva laughed at how poor she was; then her voice became heavy and slow. In the distance, a baby cried and children played. There were many unidentifiable squeaks and clatters. Vani and I did not discuss our feelings. We didn't have to. We shared a profound sense of indignation, and a passionate respect for the women.

I could not help but wonder which of the children in Kalyana's holakeri would end up in Mumbai brothels. My thoughts drifted to the two sisters I glimpsed from time to time. They seemed to run wild. No one wiped the snot from their blackened faces; no one brushed their hair. They wore filthy rags. Perhaps their mother had died, or had too many troubles of her own to look after them. I wondered if this was how Rukmini's mother and aunt had grown up. The older sister—she must have been seven—already had the matted locks of Yellamma's servants. I fascinated her, and she stopped to stare whenever I crossed her path, yet she never approached or sat in my lap like the other children. She had probably suffered a few beatings at the hands of an adult, perhaps for stealing food.

It suddenly occurred to me that I had never heard her speak. I had been afraid to look at her, afraid of what I might see. I had blocked her out, but now she came back to haunt me. One day, the distant relatives in charge of her would gather her up, confine her to the house for a week, bathe her in neem water, give her new clothes and fatten her with sweets. Too young to understand what was happening, she would be grateful for the attention she was receiving. There would be a big feast in the village, and she would be handed over to whomever offered the highest price for her virginity, perhaps a gharwali from Mumbai or a local landlord.

The government had set up boarding schools for such girls in an attempt to thwart their fate. Vani and I visited one such institution near Belgaum at the outset of our trip. When we arrived, seventy barefoot girls in pleated blue tunics were eating their lunch, a burnt roti and a spoonful of watery lentils. Vani bristled as she remarked that it was not a regulation lunch—someone was skimming off the food budget. The girls sat almost paralysed with fear. 'Who are you?' their frightened eyes seemed to ask. 'Why are you here?' Our request to visit the premises and speak with the girls was denied. The girls were playing in the yard when we took leave. Although forbidden to do so, Vani could not help herself. She stopped near a group of girls and asked, 'What is your name? Where are you from?'

A frail, doe-like creature raised her eyes to Vani's. Her small chest heaved; her breath was laboured. 'My name is Sushma. I am from Rangund, please go there and tell my mother to come get me.' She seemed to pin all her hopes on us.

'Please take me out of here,' requested her friend.

I looked to the third girl standing before us. She stiffened and dropped her gaze to her feet. Perhaps she had lost her mother, or no longer remembered the name of her village. The bleakness of the place weighed upon me. I couldn't think; I couldn't breathe. Lying on my hotel bed, just thinking of those young girls made my throat tighten. I wondered if they would receive enough education or training to tackle the world later in life. Some of the girls, although they would escape becoming devadasis, would nonetheless end up in brothels.

I wondered if the two wild sisters of Kalyana would be better off in a boarding school. But they were not the only girls in Kalyana destined to become devadasis. Although the women didn't volunteer information about upcoming dedications, and we were careful not to ask, the signs were in evidence. More than a few girls, while otherwise carefully groomed, had a single lock of matted hair woven into their pigtails, a sign that Yellamma had called them. I noticed that, although her father said she would be married, Renuka was helping Sumithra with her ritual duties. The villagers insisted that once a girl had been promised to Yellamma, her fate was sealed. If a vow to dedicate is broken, they said, the goddess will visit the village with death and destruction. I wondered about Ella's daughter. Would she end up a devadasi after all?

I suddenly felt exhausted and overwhelmed. After a day in Bangalore, I was scheduled to fly to Delhi and spend a few days with a friend before returning to Paris, but I was gripped by a sudden need to be alone. I didn't think I could manage the cheerfulness required of a houseguest. I looked around the room. There were two single beds, a desk, an armchair, and a coffee table. For two hundred rupees, five dollars a night, I couldn't do better. It was just what I needed. I let Vani know that I was going to stay behind in Belgaum for a few days.

For the next three days, other than for a morning walk and a few telephone calls, I didn't leave my room. I lay on the bed watching the ceiling fan spin, and occasionally rose to write in my journal. I let my mind wander, trying to make sense of everything I had seen and heard, hoping my thoughts would come together. I felt numb, sickened by an oppressive sense of injustice. Images of my adolescence in upper Westchester came to mind: the white clapboard house with green shutters, deer grazing at the edge of the wood. I had led such a sheltered existence. I had never known people who had to struggle. I had been handed everything on a silver platter. Private school, boarding school, and, with a little effort, a good college education. Other than in books and distant places, injustice had never been a part of my world.

I suppose I was in shock—shock that the Yellamma cult did indeed exist and was still going strong; shock that people still lived their lives according to myths and rituals; shock that all this was still happening, right out in the open.

*

When I rang Dilip in Paris, I learned from his wife that he was travelling in Orissa; an extraordinary event had taken place there. Priests at the Puri temple had announced that they were going to receive the women who had petitioned the temple, five years earlier, to become devadasis; they were planning to induct new recruits into temple service and revive the tradition. Every major English-language daily, none of which were available in Halamid, had been chronicling the scandal. Several prominent politicians, including the Minister of Law and Justice, Narasingha Misra, supported the temple's decision. Dance-worship, they reasoned, had been performed inside the temple for almost one thousand years. Donations to the temple provided for the fulfilment of devadasi rituals in perpetuity. 'How can dance rituals be stopped?' they asked.

Women's groups across the country were up in arms. Protests were being staged outside the temple; altercations had taken place. The political party, Janata Dal, had threatened to 'launch an agitation' in Puri if the temple administration went through with the selection process. They denounced the tradition as a system that reduced women to sexual slavery. Look at our sisters in Karnataka, they said. How could anyone want to bring the system back to Orissa?

I called Dilip in Bhubaneshwar; he had managed to meet with four of the five women who had applied to the temple. 'At least two of them are prostitutes,' he said.

'And why do the others want to become devadasis?' I asked.

'Religious devotion,' said Dilip. 'I know it's hard for you to understand . . .'

'Did you meet any of the surviving older devadasis?'

'No. I didn't have time. It was crazy there. But the houses in the lanes around the temple are full of prostitutes,' said Dilip. 'I'm sure they're descendants of devadasis. We may find a few devadasis from the old generation . . . Puri has been an important pilgrimage site since the twelfth century. The Chariot festival, when the god travels to his summer residence, draws three hundred thousand pilgrims every year.'

An anthropologist who did research in Puri in the 1970s, when a dozen or so devadasis who had served in the temple in the twenties were still around, wrote that, once upon a time, devadasis had been the festival's main attractions. Temple priests used to arrange for devadasis to visit the pilgrims at their hotels. Sometimes devadasis developed relationships with pilgrims who came year after year and always asked for the same woman. Temple priests kept detailed records of the pilgrims and the amounts of the offerings they made. Superintendents monitored devadasis' sexual relationships, and the latter were not allowed to leave the city without the king's permission.

In the nineteenth century, arguing that the tradition was forcing young girls into a life of prostitution, British and Indian reformers joined hands in an attempt to abolish what remained of the tradition (which began its decline with the Mughal invasions). But because the tradition was protected under 'customary law', few reforms were instituted before the twentieth century. Pan-Indian legislation officially banning it was not introduced until Indian Independence in 1947. Reforms, however, only served to worsen the devadasis' lot. Devadasis were essentially stripped of their only resource other than sex work. Their role in the temple as 'ritual specialists' had provided them with a certain social status, and their dances, required at auspicious ceremonies in the community, such as the birth of a son or a wedding, had been a source of income. With the reform movement, devadasi entertainment became disreputable. While devadasi women were shunned, their dance, purged of its overt eroticism, was reformulated as Bharat Natyam or Indian classical dance, and was taken over by 'respectable' middle- and upper-class women. With the advent of gramophones and cinema, a few women from devadasi backgrounds, such as Madurai S. Subbulakshmi, Bangalore Nagarathnama and Tanjore Balasaraswati went on to become famous classical performers.

Despite losing its devadasis, the Puri temple was still bubbling with activity and devotees. 'The god has over six thousand servants to care for him,' said Dilip. 'They're divided into thirty-six orders and perform innumerable daily ceremonies, including teeth cleaning, feeding, making offerings, dressing and undressing, and putting the gods to bed for their afternoon nap . . . before devadasis were expelled from the temple, they performed many of these duties. The most prestigious was the evening dance-worship. It is engraved into the temple wall that devadasis must enact scenes from the *Gita Govinda* [a mystical poem based on Krishna's love affair with the cowherdess Radha] . . . Can you imagine!'

'Dilip,' I asked, 'what do you think about the news?'

'I don't know what to think. Devadasis were not as badly off as you seem to think . . .'

I felt lightheaded and didn't have the strength to argue. I made up an excuse and got off the phone. I was overwhelmed by a deep sense of alienation. The problem was so vast and the devadasi system so entrenched, I felt helpless. How could I witness such injustice and not do anything about it? But then again, what could I do? And who was I to presume that I could do anything? What right did I have, after all, to interfere with another culture? I didn't have much faith in television as a medium, but perhaps by making a documentary film, by bringing attention to their plight, I could make an impact on the lives of even just a few women. If we could follow a few devadasis with a film team for a few months, and bear witness to the unfolding drama of their lives . . . if we could capture their wit and wisdom on camera, then this film would be an extraordinary document, a tribute to the strength and vitality of devadasi women. Making this documentary became a necessity for me.

My last night in Belgaum, I dreamt about a teenage girl with long brown hair. She was bouncing in slow motion on the edge of a diving board at an outdoor swimming pool. The sun blazed, and time slowed further still. Bending her knees then jumping up, she sailed into the air, arms raised and face tilting as if to embrace the sun. Floating down again, arms falling gracefully beside her, golden rays now glancing off her hair and teeth, she smiled, and then laughed, but there was no sound. The diving board bent under the impact of her weight, and she jumped again, ever higher. Carefree, glancing over her shoulder to smirk knowingly at those observing, she prepared to dive. Lost in the beauty of the moment, I now suddenly became aware that there was no water in the swimming pool. It was dry and cracked. The pale blue paint was peeling. I called out to warn her, to stop her, but no matter how loudly I screamed, no sound came. I watched, powerless, devastated by my powerlessness.

*

As soon as I was back in Paris, I set up a meeting with executive producer Estelle Bergen. I had not spoken to Dilip since Belgaum. Although it was supposed to be an informal meeting regarding the film we had proposed in northern Karnataka, Dilip brought with him a carefully prepared presentation for a film based entirely in Orissa. Estelle seemed as surprised as I was. Certainly, Orissa was a theatre for a compelling drama. This new film, he proposed, would centre on a woman who wanted to dedicate herself as a devadasi. The camera would follow her in her dealings with the temple authorities and as she defended the system against its detractors. Viewers would have an opportunity to explore the history of the tradition as well as the debate surrounding the proposal to revive it. Although he was careful not to take sides, I knew Dilip favoured a revival of the tradition.

I had to think quickly. I did not want to risk losing my project. Although the obvious approach to a film in Kalyana was to follow a girl as her family prepares her for dedication at the main temple during the pilgrimage in January, I had not made the decision to propose this. It seemed too dangerous. I had wanted to discuss it with Dilip first. Would we be able to get close to a girl slated for dedication? And if we did, would we be putting her and her family at risk? Even as these thoughts ran through my mind, I could hear myself confidently asserting that we could indeed centre the film on a girl's upcoming dedication. 'Lie, and then make the lie come true,' Dilip had once advised me with regard to film proposals. I showed pictures of the few girls in Kalyana and Lagoli who were slated for dedication.

'We'll explore the reasons for her dedication, and follow the attempts of reformed devadasis to avert this fate . . . in the process we would get to know several devadasis and try to understand what their daily lives are like,' I heard myself saying. In order to cover myself, I emphasized that dedication was a sensitive subject. 'Earning the women's confidence won't be an easy task. We'll need at least two months shooting time in the field.'

Estelle called several days later to say that the BBC wanted to move forward with the project about modern-day devadasis in Karnataka. She asked me to write up a new proposal based on my on-site research. All that remained of the history of the tradition was the opening sequence of the film, a dancer performing dance-worship in a medieval temple.

Dilip was disappointed. The Karnataka side of the devadasi system was not what he wanted to show. 'Before the Mughals, devadasis were wealthy and had a high status,' he argued. 'They didn't suffer the ills they do today. Any film we make about modern devadasis will be a misrepresentation of the tradition,' he lamented. Although I did not entirely agree, I, too, regretted that we would not have more opportunity to explore the artistic heritage and history of the system. 'The image of India in the West is so distorted,' he complained. 'We only see the most terrible things, never the good things.' On this point, I agreed.

'Why don't you take over the project? You can direct this film alone,' he said. But I needed him. I didn't feel ready to direct a film in India on my own.

'If you drop out,' I said, 'so will I.' Dilip and I both knew that if he backed out of the project now, after the

BBC had committed to the film, he would lose all credibility in film circles.

Dilip resigned himself to making this film in Karnataka with a heavy heart. Although I was annoyed that Dilip had not told me that he had prepared a separate proposal for a film in Orissa, I let it go. It was a hard enough blow for him that my proposal had been accepted, and not his. As for his idealization of the devadasi system, I felt certain that once he was in the field, once he had had a chance to hear out the women, his views would change.

Had I not been so desperate to make this film, I would have realized that no good could come of our collaboration.

PART TWO

FOURTEEN

Gods, gods, there are so many, there is no place left for a foot.[22]

—Basavanna

IN NOVEMBER 2002, THREE months after my research trip with Vani, Dilip Patil and I flew to Mumbai to prepare for the shoot. Maneesh Nair, our 'fixer', in charge of logistics, picked us up at the airport in his banged-up Suzuki. Nearing his fifties, Maneesh was short, chubby, and wore the few wisps of hair he had left combed sideways over the top of his head. Prodigious bags under watery eyes and a gluey smile gave him a toad-like appearance. One arm thrown nonchalantly over the back of the passenger seat, he twisted around to chat with Dilip as he threaded his way recklessly through traffic, averting collisions only by the thinnest of margins. An incessant stream of Hindi, punctuated by an occasional high-pitched titter, spewed from his lips. I tried to catch Dilip's eye, but he gazed out the window and sighed nostalgically, seemingly unaffected by Maneesh's eccentric driving style.

'Home, sweet home,' Dilip said as we took the six-lane flyover marking the entrance to central Mumbai. He was thrilled to be back in his own element and speaking his own language. I listened to the bubble and flow of their conversation, willing myself not to be carsick and watching the sunrise through the soupy haze of fuel hovering over the sea of cars converging upon the city.

We arrived at Janmabhoomi Marg, near Horniman Circle, at around nine o'clock. This was Mumbai's bustling business district, where Dilip kept a tiny office. Every few minutes a Redline bus, it's warped metal frame bulging with passengers, would barrel by, slowing to disgorge a cluster of workers, and departing in a thick cloud of diesel exhaust. Workers, mostly men, streamed through the streets forming conveyor belts of humanity, heading this way and that, swelling before a street vendor or ebbing into an office building.

Modern concrete buildings, eight to fifteen storeys high, in various states of decay, wore their monsoon damages proudly. Beneath dangling electric cables, multicoloured mould stains could occasionally be whiffed despite the smells of bhel puri being hawked on the street.

Atlas Films was more of a storage space than a production office. A layer of soot covered the desktops and bookcases; stagnant, musty odours filled the air. Dilip cracked a window giving onto a tiny, blackened courtyard, dumped his duffel bag in a cupboard on top of a stack of suitcases and switched on the answering machine. Sagging shelves were crammed with books, ring-binders, folders, stacks of framed prints, videotapes, postcards, and boxes of cheap mini-statuettes of Indian gods, a few of which I had received as gifts over the years of our acquaintance.

While Dilip shot instructions at Maneesh, I browsed the bookshelves until I came across a copy of a book entitled, *How to Win Friends and Influence People*. Intrigued, I pulled it down. Reading through the passages highlighted with yellow, I became embarrassed and stuffed it away.

The shoot was scheduled to span the full-moon festivals marking the death of Yellamma's husband, Jamadagni, and his resurrection a month later. The first festival, Randi Hunimae, was set for the fifth of December; we had only a month to set things up. In the proposal, I had promised a girl slated for dedication and women who would speak openly about their lives. The executive producer had announced the budget of over three hundred thousand dollars. Despite the considerable amount of money raised, we were accorded only five weeks for the filming—very little considering the sensitive nature of our subject and the foreseeable difficulties of getting the women to come before the camera. I was terrified that we would not be able to deliver all I had promised. I remembered Dilip's words, 'lie and then make the lie come true'. *Was it so easy*, I wondered? I was unsure, excited, and scared all at the same time.

The plan was that I would take the sleeper train to Belgaum as soon as possible and meet Vani. Dilip would join us in a week's time, as soon as the film team was finalized. Although the cameraman had been booked, we still had to hire the rest of the crew and rent the equipment.

After a day spent zipping around the city running errands in Maneesh's Suzuki, we pulled up outside the apartment of Ravi Gupta, the cameraman. His windows

overlooked Shivaji Park where schoolboys in short pants
played cricket. Ravi greeted us at the door. As soon as he
opened his mouth, I knew he had been raised in Mumbai's
elite circles and attended English-language schools.
His mellifluous, only slightly lilting English and closely
trimmed beard lent him the air of an academic. At the
time, he was one of the few Indian cameramen shooting
documentaries for European television.

As we entered the velvety silence of Ravi's apartment,
Dilip's bubbly enthusiasm was replaced by gravity. I
expected the two to have a warm relationship, but Ravi
received all three of us with the same formality. He led
us to the sitting room, where two low sofas had been
placed kitty-corner around a square wooden coffee table.
He seemed not so much to look at us, as to glower. I was
intimidated and kept quiet. Ravi, Dilip and Maneesh
reviewed the equipment list, while I let my eyes wander
over the austere interior. Friends had told me that he
was fiercely passionate and often worked pro bono on
documentaries about social issues.

'So tell me,' Ravi said, trying to drill me, 'you've
actually *been* there. What's it like?' I described to him as
best I could the small, dark, windowless houses, the lack
of electricity. Peering thoughtfully at me over interlaced
fingers, he cocked an eyebrow.

'Dilip, are you sure you want to shoot this on film?
Digital would give us so much more flexibility,' he asked,
shifting his attention away from me.

'No question,' said Dilip. I pressed my lips together
and shrugged. Dilip and I had been through this before.

Although 16 mm film was far more pleasing aesthetically than digital, digital was more versatile in low light situations, and, as tape was cheap, we could let the camera roll during interviews. Digital made it easier to take risks. I had begged Dilip to consider its advantages several times, but it was a breaking point for him.

'Perhaps I should bring along my mini-DV camera just in case,' said Ravi.

'No need. I'd sooner not make this film,' said Dilip.

*

Thirty-six hours later, the Udyan Express delivered me to Belgaum at eight in the morning. Vani was supposed to have arrived at six, but was nowhere to be found, nor was there a message at the Sanman Hotel. I had tried calling her several times from Mumbai, but hadn't been able to reach her. I was worried. This time a woman whom I presumed to be her mother-in-law, in whose apartment the joint family telephone was located, answered, but she spoke no English. 'Vani nahi hai,' she repeated over and over.

I called the production offices in Mumbai, but was told by the new temp secretary that Maneesh had just taken Dilip to the airport.

'Airport?' I asked.

'Yes, madam,' the secretary chirped.

'Do you happen to know where he's going?' I asked.

'I did hear something about Rajasthan, but I can't be sure,' she replied cheerfully. I was alarmed. I had wanted

Dilip to come to the field as soon as the crew was hired. I didn't mind him working on another project, but not if it took him away from our film.

'Can you please ask Mr Nair to call me as soon as he gets in? It's urgent.'

*

I spent the night attempting to either read or sleep, and succeeded at neither. As soon as the restaurant opened, I took a booth with a clear view over the patio, holding my breath in anticipation each time a car or a rickshaw pulled up. But Vani did not show. The daily train from Bangalore usually arrived at six-thirty, so by ten o'clock I had given up on her. I began to fear that our film was doomed.

On my way through the lobby to try Dilip again, nose buried in my notebook, I felt an arm slip through mine. Vani, her sari ruffled from the night on the train, was beaming at me.

'Catherine, it's so nice to see you. How are you?' she said.

'Vani,' I said, startled. I was so relieved to see her, I swallowed my annoyance as best I could.

'Why don't you have a shower and rest up in my room? I'll ask the concierge if Iqbal is available and wait for you in the restaurant,' I said.

*

'Catherine, there's something important I want to tell you,' said Vani, sliding into the booth next to me. 'I've been hired to head a research project in Bellary district. The start date is 15 December. I'm only going to be able to stay with you for a month. It's a very prestigious appointment for me; I couldn't turn it down. I've been hoping for something like this for a while.'

'Oh,' I said. 'Congratulations, though it's terrible news for me. What am I going to do without you?'

'Don't worry; I've already lined up someone to replace me. Her name is Amrit. She's a graduate student who has been working with me for years. She's very good in the field.' Vani reached for my hand and squeezed it. I could see from her face that there was no changing her mind. 'I'm sorry,' she said. 'It's too important for my career.'

'I'll never find someone like you, Vani,' I said, and right I was. Vani was the first of six interpreters that I would work with on different documentary projects over the next five years; I never found anyone as intelligent, as compassionate and as talented as she. She took the time to listen, and understand what I was looking for. She explained to me the intricacies of the mentality of the people I was trying to communicate with. 'I'm going to miss you,' I said. 'How am I going to manage without you?'

'I told Amrit to be ready by early December,' she answered, her eyes pools of apology.

'Let's call her later—I think she should come as soon as possible. I want her to have the time to see how you do things.'

FIFTEEN

Each place they touched one another,
became a secret point of pleasure;
whichever lip grazed the body,
there was the taste of jaggery,
every word spoken,
held the essence of the divine;
however they were together,
delight and beauty were there;
each movement made,
was an act of love.[23]

—Dhurjati, sixteenth-century Bhakti saint. This poem is
about a devotee of Basavanna.

OUR DRIVER DURING THE research trip, Iqbal, was
unavailable, so the concierge arranged for another equally
discreet driver, Shiva. By mid-afternoon, we turned onto
the now dry rutted road that led to Kalyana. I noticed for
the first time how perfect the weather was. We were in that
period of grace just after the monsoon, when the storm
clouds disappear and the sun shines. Wildflowers grew
rampant in the fields, trees blossomed and crops flourished.
The sky was a brilliant blue, and the fields, dotted by

flowering fruit trees, were velvety with new growth. The sun, which in a few months' time would scorch the earth, turning everything to a dusty brown, was still mild.

Less than a mile from Kalyana, we crossed five villagers on their way to the fields. I recognized a woman whom I had photographed with her child. The driver stopped the car. The villagers peered through the window as I flipped through a stack of photographs looking for the woman. When I came across a portrait of Rukmini, they laughed and pointed to a boy amongst them. I knew immediately who he was: 'that scoundrel', as Rukmini's aunt Ella called him; 'that scoundrel who refuses to help Rukmini with her son's medical bills'. We looked at each other in astonishment. Before me stood a boy of sixteen. His cheeks were soft and downy; the few tentative hairs above his upper lip had been parted and combed. Beneath his thick, wavy hair were a broad forehead, large velvet eyes and a delicate nose. In an instant, anger was replaced by confusion. He was a boy—a sweet, handsome boy, who surely loved Rukmini as much as she loved him; I could see it in his eyes. Hadn't she once said that his parents refused to give him money? We looked at each other in silence, and, resigned, I smiled. He smiled back, tentatively. I held out a portrait of Rukmini; he took it and, blushing, fell away from the car window.

In the village, the muddy lanes had hardened and the houses opened outward. Saris hung out to dry in the sun, and women sat on their stoops. Children ran to greet us, screaming with delight.

As Vani and I walked through the lanes, women called

out, 'Vanibhai, Catrin . . . namaskar.' The 'bhai' now appended Vani's name was an affectionate term of respect, usually reserved for men.

Rukmini came flying down the stairs of her house and almost knocked me over. She took hold of my arms and pulled me towards her in an embrace that resembled a French greeting, only without the kisses. Women, many whom I didn't know, gathered in a circle around us on Sumithra's terrace, laughing and smiling. Ranavva took hold of my chin and looked me in the eye. Shaking her head in disbelief, she said to Vani:

'Tell her I'm at a loss for words. I was *sure* you would never return.'

'Ranavva the chatterbox, at a loss for words!' I teased her.

'This one calling *me* chatterbox?' Ranavva shot back. 'Now isn't that a case of the pot calling the kettle black!' She threw her head back and laughed heartily. I was moved to see Ranavva again. We shared a certain offbeat sense of humour that transcended language and enabled us to discern, to a certain degree, each other's thoughts and feelings. We had a special bond.

I had taken portraits of her nephews and nieces, which I now fished out of my bag. 'Catherine akka,' she said, wiping away a tear. Other women now gathered around me to wait for their photographs. The children turned the group shots this way and that, trying to figure out which way was up. Unfamiliar with photographic images, they were unsure how to interpret them.

Our return was seen as proof of true friendship and

commitment. Sumithra performed a puja in our honour. She lit incense and waved a camphor flame before the goddess. Yellamma predicted that our plans for the future would go well, and we promised to offer the goddess a sari. Vani reconfirmed the dates of the various festivals, and then took Sumithra aside. A few minutes later, Vani came back looking shocked, and said under her breath, 'She let out that she plans on dedicating Renuka this January at the full-moon festival.' Vani and I stared at each other, incredulous. In that instant we knew that Sumithra and Renuka would be at the centre of our story.

'She admitted it, just like that?' I asked, in shock.

'I think she let it out by mistake, but I'm not sure. I didn't dare say anything. I think it's better that we don't bring it up for the moment. We'll have to come up with the right strategy for dealing with this.'

'Right,' I said, glancing over at Renuka, who stood silently by the entrance, her chin tucked to her chest and her eyes wide. I wondered if, for young girls, there wasn't a certain mystique to the life of a devadasi. Devadasis perform powerful rituals and are close to the goddess. They have a role of honour in village festivals and relationships with high-caste men. They travel far and wide, and come home with fancy clothes, jewellery and perfume. In the eyes of a young girl, the life of a devadasi may seem far more glamorous than that of a married woman in the holakeri, slaving in the fields for a meagre wage.

The women of the holakeri now gathered on Sumithra's porch. The press of bodies and the noise of everyone talking at once overwhelmed me. 'Vani, let's call a meeting tonight at the temple so we can explain once and for all why we're back.'

'Okay,' said Vani. 'But first, let's pay a visit to Kalyanappa, the village chief. We're going to need his cooperation, so we had better start playing by the rules.'

✳

That evening at the Yellamma temple, waiting for the women to gather, Vani and I handed out pens and notebooks to the children. Tamana, the priest, fussed over us, obliging us to sit on mats. Sixty people teemed onto the temple platform, mostly women, but a few men as well. Ganga and Ranavva squeezed in next to Vani and me.

'Where's Sumithra?' I asked.

'Look over there,' said Ranavva.

Yellamma was floating above the crowd, moving towards the temple. As the jagha ascended the steps, I saw that it was Renuka, still wearing a long skirt, who was carrying it. She placed the shrine near the inner sanctum and sat down. Vani and I exchanged looks.

Vani turned to Ranavva and asked, 'Who is allowed to carry the jagha?'

'Only women who have been tied with the beads,' she replied.

'Does that mean Renuka has been tied?' asked Vani.

'Oh . . . well, no,' said Ranavva, looking uncomfortable. 'Renuka has not been tied. She's an exception.'

'An exception,' Vani whispered to me, 'because she is about to be tied.'

A wave of disbelief, followed by a wave of relief, washed over me. If we could film Renuka carrying the jagha—or helping her mother in her ritual duties—then we didn't need to find a woman who would openly admit she was dedicating her daughter; it was implicit. Not only had we found a girl slated for dedication, we already had a good relationship with her mother. All my sleepless nights had been for naught. Sumithra was preparing Renuka for the day she would inherit that jagha. I had been thrown off track by the talk of marriage.

Sumithra arrived at the temple and squeezed in next to Renuka. In my head, I revised the speech I had planned to make to take into account the turn of events. Once the crowd had quieted down, I began, 'We would like to make a film about the goddess Yellamma and her devotees. A film team that works with me will be coming in three weeks' time. We will film the full-moon festivals of Randi Hunimae and Muthaidu Hunimae, marking Jamadagni's death and resurrection. We want know all about Yellamma's life and trials. We will film all the rituals—the blessing of crops, new homes, buffalo milk, the puja in the high-caste houses on Tuesdays and Fridays. With your permission, we will also ask questions about your lives. Those of you who don't want to participate in the film will not be obliged to do so.'

Vani spoke for some time. It wasn't an exact translation. I could see her miming what a film team was—the soundman with his boom, the cameraman, making pictures that would be shown on television, which people had heard of, but rarely seen. A few women lobbed questions at her, which she answered. I noticed that Sumithra looked anxious. She sat staring, immobile and tightlipped, at the ground.

Renuka sat beside Sumithra, staring into empty space. Her thoughts were difficult to parse. She blended into the background, quiet and distant as a wallflower. She rarely took much interest in our conversations and looked perpetually bored. Although I didn't see pain in her dreamy absences, I found them disconcerting. Unlike Rukmini's furtive flights, they remained opaque to me.

Compared to many devadasi children, Renuka had a charmed life. She had the privilege of knowing and growing up with her father; she had never known hunger or experienced any major trauma. Nor did Renuka have any cause for concern about her future. She would one day inherit the jagha; she would be economically independent. Renuka's parents were not pressed by economic need; for them to auction off Renuka's virginity was unthinkable. They would select a good match for her, a man from her own community. Like her parents, she might even get a say in the matter. She didn't have to worry about ending up in a brothel. But what had happened to her father's plan to marry her off?

Vani noticed me studying Renuka. 'The villagers are too afraid to marry their son to a girl destined to carry the jagha, especially if she is still a virgin. They're afraid the goddess will strike him down for impudence.'

*

Shanti, who had lost her joolwa husband during our last visit, was sweeping up the chewed bits of sugarcane scattered over her patio when Vani and I arrived. With a few strokes, she cleared the pile before the door, then beckoned us inside. She was now five months pregnant. Her two-room house was large by village standards and the walls were in good condition. She had a real fireplace with a flue, rather than an open hearth like most houses. In the centre of the room, hanging from thick hemp cords, was an elaborately carved wooden crib, identical to the one I had seen at her lover's wife's house.

Shanti covered the smouldering embers in the hearth with ash and gestured for us to sit down. 'Every morning I wake up and wonder where he is. *Why is he not lying next to me?* I ask myself,' she said. Her face was blank, as if she were too exhausted to summon up any emotion. 'Then it hits me. It all comes crashing down upon me again. Even after all this time, I forget. I expect him to walk through the door at any minute.'

'How are things with your parents?'

'My mother and my sister have been helping me some. My father has only one god—his drink. Nothing else matters to him.'

'What will you do next?' asked Vani.

'What choice do I have?' said Shanti, resigned. 'I belong to the goddess, after all.'

'That is not what the goddess wants . . .' Vani said.

'Shanti,' I said, taking her arm and looking her in the eye. Vani translated as I spoke. 'You weren't at the temple last night. We're going to make a documentary about the goddess. We'll show her festivals and her rituals, but we also need to show how women like you are forced into dhanda. We need to show it so people can understand. It's not right; it's not fair; and many people will be angry to see that this is still happening. We need to show this so that the government will do something to change the system.

'In a few weeks' time, the film team will be here. I hope you will talk to us . . . I hope you will tell us about your life. We'll change your name and the name of your village. The film will never be shown in India. Nobody here will see it. We'll be sure not to show anything that might get you into trouble.'

'In Mumbai, people like you came to the women's clinic to talk to us. They told us about AIDS. Sometimes in Mumbai, I watched television . . . It will only be shown in Catrin's place?'

Vani nodded yes.

'Why not, then?' said Shanti. 'What have I got to lose? Some women who never left this village are telling us not to talk to you. They say you're going to take us away, but I just laugh at them.'

Shanti's consent to be interviewed meant so much to me. I was convinced that if we could earn the women's trust and get them to bear witness, we would have a very powerful film on our hands, a film that paid homage to the strength and resilience, not only of the women of Kalyana, but of women everywhere; a film that would bring to the forefront the injustice of the devadasi system and be the first step on the path to change.

At thirteen, I had been deeply affected by Upton Sinclair's 1906 novel, *The Jungle*, in which he exposed the desperate poverty, the scandalous working conditions, and the hopelessness of Chicago's meatpackers. Sinclair's book resulted in a series of labour laws, which ultimately ushered in an era of profound social change. In my absurd idealism, I saw myself as continuing in this tradition.

In the meantime, I had to figure out how to construct the film. I imagined parallel editing with, on the one hand, Sumithra teaching Renuka on their ritual rounds, and on the other, a group of reformed devadasis campaigning for the eradication of the system. But to oppose the two would not work. The devadasi system as exemplified by Sumithra's life was benign. She lived peacefully with her husband and spent her days fulfilling her ritual duties for the villagers. Because she was married and because of the income she earned from the jagha, she was not subjected to the vicissitudes that most devadasis were. In order to illustrate the mechanisms of exploitation and violence that trap devadasi women in a vicious circle, we needed to contrast Sumithra's life with those of less fortunate devadasis. I knew that if I could get Shanti, Rukmini and Ranavva to bear witness, we could make a powerful documentary.

SIXTEEN

Seeing a courtesan is auspicious;
her touch destroys all evil.
Her bed is the abode of all sacred sites;
making love to her is the way to release.[24]

—Purushottama Dikshitudu, a seventeenth-century
Nayaka court playwright

'I'VE BEEN VERY SICK,' Dilip said. Standing in an STD booth in Halamid, I remained silent. 'Very, very sick. The air in Mumbai does me in.' His voice, over the phone, was thin and weak. I had not been able to reach Dilip since I had left Mumbai, ten days earlier. Whenever I rang, I was told, 'He just left,' or 'He'll be back in an hour.' I was certain that he had been working on another project, but, I reasoned, it didn't matter. Things had gone exceptionally well. The women had welcomed us with open arms and, although the matter had not yet been put before the grampanchayat, the village elders had responded positively to our request to film in the village. As it turned out Dilip's presence was unimportant. The arrival of the crew and the equipment would be the real test.

'I need a few more days in Mumbai,' continued Dilip,

'I'll come once we have a soundman . . . Tell me everything.'

*

Over the next week Vani and I had a wonderful time. I prepared the women as much as possible for the arrival of the crew, but there was not much we could do but sit back and wait. Not wanting to press the women with too many questions for fear that the on-camera interviews would not be 'fresh', Vani and I devoted ourselves to recording as many myths and folktales as possible. This gave us a mission and an excuse to spend a lot of time with the women, who, we soon discovered, loved to recount Yellamma's stories. Embedded in these tales—and the discussions around them—were the worldviews of the women. Ranavva, it turned out, was an avid raconteur. She picked up many stories in Pune.

In one folktale, she recounted the trials and tribulations of an evil landlord who violates the laws of dharma by forcing himself on a devadasi girl who is in fact his daughter. The girl's mother, no longer able to bear the pain of life, prepares to commit suicide, but in a final slapstick twist of fate, turns her knife against her tormentor by mistake. As Ranavva described his gruesome demise, the women reeled with laughter. But there was no mistaking it, the folktale addressed issues such as exploitation, violence against women, rape and incest. Other stories were trenchant indictments of caste and the devadasi system. Folk traditions have always been sources for—and expressions of—positive self-images of oppressed peoples, but they also have the power to be a political tool. Folktales subtly challenge the values of the dominant society, enabling the oppressed to articulate resistance, and then raise their voices and their arms when other forms of protest become possible.

In these recording sessions, I also discovered that the women were inveterate gossips. They had no qualms about trotting out the most intimate details of each other's lives, as long as not too many people were around. Although Rukmini had not wanted to discuss the matter, Shanti confirmed to us that Rukmini's relationship with her lover was on the rocks. In order to 'break the spell' that Rukmini had cast on their son, her lover's parents had decided to get him married as quickly as possible. Rukmini, she said, had threatened suicide.

*

Skirting the buildings of the neo-Gothic British Raj cotton-mills, we turned a corner, climbed a short staircase and found ourselves at the entrance of a hanging bridge spanning the majestic Ghataprabha river, 600 feet across. Rukmini's childhood friend Mariamma, whom we had met on our first day in the village, was home from Goa for a short visit, and Rukmini wanted to mark the occasion with a special trip. Vani and I decided to take them to Gokak, famous for its magnificent waterfall. To our left, beneath distant hills, the reddish-brown river meandered quietly through the black soil plains. Its easy flow was broken when it hit Gokak's rocky belt, a few hundred yards upstream. From there, the river raced, churning and violent towards the sandstone cliffs to the right of the bridge. With a deafening roar, it plunged 170 feet below into the neighbouring valley. Rukmini and Mariamma inched out onto the creaking planks, gripping each other. Standing at the entrance to the bridge, I could see them laughing and screaming in the spray of the river. Rusted metal stays connected the thick twine rope to the wooden planks underfoot. Stepping past Rukmini, I advanced over the churning waters, feeling a rush of adrenaline. Glancing back, I beckoned for Rukmini to follow me to the middle, but clutching Mariamma, she refused. Vani didn't budge from the entrance of the bridge.

A path along the riverbank led us to the head of the waterfall, and further along, to several eleventh- and twelfth-century Chalukyan temples that dot the area. Mariamma, Rukmini told me, was her little sister. She looked not more than thirteen years old. On our first day in the village many months earlier, I had been shocked to see her nursing a newborn. Rukmini and Mariamma were neighbours in the village and had stuck together for as long as they could remember. Mariamma was small, delicate and timid. Rukmini had always protected her from the village bullies. She had luscious shining hair and eyes, high, prominent cheekbones and silky, dark skin. When she smiled her large lips blossomed pink. She was stunning. We sat on the steps of one of the temples and pulled out the cucumber and chutney sandwiches that the chowkidar's daughters had prepared for us. I set up my recorder.

'My [joolwa] husband rents a room for me in a house

in the city. I live in Goa now,' said Mariamma. 'There are six other girls in our house and the gharwali is from these parts, that is how my husband found me, but she leaves me in peace and I do what I want. No one bothers me or expects anything from me. I just take care of my little boy and I miss the village, but it's not so bad there, I'm getting used to it. It's not like the village here where we can wander wherever we want, to the river, or the forest. The city is there and I went out once but I'm too afraid, even if I go with the other girls, so whenever my husband goes on a long haul—he's a truck driver—and will be away more than a week, I come home. He doesn't mind, sometimes he even drops me in Halamid. Our village is very beautiful and I am always happy to come here.'

'Your parents are here?'

'My uncle's family and my friends—Ruki and I have been close since we were very young. We are like sisters. My mother died when I was small. I don't remember her. I was brought up first by my grandmother and after she died, by my uncle and his wife, here in the village only.'

'Are they nice to you?'

'They took care of me from my very young age; they look after me like their own daughter. Even after my aunt had two children, still she doted on me.'

'Did you go to school?'

'No, I never attended school.'

'Why not?'

'My cousin brothers were born around the time I should have been entering first grade, so there was too much housework to be done.'

'Did you want to go to school?'

'I wanted to be helpful to my aunty who is so kind to me.'

'How old are you?'

'I don't know.'

'I think she must be around two years younger than me,' interjected Rukmini. 'I was always bigger when we were growing up, so maybe she is twelve or thirteen?'

'When were you dedicated?'

'I was promised to the goddess when I was very young, I don't remember my first pattam.'

'How did you meet your man?'

'My uncle took me to a nearby village where the gharwali was waiting to meet me. She looked at me and then the next time my uncle took me, the man came to see me. And there was a small ceremony at the temple with some other devadasis. They tied the beads and then I went to live in Goa. They told me that the man was my husband and that I must treat him like a god and do everything he asks. That was about two years ago.'

'Did you have any idea what would happen to you that night, the night of the girl virgin?'

'No, I did not. No one told me a thing. Who would have told?'

'You mean you knew about being dedicated to the goddess, but you didn't know about dhanda.'

'That's right.'

'How did you feel about it when you found out?'

'How do you think I felt?' Mariamma scrunched her brows together and stared at her hands. Her lower lip quivered. There was a long silence. The distant roar of the falls seemed to grow and threaten us. How could I go on with my questions? I wanted to stop, to take her away from this pain, but I continued.

'Did you feel betrayed?' I asked, hating myself.

Vani took a long time to relay the question. I could see that it was not understood.

'Betrayed? Betrayed by whom?' Mariamma looked from me to Vani, confused.

'Betrayed . . . tricked by your uncle and aunt . . .'

'How could I have felt betrayed by them? They have been good to me. This is the life that God has given me. This is my fate. There is no escaping that . . .' Mariamma at this point briefly rotated her hands in her lap and glanced down at her wrists. They were crisscrossed with keloid scars. She had slashed them deeply. My heart skipped a beat. Lightheaded, cheeks burning, I clenched my teeth. Fortunately, Vani hadn't noticed anything and continued the conversation.

'Did you have your first menses at that time, when you were given to your joolwa husband?' Vani asked.

'No, I did not.'

'How old is he?'

'I don't know . . . to me, he seems old, older than my uncle.'

'Does he have a family?'

'I don't know. He doesn't talk much. He comes and I prepare dinner for him and serve him. That is all. He comes twice, maybe three times a week, sometimes he comes with his friends and they are drunk and smelly and I must obey them too and I don't like that, but what can

I do? I must serve and obey. My husband doesn't beat me, I should be thankful for that. Some men are violent. Dodavva [Big Mother] tries to keep them out, but once it starts, it's already too late. There are a few men—Dodavva won't let them near the house, she says they damage her girls. When they come she pretends we are busy and locks the door. But my man has never raised a hand on me and I am thankful for that.'

'How much are you paid?'

'I don't know. Dodavva gives the money to my uncle, but my husband gives me gifts—a new sari or bangles—or money to go to the movies with. He's always telling me to get out and go to the movies. There is a theatre not far from our house, and the other girls take me along . . .'

My attention faded in and out of the conversation. I was incessantly pulled back to Mariamma's wrists, which she kept carefully turned inwards. How could I gently broach the subject? Finally I leaned over and pressed the inside of her wrist. 'What happened, why did you do this?' I asked. Mariamma bit her lip, and Rukmini looked away, pained by the question, or perhaps by the memory of Mariamma's suicide attempt, as if it were her fault, as if she had somehow failed to protect Mariamma.

'It was very hard for me when I first went to Goa. I had never been away from the village before and suddenly I found myself in a house and I was too scared to go out and the other girls, they were not nice to me, because maybe they were jealous that I had my own room and Dodavva gave me special attention and did not make me go with other men. And of course there was my husband . . . it was so painful, I hated him though he was kind to me and hated myself for not being grateful. I could not get used to him at first. For months my only thought was to end my life and then Dodavva went away . . . but the other girls, they found me and took me to the doctor and got me stitched up. After that the other girls were nicer to me. They call me "little sister" and they watch over me. Now, I have my son and I look at his face and I know I could never do that again. I have a reason to live now.'

'In Kamathipura, not a day goes by without some drama like that happening,' said Rukmini. 'There is always some girl with a broken heart slashing her wrists or swallowing poison, but it's hard there, there are so many people, someone will almost always find you before it's too late. Better to come to a place like this where there is no one to stop you,' said Rukmini, glancing over her shoulder at the river.

SEVENTEEN

I saw the fragrance fleeing when the bee came,
what a wonder!
I saw intellect fleeing when the heart came.
I saw the temple fleeing when God came. [25]

—Allama Prabhu, twelfth-century Bhakti
saint close to Basavanna

DILIP ARRIVED TWO WEEKS late, with only a day to spare before the official start date of the shoot. Vani and I returned to Belgaum to meet him. We whiled away the time playing crazy-eights in the hotel lobby while our driver went to pick him up at the train station. The early morning rays glanced through the plate-glass windows and heated the black vinyl couches. Soon enough, I spied him striding across the hotel lobby, his suitcase rolling behind him. His hair was starting to grow long, and he had slicked it back, making him look older than his thirty-four years. With his black jeans, button-down shirt and aviator sunglasses, he was the picture of an 'NRI', a Non-Resident Indian, a class of persons—revered in India—who sought their fortunes abroad. When I introduced Vani to him, he gave a tight smile but did not remove his sunglasses.

'I've reserved a room for you, why don't you go have a rest,' I said since he looked exhausted.

Dilip hesitated, and then sank into the couch. 'I'll just sit down for a minute,' he said, pushing up his aviator glasses and rubbing his eyes. He looked strained and vulnerable.

'My asthma's been very bad,' he said quietly.

The next few days were lost to a flurry of boring, but necessary, formalities. Vani and I took Dilip to Kalyana to introduce him to the villagers. I had always thought of Dilip as a friendly, outgoing person, yet I now discovered a formal, reserved side. Villagers treated him like a visiting dignitary. When Kalyanappa heard we were looking for lodgings for the film team, he proposed two rooms in the compound of the high-caste Hanuman temple. I looked at Dilip, thinking this would be the last thing he wanted, but his eyes lit up with delight and he thanked Kalyanappa for his generous offer. But then his face clouded over and he pointed out that there would be three women on the film team, and that we would be staying for over a month. Dilip didn't need to say more: menstruating women are not permitted to enter sacred grounds. Kalyanappa thought better of his proposal. I was both impressed and taken aback by Dilip's deft manoeuvring.

That evening, Maneesh, the crew, and the equipment arrived from Mumbai in a red Suzuki van. Dilip, Vani and I stood in the parking lot as Ravi supervised the transfer of twenty-two black metal-edged cases of equipment— the camera, lenses, sound mixers, microphones, booms, lights and raw footage. were moved from the back of the Suzuki to the hotel room. The first case had hardly touched the pavement, and already Ravi was pacing up and down, barking orders. The cases were sorted according to function and counted three times. Ravi shouted at the gaggle of wide-eyed bellboys who were eagerly waiting to transport the magical boxes, which, it had been rumoured, had something to do with Bollywood. The restaurant staff stood watching through the plate-glass windows, and even the concierge and the hotel owner came out.

Vani soon arrived with our new translator, Amrit, and yet another round of introductions ensued. At the dinner table that night, the polite exchange of essential details that would have taken place in the States or in France was eschewed. The women, myself included, might as well have been sitting in a curtained off 'family booth'.

Amrit had a small, sturdy build and wore a hand-woven, block-print sari, which seemed to denote a certain pride in her Indian heritage.

'How was your trip?' I asked.

'How was my trip? Oh yes, my trip. Fine fine fine, yes, thank you,' she replied, clutching her purse so hard her knuckles turned white.

*

Vani was scheduled to depart in ten days, leaving us with only one interpreter, so Dilip put an ad in the local paper. The first applicant for the position was a housewife named Malika. She had jet-black eyes, soft, pale skin, and dark brown lips. She was pleasantly plump like women in ads for kitchen appliances in upscale Indian magazines, but her eyes sparkled with intelligence. She arrived escorted by her husband, Nikhil, a tall, barrel-chested man with a bushy mustache and small nervous eyes. I expected him to wait in the lobby while we interviewed his wife, but he tagged along and sat down with us at the booth in the restaurant. Throughout the interview, which took place in English, Malika's husband answered the questions. When I addressed a question directly to Malika, she would turn to her husband, and wait for him to answer for her, occasionally stealing a glance at Dilip to gauge his reaction. Malika's husband looked exclusively at Dilip; I may as well not have been there. *Why didn't she answer the questions for herself?* I was flabbergasted. It was almost comical. Did they not look at me because I am a woman and therefore unimportant? Was it a cultural thing, the symptom of a society where the status of women was so low they were not even to be included in the conversation?

At one point I tried to think up a question that only Malika could answer. 'Malika,' I interrupted, 'what were your favourite subjects in college?'

'She has degrees in law and personnel management,' said Nikhil. Malika turned to gaze upon her husband lovingly, drinking up his words.

'Oh . . .' I said. 'Personnel management is . . .' I saw Nikhil preparing to answer the question so interrupted again, 'Malika, maybe you could answer this question?'

'Oh, no it's okay, really, he knows all this so much better than I do,' she said, not taking her eyes off her husband. Thinking it was a joke, I laughed, but he proceeded to reply for her.

At the end of the interview, Nikhil and Dilip agreed that Malika would accompany us to the field the following day for a trial. I was appalled. I didn't want to have anything to do with her.

'Personnel management, what's that? So she can give orders to her servants? She's a parody of a submissive, retiring housewife,' I said to Dilip after they left.

Dilip laughed. 'I wouldn't underestimate Malika. She seemed smart to me. Besides, she was the *only* applicant for the position. Welcome to the provinces, Catherine! In Belgaum, families don't want their daughters to work—especially with foreigners.'

∗

Belgaum's avenues, canopied by trellises of aerial banyan-tree roots, soon gave way to farmland and forest; trucks and cars gave way to bullock carts and bicycles. The roads became increasingly narrow and rugged. Travelling in a three-car convoy, the film crew snaked its way through the rolling green hills of the Western Ghats. The terrifying scarecrows menaced us from their posts in the fields. On the outstretched arm of one monstrous witch, her profile crudely sketched on a panel of whitewashed wood, sat a row of large black crows. Ochre dripped from her black gash of a mouth; strips of cloth and tufts of long, tangled hair fell from her battered tin hat. The close, bouncy foothills of the Western Ghats flattened out into a more arid, undulating landscape.

When we turned onto the dirt track that led to Kalyana,

I felt my adrenaline surge. This was the technical crew's first time in the village. I knew that the villagers had no real sense of what a film shoot entailed. We parked the cars on the outskirts and unloaded the equipment. Dilip and Ravi, camera on his shoulder, walked down the central lane towards the ooru's Hanuman temple in the main square. The interpreters and I trailed behind the camera assistant. We had decided to immerse ourselves gradually into village life; on the first day we planned to shoot only exteriors and capture the general ambience of the village.

By the time we reached the main square, a handful of people had joined us. Ravi set the camera on the tripod and looked through the viewfinder. A group of men gathered around him. Speaking through Amrit, he explained how the camera worked. He invited several young men to look through the viewfinder. It seemed so strange, so brazen, just to drive up, take out the camera equipment and start shooting. I wondered whether we shouldn't have knocked on Kalyanappa's door first.

The soundman waved the microphone above the heads of the small children. Enveloped in a furry windscreen, it looked like a stuffed animal and made the children giggle. Soon twenty or so villagers gathered. Ravi sat down on a lens case to smoke a cigarette, then looked over at me and smiled. 'Don't worry, Catherine,' he said. 'It's like this every time. In a few days, they'll get bored and leave us in peace.'

Vani took Amrit to the holakeri to introduce her to the devadasi women. No sooner had they left than a motorcycle barrelled into the square at high speed, skidding to a halt a few feet away from the camera, sending a cloud of dust over the assembled crowd. A large, beefy man jumped off and, feet wide apart, hands on his hips, stared at us. Lowering his chin, a lock falling over the middle of his forehead, he looked as if he was about to charge. The crowd seemed to have stopped breathing. Regaining his composure, Ravi crushed his cigarette underfoot and stood up slowly. No one moved or spoke. Seconds plodded by, each separated from the next by an eternity. Then the man started shouting at us and it seemed that he would never stop; spittle flew from his lips, he foamed at the mouth.

Once the initial shock had passed, Malika bravely stepped forward, bowing and scraping. Raising her voice, she explained to him that we didn't speak Kannada, and that she was there to interpret. He was so surprised, he fell silent. She introduced Ravi, Maneesh, Dilip and myself, telling him who we were and why we were there. She turned to me for Kalyanappa's name. The flow of mellifluous words was gentle and calming. By the time she had finished, he had no questions left. He glared at us and marched off in the direction of Kalyanappa's house. The children were quiet.

'Why don't we go over to the holakeri?' I suggested.

The crew picked up the equipment and we walked in silence towards the Yellamma temple. No one said a word.

'Hey, Maneesh, where's the coconut?' Dilip cried buoyantly when we were in sight of the temple.

'Coconut?' asked Maneesh

'What do you mean? We don't have a coconut? How can we do *mahurat* without a coconut?' he demanded to know. A mahurat is a special offering made to the gods at the start of each new endeavour. 'You better find one . . . where's the priest of this temple?'

Vani and Amrit soon arrived with Ganga and Ranavva. Children were sent to summon inhabitants of the holakeri. By the time Maneesh returned, over forty people had gathered. Maneesh had brought not only a coconut, but also huge bags of sugar candy, bananas and flowers. Ravi set up the camera before the inner sanctum. Tamana rang the meditation bell, waved a flame before the goddess, lit the incense and intoned a mantra. Smashing the coconut on the base of the shrine, and placing a flower inside, Tamana returned it to Dilip. The candy and bananas were blessed and distributed to the crowd.

'Okay, time for a group portrait,' said Dilip, clapping his hands. 'Vani, please ask everyone to gather around the inner sanctum . . .' Dilip handed his Nikon to Chandi, the camera assistant, and stood next to Tamana, near the goddess. Bewildered villagers chattering about their odd guests quickly filled the platform. Dilip made room for Ganga and Ranavva.

'Ravi, Catherine, everybody in!' cried Dilip. Dadar, Chandi, and even the villagers were laughing now. Dilip had transformed a tense moment into a joyous occasion.

'Great idea,' I said, squeezing in near the goddess.

'I grew up in a village like this; I know how to speak their language,' said Dilip.

'What did your father do again?' I asked, as ever more people piled onto the temple platform. I knew he had come from a modest background. His father, he had once told me, renounced his inheritance after a family dispute and worked in the restaurant service of the Indian railways.

'He was a tea vendor at a deserted railway post. I worked with him from the age of six, peddling tea inside the wagons,' Dilip said, shooting me a sideways glance.

The white light of Chandi's flash filled the temple three times.

*

Although caste was a problem for Malika, an hour in the field confirmed that she was a brilliant translator. She was fluent in the local dialect and could give a running translation in both directions without interrupting the flow of conversation. The coy timidity she displayed around her husband disappeared without a trace. She was bold, confident and eager to work with us. Dilip told her that if she could learn to work with untouchables, the job was hers.

Maneesh had not yet found housing for the crew in Halamid, the local market town, so after the mahurat ceremony, Dilip and Maneesh went to explore the possibilities while Vani, Malika, Amrit and I paid courtesy visits to our friends in the holakeri. Driving back to Belgaum, Malika, excited by the prospect of working with us, proved talkative.

'Catherine, it must be hard for you to understand. I don't have much freedom. After I was married, I was offered a job as a lecturer in the university, but my husband refused to allow me to take it; he won't let me work! Now that the kids are older, I get bored sitting at home with my mother-in-law. You can't imagine what it took for me to be allowed to interview for this job! I had to threaten him with divorce!

'My father is very progressive, and when I was growing up, he encouraged me to study, to go out into the world, but my husband doesn't see it that way. As far as he is concerned, for me to work is a blow to his prestige. He wants me to sit in the house all day next to his mother . . . he was very impressed with you, Catherine; that's the only reason I'm here. If it had only been Dilip, I never would have been allowed to come. I want to thank you for that. My husband and I don't have the same level of education. It's hard for me, he won't even let me read books! I have to sneak them into the house and hide them under the children's beds. . . I'm so much more intelligent than he is. We just don't have the same level of education! What to do, what to do . . . "Malika, I don't want you reading those books," she mimicked her husband, sticking out her chest and rolling her eyes. "They're bad for your health!"' We shrieked with laugher, tears running down our cheeks.

'You see Catherine?' said Vani, 'This is the situation of so, so many women in India. Even Amrit has a hard time with her husband, don't you, Amrit? Her husband is very irresponsible. Her parents gave her money, but he took it from their account and spent it on his mistress. She's been thinking about divorce.'

'So have I,' said Malika on a more serious note, 'but it would mean being outcast from my community and disgrace for my children and my parents. Maybe in a city like Bangalore it's easier for a woman, but in Belgaum, it's social death.'

'What, what?' asked Amrit, who was sitting shotgun. She was barely proficient in English; I shot Vani a look.

'Give her some time,' she whispered back. 'She needs to get used to the local dialect. Ganga, Ranavva and all the rest liked her a lot. She'll know how to gain the women's confidence, and that's important. Trust me on this one.'

*

In Belgaum, we found Malika's husband Nikhil pacing up and down the hotel lobby, wringing his hands. We sat him in the restaurant and ordered tea. 'What will your housing arrangements be?' Nikhil asked in a whisper, cringing anxiously. 'I know that area. There are no decent hotels.'

'We're looking into renting a house,' Dilip assured him. 'We visited a house today in an upscale colony just outside Halamid, but it seems there is some problem with water supply . . . we're supposed to look at another one tomorrow. As far as catering is concerned, I spoke to the owner of the Sanman, and he has promised to arrange a cook for us. I'm a vegetarian, and I'm *very* particular about food,' said Dilip. Although the word 'caste' had not been uttered, the discussion was about just that. Dilip was letting Nikhil think that he, too, was high caste, and shared his concerns. 'Unless and until we find something decent, we'll be staying right here at the Sanman,' Dilip assured Nikhil. Malika eyed her husband, then beamed at him when he glanced in her direction.

'There is a landowner in Halamid, a former member of the state parliament, perhaps he would know of something. I can provide his contact numbers, we have friends in common,' proposed Nikhil.

'Yes, that would be helpful. I'll have Maneesh call him,' said Dilip.

Malika adjusted the cushion behind her husband's back and gazed upon him as if he were a god, lapping up his every word. After what she had said in the car, I was intrigued. I studied her behavior with great attention, searching for the slightest sign of exasperation, the slightest chink in her armour. She played the role of the devoted housewife to perfection.

I tried to mesh what I knew about Malika with what friends had told me about the traditional world of arranged marriages. Mothers-in-law are expected to be cruel to their son's new wife, and sisters-in-law to cordially detest her. A young bride remains the lowest-ranking family member until a new wife comes into the house, or until she bears a son. With the passage of time and the birth of children, women gradually integrate into, and come to identify with, their husband's family. Most women, when they in turn become matriarchs, expect of their sons' brides the same back-breaking services they once provided. I tried to imagine Malika forced to cater to a dim-witted, capricious old witch. I didn't envy her.

For women who are unhappy in their marriages, divorce is not much of an option. It usually means being outcast from their communities, and disgrace for their children and their families. Women who flee abusive husbands are sometimes turned away by their own parents, who fear damaging the marriage prospects of younger siblings. Women usually lose custody of their children. Without the support of a community, it is difficult for a woman to survive alone. It is no coincidence that, in many Indian languages, the word for 'widow' and 'prostitute' are the same. In such circumstances, it is not surprising that some women develop highly compartmentalized personalities. Perhaps it is a strategy that enables them to cope with the pressures of the extended family, while retaining a sense of self-worth.

In Malika's case, the role of the devoted housewife was an act she adopted for the general public—to keep up appearances, to cajole her husband. But if she had threatened him with divorce, they must have their rows, at least in private. I now understood why women had a reputation for being manipulative: people—men and women—unable to pursue their needs and desires openly learn to manipulate. And since women are, by and large, far more constrained by the societies they live in than men are, wouldn't they earn this reputation? *Some raise this skill to the level of an art,* I thought, glancing over at Malika. I cringed to think how I would fare in a society where a woman's needs and desires were beside the point. My mother, who rebelled against her aristocratic French upbringing, had taught me to express myself openly—too openly, perhaps, for my own good.

Nikhil and Dilip were now negotiating details. 'Five straight weeks is a long stretch,' said Nikhil. 'Can she have one day off a week?'

'Oh, dear,' exclaimed Malika, beaming at him wide-eyed, 'I'm not sure that I could manage more than one week without seeing my husband!' Turning away so he could no longer see her face, she gave me a smirk and a wink.

EIGHTEEN

Our sole duty is joyfully to sing
the glory of him who manifests himself
as the moving and the still,
as earth, water, fire, wind, and sky,
as the small and the great,
as hard to reach, yet easily attained by his lovers,
as the highest reality, immeasurably great,
as infinite Sadasiva, as you and me. [26]

—Appar

AS OUR THREE-CAR CONVOY headed down the last stretch to Kalyana for our second day in the village, an old man walking alone along the vast expanse of fields stepped into the middle of the road and held out both his arms. Our driver jammed on his barely effective brakes and eventually came to a halt. The old man's close-cropped beard accentuated his stern, angry features. Strutting up to Vani's open window, he shouted, 'Turn your cars around and go away.'

'Continue on to the village,' Dilip, seemingly unruffled, said to the driver. Instead of parking on the outskirts of the village as we had the previous day, Dilip told the drivers to turn down the main street of the ooru and park in the square near the temple. It was a statement, a demonstration of our wealth and power.

Kalyanappa and a handful of village elders came to greet us, inviting us to sit with them under the banyan tree. The tension was palpable. I felt uncomfortable and slipped away to the holakeri with Amrit, but the insecurity that beset the upper castes was now spreading to the devadasi community.

Amrit and I sat with half a dozen women on Sumithra's terrace. In addition to the longstanding speculation about our collusion with government agents and/or Mumbai gharwalis, it was now rumoured that we were CIA agents, although no one could explain precisely what the CIA was or why they would be interested in spying on Kalyana villagers.

'It's Balram,' said Ganga. 'He's stirring up trouble. He says you are just going to exploit us.'

'Who is Balram?' I asked.

'Kalyanappa's nephew,' said Shanti. 'He's young, but he already counts for something in the village assembly. During the harvest, he has almost a hundred men working for him.'

'Is he one of the village elders?' I asked.

'His father is,' said Ranavva. 'But he'll be one soon. He's a big man.'

A bent old woman, her lips curling in over toothless gums, her face as wrinkled as an elephant's knee, hobbled up and started screaming at us, 'These people are evil. Why are you speaking to them? They are nice to you now, but later they will take you away. By talking to them, you are jeopardizing the whole village! Tell them to go away.'

Shanti took up our defence. 'Get out of here, you stinking, stupid old lady!' she screamed. 'Can't you see they're women just like us? They're good to us, they care about us, they're here to help us! They are our sisters!'

Ganga, Ranavva and Sumithra joined together in objecting to Shanti's insults.

'I'll say whatever I want,' Shanti shouted back. The old lady, outraged, ambled off.

Before anyone could say a word, Maneesh sauntered up sporting a pair of mirrored sunglasses and a leather jacket. This was the first time many of the women had laid eyes on him. Short, balding and dressed in the trappings of material wealth, he looked like a villain straight out of a Bollywood movie.

'Everybody run!' Shanti gasped, jumping to her feet. 'He's got X-ray glasses. He can see through our clothes! He's deciding who to kidnap!' Shanti and Rukmini bounded off like a pair of gazelles.

Luckily, it was an easy rumour to dispel: I took hold of Maneesh's sunglasses and made the women who remained look through them. They laughed heartily at Shanti's expense. But Shanti's vacillation between fear and support was indicative of the mood in the village. On the one hand, the women were drawn to us and intrigued by the fact that we seemed to genuinely sympathize with them; on the other, they were terrified by the film crew and the equipment and subject to fits of paranoia.

*

Almost two hours later, Amrit and I returned to the ooru. The meeting was still underway. The discussions were tense. Although the village chief, Kalyanappa, was on our side, many other elders were not. Balram was shouting. The village elders argued amongst themselves. All previous agreements were called into question. 'You're just interested in the women's sex lives,' accused Balram. He swore he would get the police to come and arrest us unless we showed him written permission, not only from the government in Delhi, but also from the district and taluka heads. When Dilip replied that we had all the required permissions, Balram's face distorted with anger. He lunged at Dilip, but the villagers caught him and held him back. Dilip looked bewildered and terrified. Kalyanappa suggested we return to the village tomorrow.

'Don't worry,' he said. 'We'll contain this problem.'

I was seized by anxiety. Perhaps I had underestimated the difficulties in shooting a subject such as devadasis. The arrival of two women in the village had not been threatening, but the film crew with their fancy equipment were a different story. I empathized with the villagers. I didn't like the way we had driven into the village square. It felt so intrusive. Shouldn't we have introduced ourselves to Kalyanappa and the village elders first? But Dilip was far more knowledgeable than I about village life. Perhaps aggressive intrusion is an unpleasant yet occasionally essential aspect of filmmaking—and of journalism in general.

Everyone was shaken. Dilip and I walked back to the Ambassador in silence. His eyes were wide and his breathing became increasingly constricted; I thought he was having an asthma attack. 'Are you okay? Do you have your ventilator with you?' I asked. Vani took one look at Dilip and decided to ride in the Sumo.

Once we were inside the Ambassador, Dilip, between ever sharper intakes of breath, finally managed to spit out a few words, 'I'm calling Estelle; we're cancelling the shoot.' Panting, his breathing ever shorter and more violent, his pitch rose, 'In all my time in India, I've never seen anything like this! They're completely mad, impossible to talk to! We're never going to be able to make this film—'

Worried that he was going to hyperventilate, I interrupted. 'Don't be silly,' I said. 'Everything is going to work out, trust me. We're like some sort of UFO that has landed in their village. What would you make of us if you were a villager? Once they get to know us, once they realize we're not here to make trouble, they will accept us.' I don't know how I managed to sound so calm and confident. Truth be told, I was almost as worried as Dilip, and he was having a panic attack.

'I'm calling Estelle,' said Dilip, barely able to squeak out the words.

'Dilip,' I interrupted, 'trust me. Things will calm down in a few days. It's only normal. All is well in the holakeri. The women are still with us, they call me their sister, they trust me and we can trust them.' My words seemed to have a calming effect on his breathing so I kept talking in that vein. Privately, I reasoned that we might as well persevere now that we had come all this way. Cancelling the shoot a few days sooner wouldn't save a significant amount of money, and informing the executive producer would only put her into a panic.

Dilip's breathing gradually returned to normal, and I fell silent. As we approached the main road, we came upon a bullock cart. On the flatbed of the cart were three women surrounding a woman in labour. The road was too narrow to pass them, so we followed behind the bullock cart, waiting for the driver to find a place to pull over.

'Where do women usually give birth?' I asked Dilip, transfixed.

'At home,' said Dilip. 'The labour must not be going well. They're taking her to the doctor.' As we drove by, I caught a glimpse of the pregnant woman's face—it looked grey and slack. Her companions looked grief-stricken. Suddenly, the woman was seized by a contraction. Her arms and face tensed, and her back seemed to arch upwards. She dug her fingers into the side of the cart but didn't utter a sound.

'We have to do something,' I said. Now it was my turn to panic. 'Let's take them in our car.'

'They'll never fit,' said Dilip impatiently.

'They'll fit in the Sumo.'

'Come on, Catherine, these are village women; they're used to it.'

'But the bullock cart is so slow . . . this could be a matter of life and death!'

'Look, we can't risk taking them in our car,' insisted Dilip. 'If something goes wrong, we'll be responsible. They'll get us for everything we've got.'

I turned to stare at Dilip, shocked by his heartlessness. The bullock cart finally pulled over and our driver passed him. Vani was in the Sumo just behind us. As I peered out the back window, she stopped to talk to the bullock cart driver who shook his head and waved her on, refusing her offer of help. I sat back in my seat, fuming.

*

At noon the next day, yet another meeting had been arranged at the ooru's temple. Vani, Dilip and I sat under the pavilion facing twenty village elders, many more than the previous day. They wore ankle-length dhotis and white starched caps. Their faces were grim. Balram was nowhere to be seen. I sensed that this was the critical meeting. Once again, Dilip and I tried to make the project acceptable to the village elders. Frustrating though this process was, my conviction that this was an important film to make gave me limitless energy. I drew my inspiration from the strength and courage of the devadasi women. Although they had difficult lives, they were proud and independent, and they resisted the degradation imposed upon them. They survived terrible abuse with such wit and wisdom, I could not help but marvel at their resilience. Their lives were tragic, and yet, paradoxically, life affirming. If we could capture this on film, we would have a powerful document on our hands. Anti-Slavery International had filed a report on the devadasi system to the UN Commission on Human Rights, but with no results. I didn't have much confidence in television as a medium, but reasoned that this was a film for the BBC. In the past, some documentaries had had an effect on government policies.

Dilip concluded by reminding them that we had allocated a sum in our budget for a donation to the village. This certainly had its own persuasive power.

'We have been raising money to build a new schoolhouse; it should cost one lakh and fifty thousand rupees [$3,750] and we have already raised thirty thousand [$750],' Kalyanappa said. 'Perhaps you could contribute something to our fund? We only have two rooms and one teacher for all the grades. We plan to replace the west wall of the temple compound with a two-storey school building with a room for each grade. We have also requested a second teacher.'

Dilip listened to Kalyanappa, but his face was closed and his arms folded.

'Is it so bad to have to make a donation to their schoolhouse?' I whispered to him. 'With the twenty-two thousand dollars that we budgeted for gifts to the village, they'd be most of the way there. What better cause could we find?'

'I hate to disillusion you, Catherine, but the schoolhouse is merely a pretence to milk us for everything we have. The village elders are just going to pocket the money!'

'Kalyanappa seems sincere to me. The devadasi women speak highly of him . . .' I ventured.

'Even if Kalyanappa is sincere, by the time the other village elders are through with him, there'll be nothing left for the schoolhouse . . . look, these negotiations don't concern you. It's better you stay out of them. I'll tell you this: If they ever do build that schoolhouse, we'll deserve a plaque outside with our names on it!'

'Well, with all we're saving on hotels and domestic flights, we can easily afford to pay for the whole thing,' I snapped.

After the meeting was over, Vani, Amrit and I went to the holakeri to find Sumithra, and ran into Ranavva in the lanes.

'Balram's child was stillborn. It was a boy,' she said. 'The labour was difficult and they let it go on for too long before taking her to a doctor. He's lucky he didn't lose his wife as well.' *It was Balram's wife we passed on the way home last night,* I thought to myself. *He delayed taking his wife to the doctor because he was in the village arguing with us.* I feared that we might be blamed, but the contrary was true. 'The goddess's will has been done,' Ranavva said with a shrug. The goddess had punished Balram. No one will dare oppose us now.

The following day, we moved into Mr Patel's brand new guesthouse. Mr Patel was the Congress Party member that Malika's husband had mentioned. His property was located down a dirt track, just off Halamid's main street. I was surprised to discover such a luxurious estate nestled in the town's centre. The two-acre property was carefully landscaped. Ancient trees, flowerbeds, bushes and vines masked the surrounding wall with its broken glass and barbed wire protection. The driveway led through the lush garden to a large patio where Mr Patel received petitioners. The main house was an elegant, two-storeyed octagonal structure built around an impressive translucent dome.

The guest house, near the gate, consisted of two large rooms, a kitchen and a bathroom. Maneesh had furnished them with cots, tables and chairs. The rooms were large, and had windows facing east, over flowerbeds, and west, over a wooded area. We squeezed a table and a few garden chairs onto the patio so we could have our dinner sitting down.

NINETEEN

O devotees who have joined our group out of love,
Dance, weep, worship him,
sing his feet,
Gather at Kurankatuturai [temple], place of our lord.[27]

—Appar

TENSIONS IN KALYANA REMAINED high. We eased gradually
into the filming process. After shooting the exteriors of
the village and general ambience shots, we interviewed
Kalyanappa and the village elders at length about the
political, judicial and religious practices of the village.
We decided to be present with the equipment, without
necessarily filming, at every event in the community. Our
theory was that once the villagers got used to the camera
and learned that being filmed didn't hurt, they would
open up.

Whenever we heard about a ceremony or festival, we
requested to film it. High-caste villagers invariably kept
their appointments, but devadasis—even those that Vani
and I had cultivated relationships with—gave us the slip
every time. 'We'll have to adapt our technique,' said Dilip.
'We'll just go to the village first thing in the morning and

see what's happening, rather than try to plan things.' This method was far more successful.

One day as Vani and I were talking to Rukmini, I spied Renuka, accompanied by Kassi, walking by with the jagha on her head.

'I'll be back in a minute,' I said, slipping out of the house and following at a distance. Renuka walked past the Yellamma temple, then veered onto a small path that led past a series of sunflower fields to a hamlet about half a mile away. Filming Renuka carrying the jagha was key to visually identifying her as a girl slated for dedication. I ran back to fetch Dilip and Ravi, who were waiting outside the village, and within ten minutes we had caught up to her. In my absence, Kassi and three other devadasis had joined her.

Ravi ran in front of the troupe and, walking backwards, started filming. His assistant held him by the belt in case he stumbled. Dilip asked questions as Malika translated:

'Where are you going?'

'To the farm; a buffalo has been born,' said Kassi flatly.

'Why are you going there?'

'We just told you. A buffalo has been born.'

'So why go when a buffalo is born?'

'We have to make a libation to the goddess before the milk can be sold . . .'

As we approached the farm, Ravi ran ahead so as to capture Renuka's arrival. The farmer's wife rushed to greet her, poured water over her feet, then prostrated herself on the ground. In the interior courtyard a mother buffalo was licking her still wet, newborn calf. Renuka placed the

jagha on the ground, while Kassi lit incense and
The women sang devotional songs, and then the mistress
of the house fed them rice mixed with buffalo milk on tin
plates. When they had finished, Dilip, speaking through
Malika, said to Renuka:

'Renuka, I hear your father is looking for a boy for you.
Do you want to marry?'

'My mother married; why shouldn't I?' she said, and
then refused to answer any more questions.

*

Capturing Renuka carrying the jagha and performing
the buffalo milk ceremony was a major accomplishment.
In the editing room, if we cut these images back to back
with the reformed devadasis discussing the dangers of
dedication, we had the beginnings of a story. That night
after dinner, Vani, Dilip, Ravi and I sat on the patio and
discussed the film.

'The devadasi system as exemplified by Sumithra's life is
benign,' I said. 'She lives peacefully with her husband and
spends her days fulfilling her ritual duties for the villagers.
Nobody will understand what's wrong with the system
unless they see what happens to other girls. Renuka is
an exception.'

'Yes,' said Vani, 'Sumithra is not subjected to the
vicissitudes that most devadasis are because of the money
she earns from the jagha. We need to show the mechanisms
of exploitation and violence that entrap devadasi women;
we need to show Rukmini or Shanti or Ranavva—someone

like that. Someone who has been through the worst of it . . .'

Ravi knitted his brows. 'My feeling is that Sumithra is too boring to be the main character of this film. I'm looking at her through the lens, and her face is blank, almost expressionless. She won't carry our interest.' Dilip looked apprehensively at Ravi, whom he treated with deference bordering on fear. 'Many of the women seem so strong and independent; what about Ranavva? She has real presence on camera. Catherine, I've noticed that she's very affectionate with you. Can't we do something with her?' asked Ravi.

'Ranavva is highly intelligent, but very careful about what she says,' I said. 'Besides, there's no unfolding drama in her life right now, like there is in Renuka's . . . or Rukmini's. What about Rukmini?' I looked up, stealing a glance at Dilip. I had felt all along that she would be great on camera, but Dilip showed no interest in her; I knew that if I pushed her too hard, it would be counterproductive.

✳

Filmmaking requires a great deal of patience. After college, I had worked on a number of feature films and *waiting* had seemed to be the main activity on a shoot. *Waiting* for the director of photography to get the lighting right, *waiting* for the cameraman to frame the shot, *waiting* for the actors to get through hair and make-up, and last but not least, *waiting* for the director's approval. And sometimes the director would arrive on set at the last minute and scrap everything. But with feature films, there was the certainty that eventually, the sequence would be shot. With documentary filmmaking, there was no such guarantee.

Sumithra had invited us to film the morning puja, but when we showed, her front door was bolted shut. 'They left early this morning,' shouted Swapna, Sumithra's neighbour, on her way to the pump well. I sat on the wall of Sumithra's terrace and watched the crew struggle up the lane with the equipment. I was concerned that the crew was getting demoralized with all this waiting around, but Dilip laughed.

'Don't worry,' he said. 'In this country getting a train ticket can take half a day . . . Sumithra will come home at some point.'

Ravi settled onto his lens case and took out a book with a homemade brown-paper dust jacket. He must have felt me trying to discern the title through the cover, for he lifted his eyes from the page and smiled at me.

'It's a collection of poems by a Virashaiva saint,' he said.

'Virashaiva?' I asked.

'Twelfth century. The founding prophet was a poet. He led a protest movement against the Brahmin priests, though he was a Brahmin himself. He also fought for gender equality and widow remarriage.'

I thought about it for a moment, then asked, 'Would that be Basavanna?'

'You've heard of him?' asked Ravi, shocked.

'You have his collection of poems! It's out of print!'

'This is an old copy. I found it on a friend's bookshelf,' he said, passing it to me. 'It's in fragile condition, so be careful with it. Look at the page where the bookmark is;

that's my favourite poem . . . Basavanna was quite radical for his time. He was humanist. It all happened near here somewhere. I'll lend it to you when I'm finished.'

'I looked all over Delhi for this book. A few inscriptions from the ninth century mention protests against the devadasi system, but Basavanna is the first recorded activist.'

'I'm not surprised,' said Ravi, knitting his brows. I passed the book back to him and he leaned forward, 'I grew up in the city,' he began quietly. 'I went to progressive schools. I wasn't exposed to certain aspects of traditional India.' He paused again and cleared his throat. He seemed not to want to be overheard by the other crew members, so I shifted closer to him. 'Some of the documentary projects I've worked on have been a real education for me. Last year I did a film in Vrindavan—the city of widows. Several temples employ widows to sing bhajans, and widows of all ages get dumped there by their in-laws without a rupee in their pockets. You wouldn't believe what they go through. They have to survive by begging, singing and often, prostitution. Some of them are as young as six years old! Have you heard of the 'sevadasi system'? Establishments for widows take them in and require them to cater to pilgrims as a kind of penance. It's sick . . . in some ways, it's similar to the devadasi system. Some people say you can judge a society by the way it treats its weakest members . . . when I see things like that—and what's going on here in this village, for that matter—it kills me.'

Ravi looked up, and our eyes met. His face was set in anger, and for the first time I saw beyond his hot, brooding temper to his fierce idealism.

'The women will open up; it's a matter of time,' I said.

'We shot the film in Vrindavan on digital. The director was a woman and she did the sound. It was just the two of us . . . if I had known, I would have brought my digital camera.'

'Who wants some tea?' asked Dilip, walking up the path carrying thermoses and teacups.

An hour went by. The harvest season was in full swing. Only people too old to work in the fields or women with small children seemed to be around. Swapna, Sumithra's neighbour, returning from the well, set down her water jug and leaned over the terrace wall.

'You're still here?' she asked, incredulous. Then, pointing to the lens cases and microphone, she demanded, 'What's in those boxes, anyway? And what's that furry thing on the end of that pole?' She pointed to the wind cover on the microphone.

As soon as Dilip had finished explaining, a bent old man hobbled up and pointed to the microphone. 'It's a dog—be careful, it bites,' said Swapna, and everyone laughed. The old man shot back a reply, and the villagers began bantering amongst themselves about the film team.

Swapna pointed to Dadar, our linebacker-sized soundman, and said, 'He's so big. We're all afraid of him.' Durga, a beautiful young devadasi of sixteen walked by, pulling a recalcitrant child by the hand. Seeing the film crew, she stopped to glare at us, then asked, scathingly, 'What have you come here for?'

'Durga, you know why we have come, we have come to talk to you, and to learn about your lives,' said Vani.

'Why should we talk to you?' Durga demanded to know. 'If you want to know about our lives, just look around you. Can't you see? We are wretched! We have no proper clothes to wear and no proper food to eat! Without eating, how can we find the strength to work? I've had to accept the worst kind of man for just two rupees, just so I can feed my children. Is that what you're so curious to know?'

'Durga—' pleaded Vani, but she was interrupted by Swapna.

'These ladies are our guests,' said Swapna. 'If you can't manage to speak to them nicely, then go crawl back into your hole.'

'Durga, we are here to try to help you,' said Vani, rising from her seat, but Durga was now enraged.

'Some people look down on me because I don't know who the fathers of my children are,' she said, glaring at Swapna. 'They think they are better than us, but they're not. We, too, are human beings!' She stomped off down the lane. Vani ran after her. Dilip and I exchanged questioning looks. Neither of us had understood a word, but there was no missing the intensity of the exchange.

'She's beautiful. Is she a devadasi?' asked Dilip, who had never met her before.

'Yes,' I said, running down the lane after Vani and Durga. By the time I caught up with them, they were outside Durga's house. Big fat tears were streaming down Durga's cheeks. Vani was holding her hands.

'I have no strength, no energy. I only have rage,' she said, hanging her head in shame. 'My father can still work in the fields, but what will we do when he is old? When they have their own children, my brothers won't support me, yet I'm supposed to be supporting them—making money so they can get married.'

'Have faith; we're here to help you,' said Vani.

Durga's father came out to see what the commotion was about. 'Get out of here. I don't want to see your faces near this house again,' her father shouted at us. Durga ran inside and slammed the door shut.

Vani and I stood in the lane, stunned. 'Look,' I said, spotting Rukmini peering around the corner of her house 30 feet up the lane. Vani and I went to her house and, as Vani translated Durga's words, I wrote them down in my notebook. 'We, too, are human beings, I repeated to Vani. 'What does she mean by that?'

'It's a common phrase used by Dalits struggling against the injustices of the caste system,' said Vani. 'She's something, that Durga. The questions she asked— "Why should we work with you? What are you going to do for us?"—I ask myself the same questions.'

Vani and I had already told the women that we hoped that our film would call attention to their plight so that the government would help them, but that this would take time. We also promised to compensate them for the wages they lost in the fields by spending time with us. This seemed to satisfy them, but it didn't satisfy Vani or me.

'I understand that it's impossible to pay people, because then they'll say whatever just for the money,' said Vani. 'But in this case, I think it's unethical not to pay them.'

'Dilip and I have discussed this. We're going to give the women something at the end of the film—that way it can't be considered unethical. With what we're saving on our budget, we can afford to be generous.'

*

Randi Hunimae, the festival mourning Jamadagni's death—the first important event in our shooting schedule— was fast approaching. On our research trip, we had met Lathamala, a dedicated and effective social worker with the NGO, Myrada. She and a group of devadasis who had renounced Yellamma were planning to hold a simultaneous alternative ceremony in which devadasis could break, rather than reaffirm, their vows to Yellamma. As we were unable to be in two places at once, Dilip and I decided to film the preparations for the vow-breaking ceremony on the eve of Randi Hunimae, rather than the vow-breaking ceremony itself. Unfortunately, our appointment with Kempavva, a former devadasi and the leader of the Yellamma renouncers, coincided with the biannual committee meeting at the main Yellamma temple in Saundatti. I was slated to request permission to film at the main temple during the Muthaidu Hunimae festival.

On Monday, 4 December, Dilip and the film team went to meet Kempavva at the NGO while Maneesh and I took the Ambassador to Saundatti. The meeting took place in the town hall's conference room. When our item came up on the agenda, I was ushered in before the temple trust, an assortment of local dignitaries, state and government authorities, and representatives from the various clans of hereditary priests. Thirty or so distinguished-looking grey-haired men in white simultaneously turned to scrutinize me; I tried not to look scared. I kept my presentation short and simple, explaining that we were making a film about the history of Indian dance and wanted to include a sequence about modern-day devadasis.

There was a long pause. The air grew thick and heavy. Finally, someone spoke up. Although he was speaking Hindi, I picked up a few key words and understood that he was expressing doubt as to our intentions and reminding the committee of the temple's past experience with the press. I rudely interrupted him. 'We have no intention of misrepresenting the temple's position on the devadasi system. I have spent months in the area doing research, and I know that the temple has been very supportive of the NGOs working to eradicate the system. I saw the video of the vow-breaking ceremony that was held here last year. As we speak, my film team is interviewing Lathamala and her group of activists as they prepare for this year's vow-breaking ceremony. We are aware of the extremely impressive work being done on the reform front; we intend to show that too . . .'

'Where will the film be shown?' asked one of the committee members.

'This is a film for the BBC,' I said. 'It will be shown on British television.' The committee members nodded in approval and then debated the issue in Hindi.

I stood at the head of the table, waiting nervously. In the morning, I had hesitated to put on a sari, but now felt relieved that I had. As I was 'properly' dressed, I could not be classified in the other category reserved for foreign women: sexually permissive barbarian. All but a few of the committee members voted in my favour. To this day, I am amazed that permission was granted. During Muthaidu Hunimae, we shot in the inner sanctum of the temple. This kind of access is exceptional. I think the committee was completely mystified: a white woman in a sari working for the BBC and demanding permission to shoot inside the temple . . . it was so bizarre and unlikely, how could they refuse?

*

Maneesh and I arrived back at the lodge after lunch. I was surprised to see that the crew had already returned. Dadar, the soundman, was transferring the morning's interview to a cassette tape so that Amrit could translate it. Dilip seemed nonplussed by what he had seen. 'There were twenty or so women there. They were packing pamphlets, bangles, and things for the puja into boxes,' he said.

I sat beside Amrit as she transcribed the tape.

'What's the first item?' I called from the patio to Dilip, who was now inside the men's quarters.

'The oath that devadasis take at the vow-breaking ceremony,' he called out.

As I listened, I thought I recognized the voice. 'Who is talking?' I asked Amrit.

'That's me. I'm reading the oath,' said Amrit. I was confused. Amrit finished transcribing and shut the notebook.

'Where's the interview?' I asked.

'We didn't do one,' she said, looking at me blankly.

'You didn't interview Kempavva?' I was dumbfounded.

I went inside the men's quarters for the first time. Dadar was lying on the floor labelling rolls of audiotape. Cases of bottled water were stacked to the ceiling. Dilip was lying on his cot listening to Bob Marley.

'Dilip,' I asked, pulling up a chair, 'why didn't you interview Kempavva?' He turned down the music.

'She got there as we were wrapping up. It was too late.'

'Too late? It's only three o'clock now,' I said, confused.

'The crew was already loading the equipment into the car. They were hungry.'

'Did you interview any former devadasi about why she is against the system?' I asked.

'Look, we have the oath, and we shot them putting stuff in boxes. That's all we need. It's not going to be a long sequence. It's just going to be shown in counterpoint.'

'But viewers aren't going to connect with someone reading an oath. They will connect to a woman explaining why she's opting out of the devadasi system. And Kempavva is amazingly eloquent.'

'I tried to get a few of the devadasis to read the oath, but they refused. I didn't get the feeling that they were invested in what they were doing. They were just trying to benefit from the NGO's money.'

'Dilip! How could they read the oath—they don't know how to read!'

'Hmm . . . maybe,' said Dilip. 'But don't worry. If you

think it's so important, we can catch them later. The troupe has three performances per week scheduled in different villages over the next month. We told Lathamala that we'd film one, so you can interview Kempavva then.'

TWENTY

Wise are they who see no difference between a learned, well-mannered Brahmin, a cow, an elephant, a dog and an eater of dogs.[28]

—Bhagavadgita

AT NOON, THE HOLAKERI was teeming with people. Randi Hunimae—the full-moon festival marking Jamadagni's death, when thousands of devadasis break their bangles and begin a yearly one-month mourning period—was to start at dusk. Buried halfway into the earthen platform in the centre of the square were two ceramic pots where, according to myth, Yellamma hid when her son came to chop off her head with an axe. Ravi and his assistant were hanging lights from a tree; Dilip measured out the generator cord. The village elders had assigned high-caste 'helpers' to 'protect' us, but by arguing with the crowd, they made matters worse. Malika, Amrit and I were sitting by the pump well with Rukmini and a few other women. I waved to Gajanan, Rukmini's boy, who ran towards me with open arms. Malika, sitting next to me, afraid that the boy would touch her, recoiled in horror. Gajanan, confused, stopped in his tracks. Rukmini whisked him away. I was aghast. This was it. This was caste at its worst—the fear of being grazed by a two-year-old.

Rukmini and Kassi exchanged knowing glances. I felt as if someone had inserted a knife into my stomach. I glared at Malika, who was now chatting away with her neighbour as if nothing had happened. 'How could you?' I murmured, but Malika, if she heard me, avoided the question. *This unspeakable person,* I thought to myself, *is in the village because of me. I brought her here.* I wanted to scream, but felt as if I might burst into tears. I jumped to my feet and fled from the square, from the film team. My feet carried me to Ganga's, where I knew I would find Vani.

Vani was sitting cross-legged opposite Ganga and Ranavva, who scooted over to make room for me. 'What's the matter?' asked Vani. I didn't know where to begin and couldn't bring myself to admit to her the scene I had just witnessed. My eyes were burning. Ganga and Ranavva looked distressed to see me so upset.

'Vani, I can't believe you're leaving tomorrow. I don't know how I am going to manage without you.' I clenched my jaws, trying to regain control of myself, and blotted my tears with the end my pallu. Vani translated what I had said for Ganga and Ranavva, who stroked my arms and reassured me that they would look out for me when Vani was gone.

'How sweet,' said Ranavva, smiling. 'She's sad because Vani's leaving.'

'Vani, I'm worried,' I said. 'I don't like Malika. I don't like the way she talks to the women.'

'So let Malika work with Dilip and you keep Amrit by

your side,' suggested Vani. While Amrit had earned the trust of the women, she was intimidated by Dilip and didn't dare speak her mind before any of the male members of the crew. She only expressed her opinions to Vani and me privately. Much to my dismay, she also refused to translate questions the women had about fertility and pregnancy. She would simply tell them to ask a doctor. The women were too intimidated to raise such issues with 'important people', like doctors, but no amount of exhortation could get Amrit to change her mind. While such subjects embarrassed Malika, she was determined to be professional and give exact translations. Where Amrit was shy and retiring, Malika was bold and authoritative. Whenever something was happening, Malika always seemed to be there, on top of things, ready to step in and help. The same could not be said for Amrit.

'It's the caste thing. I can't bear it. It kills me,' I said.

'She has the caste feeling, there's no denying it, but she's improved since she's been with us . . . consider where she comes from!' said Vani.

'I'm afraid that after you leave, Malika will assume the role of lead interpreter—what will that do to our relationships with the women?' I asked.

'You're here, Catherine! Have some confidence in yourself! Besides, Malika is hardly the only person with the caste feeling.'

'Why do you say that? What else have you seen?'

'Just look around you—the whole team is high caste!'

'That doesn't mean they're prejudiced,' I countered.

'High-caste people are not always aware of how the

postures they adopt assert their caste and reinforce the status quo. Many dismiss the importance of caste, but being at the top of the ladder and looking down is very different from being at the bottom and looking up . . . Haven't you noticed that Dilip never accepts tea in people's houses? He says, "*vraat*", which means he's on a religious fast and doesn't eat before sundown, but when we go back to the lodge for lunch, he eats. "Vraat" is just an excuse for him.'

'His health is fragile. He's probably just scared of catching something—'

'From boiled tea? I don't think so,' Vani interrupted.

I looked up to find Amrit at the doorway. 'Dilip has been looking for you,' she said. 'The villagers are saying that Randi Hunimae will be celebrated tomorrow night.'

'Tomorrow night?' Vani asked Ganga.

Ganga chuckled. 'Don't worry. It's tonight, trust me,' she said, smiling mischievously. 'They're just trying to get rid of you.'

When Vani and I arrived in the square, electrical wires were hanging off the temple roof and in the branches of the tree. The lights had been installed, but not yet secured. Ravi was leaning against the temple with crossed arms, scowling. Men were gesturing for him to pack up his lights and go. Sumithra, watching discreetly from the edge of the crowd, motioned for us to follow her. In the privacy of her hearth room, she confirmed what Ganga had said.

'They want you to think it's tomorrow so that you'll go away, but it can only be celebrated tonight. I should know,' said Sumithra.

Back in the square, Dilip gave the order to finish setting up the lights.

While I was resting in the back of the Ambassador, the situation reached a low point. One of our high-caste 'helpers' beat up an untouchable boy who was trying to help Ravi.

'Our "helpers" are so drunk, they can't see straight,' said Ravi, disgusted and demoralized. Amrit was reduced to tears by the insults of a drunken man and told Vani that she wanted to quit and return to Bangalore with her.

✳

At six o'clock, the light began to fall. Drums were warmed over the fire. A trumpet sounded and a troupe of men with discordant brass instruments set off in a procession. As they passed houses, villagers emerged and joined. By the time they reached Sumithra's house, the night had fallen. With frenzied dancing and trumpeting, men beckoned the goddess. Once the secret rites inside the house were completed, Yellamma emerged above a headless Sumithra, who now led the procession. She walked slowly—pausing with each step—making her way to the square. Her husband, carrying a torch, hovered protectively beside her. Sumithra placed the jagha on the platform next to the half-submerged, womb-like pots where Yellamma sought refuge from her bloodthirsty husband. Devotees then hoisted up Sumithra. While chanting a mantra, she rang the meditation bell, waved an oil lamp, and lit incense. After moistening the lip of the pots, she decorated them with strips of red and white powder. One devadasi fanned Yellamma with palm fronds, while another waved the horsetail whisk. Devotees stepped forward to offer garlands of flowers and cowry shells, which Sumithra draped around the pots. Sumithra then handed a brass bell to her assistant, who smashed the bangles on her arm. Ravi, who had been filming the proceedings from the ground, now climbed onto the platform beside Sumithra.

Devadasis made their way towards the jagha in small groups, carrying their shrines on their heads, to mourn the annual death of Jamadagni. Sumithra smashed the glass bangles on their outstretched arms, doing her best not to draw blood. While Indian women smash their bangles only once in a lifetime, when their husbands die, devadasis did so every year. Soon, the square was packed with devotees. Tamana, the high-caste priest, heralded in Ganga and her group. Dilip pointed them out to Ravi, who, camera on his shoulder, headed towards them, melting into the crowd. Rather than simply let them do their own thing, Tamana pushed aside the crowd and arrayed the women in a line. When Ravi reached them, Tamana stood beside the women, pointing at the lens and smiling, as if for a still photograph. Dilip rushed to the scene and tried to explain to Tamana that we didn't need him to marshal troops for us, but communicating with Tamana was difficult even on a good day—in the press of the crowd it was impossible.

Lanterns were placed on the platform alongside several other shrines to Yellamma. The villagers fell into formation according to their rank: high castes up front and untouchables behind. A procession of devadasis snaked its way through the devotees, passing before the platform where Yellamma reigned, their faces illuminated by the lamps as they approached. Ravi, with Chandi behind him, holding his belt and his shoulder, protecting him, moved through the surging crowd. Arms swooping like a watermill, Sumithra received offerings, presented them to the goddess, and smeared devotees' foreheads with haldi. One after another, devadasis exposed the tender insides of their arms to Yellamma, and waited for Sumithra to smash their bangles. The women would now enter a period of mourning which would last until the next festival, Muthaidu Hunimae, during which Jamadagni would be revived and Yellamma would be a wife again. Six devadasis were now on the platform. One of them went into a trance. With eyes shut and limp hands dangling from outstretched arms, she flopped about the stage like a rag-doll marionette. The crowd momentarily stood still, faces tilted up. The voice of the goddess rang forth: 'Tonight we have guests from faraway lands. They must be welcomed and treated as gods.'

*

The film shoot had been scheduled to start ten days before Randi Hunimae, the first important event in our story, so that by the festival, we would be up and running. Although the shoot seemed chaotic, Ravi assured us he had 'covered' the event; we had what we needed to make a sequence in the editing room. I breathed a sigh of relief: Randi Hunimae had gone well; we had even received the blessing of the goddess. The villagers would trust us now, I thought; our relationship would finally improve. So far, we had shot only about forty minutes of film, approximately fifteen per cent of our total stock. Although the women were not yet comfortable in front of the camera, they were learning that being filmed didn't hurt. It was only a matter of time, I assured Dilip, before they would relax and forget our presence.

How wrong I was. Ten days later, we were halfway through our schedule and had shot almost forty per cent of our film stock. Whenever we turned on the camera, the women stiffened. None of our interview attempts had been successful. Shanti, Rukmini, Ranavva and Sumithra refused to speak about their lives in front of the male members of the crew, even though none of the men, including Dilip, spoke Kannada. Every time we arranged to shoot Sumithra performing her ritual duties, she would cancel or not show up. Other than the festival, the only interesting sequence we had managed to shoot—the buffalo milk ceremony—had been a fluke.

The reasons for this rather alarming state of affairs were multiple. The divide between the film team and the devadasis was much more difficult to bridge than I had expected. Despite the fact that no mass kidnapping had taken place, many villagers continued to believe that we had an evil plan up our sleeves. In our first attempt to interview Rukmini, she started by saying, 'Everyone is scared of you. They're saying that you're going to take us away, that you are going to kill us. "Let them take me away," I tell them, "I'm not afraid, I'm ready to die." But you're not going to kill me, are you? You're going to feed me, isn't it so?'

Only those devadasis with whom Vani and I had spent time were willing to approach the film team. Though they knew we wouldn't hurt them, they couldn't help but wonder why we were spending so much money recording their daily life. 'What's the *real* reason you're here?' they would ask. Many ethnographic filmmakers enlist the cooperation of their 'contributors' and get them to participate in the filmmaking process by appealing to their pride in their traditions. With devadasis, however, these tactics wouldn't have worked; they had ambivalent feelings about their tradition. Attempts to motivate them along these lines would merely have aroused their suspicion and caused them to question our sincerity. It didn't make sense to them that people in a foreign land might be interested to learn about their lives and listen to what they had to say.

Legally and socially, devadasis were at the margins of society. Politically, they had no power whatsoever. They didn't know how to read or write and constantly had to worry about where the next meal would come from. By sitting on the ground with them, eating their food, and listening to their stories, Vani and I had played down our differences and connected with them on the level of our shared humanity. By showing respect and sympathizing with them, we won their trust and friendship. The arrival of the film team, however, brought our differences into bright, glaring lights. In the eyes of the devadasis, we, the film team, were foreign, educated, high caste and loaded with money. We came armed with dazzlingly sophisticated technology and documents from the government in Delhi. The women perceived us as being politically very powerful and thought it best to at least pretend to comply with our requests.

*

Ten days after Randi Hunimae, Ranavva let out that Sumithra was planning a special ceremony at her house the next morning. We showed up uninvited, but Sumithra didn't seem surprised. She opened the door and gave us permission to set up lights. As Dilip and Ravi got to work, she prepared the oil lamps and lit the incense. I noticed that there was a veil covering Yellamma's face and asked Malika to find out what it was. In the meantime, Kassi and several of the old devadasis arrived, sat down and started singing a devotional song. Dilip, Ravi and Chandi were still fiddling with the lights.

Malika stepped into the circle of women, waved her hands in their faces and screamed at them to stop. Kassi and the other old ladies glared at Malika behind her back, clearly annoyed.

'Tell me what's going on,' I whispered to Amrit.

'She's telling Sumithra to remove the veil from Yellamma's face. It's part of the mourning ritual.' Before I could say anything, Sumithra had removed the veil. 'Malika told her she'd give her ten rupees!' said Amrit, shooting me a look.

'Malika, what are you doing? I didn't say she had to remove the veil. The idea is to interfere as little as possible . . . you're making the women tense. Please get out of shot; we're about to start,' I said. Annoyance must have crept into my voice, for the devadasis trained their eyes on me. Malika looked mortified. Flushing crimson, she stepped over to me and put her hand on my forearm. 'The only way to get these people to cooperate is to rely on the authority of caste. My husband works with these people; he's told me about them,' she whispered quietly but firmly.

I looked at Malika as if seeing her for the first time. I thought she had made so much progress. Could she really have understood so little?

'Okay,' interrupted Dilip. 'Roll sound.' Malika and I scampered out of shot. Ravi focused the camera on the plate of burning wicks. Sumithra stepped forward to ring the meditation bell. Kassi clapped her cymbals together and the women started to sing again. Dilip crouched down behind Ravi.

No sooner was the puja underway than a heavy-set man with white hair and a handlebar mustache walked in and sat down by the door. He seemed to be more interested in the film crew than in Yellamma.

When the puja was over, he introduced himself: 'My name is Basappa. I live at the big farm on the left after the sugar refinery. I have some matters to see to with Sumithra here—but since you are here, allow me to extend an invitation to you and your team for lunch.' His starched white clothes and self-assurance gave him away as a high-caste landlord.

'Invite us for lunch? Have you seen how many

people we are?' asked Dilip, laughing. 'It is we who shall invite you!'

'Even if there were twice as many of you, there would be no problem. So tell me what will you be "shooting" today?' The villagers had apparently picked up on our lingo.

'As you can see, we came to shoot the puja this morning, but since you are here, maybe we should "shoot" you?' said Dilip.

Malika translated, but the conversation quickly slipped into Marathi, a language they both spoke. 'Dilip is teasing him,' whispered Amrit to me, 'asking him what he's doing in this part of town.'

'Business only—some say I'm a ladies' man,' said Basappa, 'but don't believe a word of it. I'm here to make sure Sumithra will come to my fields in three days' time. The green gram and sugarcane will soon be ready for harvesting.'

'Is that all she's coming for?' said Dilip.

Basappa laughed. 'If we wait too long the crop will spoil in the fields,' he said.

'Okay, then we'll come, too,' said Dilip.

'You'll be my honoured guests. My wife will be happy to meet you.'

*

When the crew returned home for lunch, I sounded out Ravi, cornering him near the kitchen when he rose to get a second cup of coffee. 'Did you see Kassi's reaction this morning when Malika interrupted the singing?' I asked.

'No. I missed that. But I did see Sumithra's face when she ordered Renuka to change her shirt,' said Ravi.

'To do what?'

'To change her shirt . . . I guess it was dirty and full of patches . . .' Ravi and I looked at each other and cringed. Up to now, Malika hadn't taken such initiatives.

'She thinks the best way to make this documentary is to exploit our position of power. She thinks we should *pay* the women.'

Ravi frowned and then said, 'That would just make our problem worse. Villagers would mob us, telling us whatever they think we want to hear. I'll talk to Dilip about it. This needs fixing now.'

Seeing us in a huddle, Dilip approached. 'We were just talking about Malika,' I said.

'Yeah, what happened between the two of you today? She was very upset.'

'Upset about what?'

'Upset about the way you talked to her.'

'About the way I talked to her? What about the way she talked to the women!'

'You have to be careful. She's a Brahmin. She's not used to getting yelled at.'

'I didn't yell at her, I snapped at her.'

'Well, be careful with her. We need her.'

'Not if she's going to screw up our relationship with the women—'

'Catherine's right about that,' interrupted Ravi.

'We only have three weeks left and we hardly have anything worth splicing together!' I pleaded.

'But we've shot lots of scenes,' said Dilip.

'But it's vapid. The women have not yet given us the kind of access we had when it was just Vani and me. Without that intimacy, we don't have a film.'

'She has a point . . .' said Ravi.

Dilip drew a deep breath, and pressed his lips together, resigned. 'All right, let's provoke a discussion after dinner tonight, but be careful not to single out Malika. She needs to be treated with kid gloves.'

✳

Variety was not the forte of our cook. Day in and day out, we were fed the same oil-drenched vegetables stewed in the same pre-prepared spice mixture. The sauce was so thick it was difficult to determine precisely what vegetable one was about to eat, and there may have been only eggplant and onion. Dilip's complaints were to no avail. We had made the fatal mistake of including the cost of the food in the cook's package, so he had a vested interest in buying as cheaply as possible. When Dilip lost patience with him, he disappeared without a word and had to be fetched back from Belgaum. He knew we had no other option.

Chubby and dark, with dimpled cheeks and a ready smile, the cook was pleasant enough to look at, but so discreet as to be practically invisible. He would emerge from the kitchen only to place tureens of vegetable curry and rice and a pile of plates on the terrace wall we used as a buffet. Seating at dinner was arranged along linguistic lines: Chandi and Dadar took their meals sitting on the stoop of the men's quarters, while Dilip, Ravi, the interpreters and I would sit in garden chairs with our plates on our laps.

'I thought the puja went well today. Sumithra finally seems to be accepting us,' Dilip said. 'We have enough material to visually describe the devadasi tradition, at least as it concerns Sumithra's life.'

'I agree,' I said, weighing my words. 'But it seems to me that we're only describing a narrow, and rather toothless, version of the system. If we limit ourselves to Sumithra and Renuka, no one will understand why anyone's trying to eradicate the system.'

'The problem for me is that Sumithra's boring,' said Ravi. 'I look at her through the lens, and I'm not sure she has enough charisma to carry this film. There are a lot of strong women in the village—I can tell just by the lines on their faces that they have interesting stories to tell. We need some of those women.'

'We've tried, but they don't want to be interviewed—or they start talking nonsense once the camera rolls,' said Dilip impatiently.

'I think maybe there is something we're not doing quite right. Maybe we should be putting more effort into our relationships with the women. Both Rukmini and Shanti have agreed to do interviews, but they're still feeling uncomfortable with the crew . . . Amrit and Malika, what are your feelings? How can we get this to happen?'

Malika snorted dismissively. 'Dilip and I were discussing it yesterday; the only language these people understand is money, that's what I think. If we pay them, they'll do whatever we want,' she said, her voice full of casual arrogance.

I struggled to withhold the many withering remarks competing for my tongue. The air around me grew thick. I was seething. I glanced around to gauge everybody's reactions. Amrit's black eyes burned like hot coals; Ravi rolled his eyes lazily. Dilip pulled on his chin, folded his arms across his chest, and stared at the ground.

'Hmm . . .' said Ravi, upbeat. 'I'm not sure that, in these circumstances, bribing them is the right way to go. I've seen people try to do it, and, well, once people start doing things for money, the situation can go haywire fairly easily. It's like opening a can of worms. I think maybe we haven't done enough to gain the women's confidence. Catherine and Vani developed sisterly relationships with the women. That bond needs to be extended to the film team. What do you think, Amrit?' Dilip considered Ravi through narrowed eyes and nodded thoughtfully.

'It's a question of time,' replied Amrit. 'Of sitting with them and chewing the fat, of sharing food with them—'

'Well, that's out of the question,' Malika said with a laugh. 'If we all get sick, there'll be no film at all.'

'I've eaten their food on many occasions, and I've never gotten sick,' I pointed out.

'We could begin by accepting the tea they offer us rather than always drinking from our own thermoses. No one's going to get sick from boiled tea,' said Amrit.

'The problem is time,' said Dilip. 'Do we have the time to take the softer route? We hardly have three weeks left.'

'Well, paying people to come before the camera is not

an option. That's not a route I'm willing to take,' I said.

'We need to remember that this is a documentary; there are certain constraints that go with that,' said Ravi. 'And anyway, it wouldn't work. You can't force people to share their intimate thoughts and feelings with you.'

'Okay,' said Dilip. 'So that's it. Let's all work at winning their friendship and trust.'

TWENTY-ONE

Hindus are not very severe in punishing whoredom. The fault, however, lies with the kings and not with the nation. But for the kings, no Brahmin or priest would suffer in their idol-temples the women who sing, dance and play. The kings make them an attraction for their cities, a bait of pleasure for their subjects, for no other but financial reasons.[29]

—Alberuni, eleventh-century envoy to India

ON THE WAY TO Sumithra's the next morning, Dilip stopped in town to buy two boxes of sweets. He offered one box to Sumithra and shared the other with whoever happened to wander by her house. Sumithra had agreed to let us keep the lights up in her house; the jagha room had been the site of many a shared secret on the research trip, and I was hoping to recreate the same atmosphere again. Malika, Amrit and I paid courtesy visits to all the devadasis we knew, and asked them to stop by. Malika made a point of accepting tea every time it was offered.

After three days, Ganga, Ranavva and Chandra showed up for morning worship. When the puja was over, the women sat down and enquired about our wellbeing; Sumithra made tea. Once Ganga had allowed for the appropriate amount of polite conversation, she let us know that they wanted to be taken on a day trip in our car. The request was well timed for we had been debating visiting Badami, the seat of kings in Karnataka between the sixth and twelfth centuries, and only forty miles away. We were looking for a place to film a dance performance—the only remnant of our intention to explore the artistic heritage and history of the devadasi tradition.

*

Badami is surrounded on three sides by soaring red sandstone cliffs. In the seventh century, cave temples built into the sheer cliffs were dedicated to Shiva, Vishnu and Indra. Later, in the eleventh century, intricately carved stone temples dedicated to Durga and Yellamma, among others, were built around a vast reservoir in the centre of the city. The first temples were founded as the Bhakti movement swept south India and the devadasi system first emerged. The later temples were built at a time when the devadasi system flourished; the number of devadasis soared and they came to be hierarchically ranked.

The power-sharing alliance between Brahmins and kings encouraged trade and economic development. Temples used their endowments to construct water tanks, irrigate fields, build and maintain roads. They were large-scale employers, landowners and moneylenders. They maintained doctors, provided beds for the sick and lodging for pilgrims. In wartime, communities took refuge inside the temple walls. During famines, they opened their stores to feed the community. In addition to devadasis, the temple maintained scholars and students, and sponsored debates. Temple festivals and rituals, in which devadasis played an important role, were essential in reinforcing and maintaining this politico-religious-economic order.

The temple was the nexus through which honours, rights and privileges were exchanged and material benefits were redistributed. By publicly making offerings and receiving honours at festivals, the elite displayed their power and affirmed their place in the hierarchy. Gifts of honour bestowed by the temple included fine clothes, ornaments, palanquins, parasols, and the right to be accompanied by a retinue of devadasis and musicians on outings. This held true right through the nineteenth century. As 'persons of consequence,' one British administrator noted, 'could not be seen in public without a proper retinue of devadasis,' the East India Company put them on the payroll and taught them to sing the national anthem, 'God Save the King'.

Notables travelled for days by bullock cart in order to attend a young girl's arungetrum, her first public dance performance. After this, bidding for the right to deflower her would commence. Notables were known to ruin themselves financially, squabbling over such honours.

A number of intriguing temple inscriptions record not only the sale and purchase deeds of devadasis, but also punishments meted out to them for running away or going on strike. One fourteenth-century inscription records a series of strikes by an association of devadasis over a twenty-five-year period which various representatives of the king were unable to resolve. They also record donations made *by* devadasis *to* the temple. I found these particularly intriguing: why would a devadasi give to the temple?

Donations by devadasis were rewarded with special privileges such as the hereditary right to perform certain prestigious duties. In return for a gift, a devadasi and her descendants would be granted the right to wave the horsetail whisk on the god's chariot during the festival, for example, or to perform certain dances during the evening puja. The nature of a devadasi's duties in the temple determined her rank in the temple hierarchy. Perhaps, just as parents today give to their alma maters in the hopes of obtaining special consideration for their children, devadasis gave to the temple to secure their daughters' futures. To see devadasis as merely the passive victims of a patriarchal system is an error. They struggled to retain their dignity, improve the material conditions of their lives, and secure the future of their progeny.

*

The stone columns of the arcade surrounding the reservoir in the centre of the city blended seamlessly with, and seemed to hold up, the cliffs in the distance. Sumithra, Kassi, Ranavva, Ganga and Tamana walked barefoot through the arcade. They were daunted neither by the beauty nor the antiquity of the site. They made their way to the mandapa of one of the temples overlooking the water, sat down, and began to sing devotional songs. They melded so perfectly with the surroundings that it was not difficult to project them back in time. On festival days, one thousand years ago, devadasis would have danced in the halls of the temples from noon to night. The royal elephants would have been decorated and the horses caparisoned while the army stood at attention outside the city. Village processions led by chieftains—similar to the processions to the Saundatti Temple these days—would have converged upon the capital to affirm their allegiance and pay tribute. Elephants, horses, devadasis, fine clothes and ornaments would have been paid in tribute. Rulers and kingdoms have come and gone, I mused, and temples are no longer the locus of power, but the deities and their rituals have survived.

After visiting the temples surrounding the reservoir, we took the troupe to lunch at the local government-run tourist hotel. It was the sort of place one is always relieved to find when travelling: simple, clean and quiet. The dining hall was empty. High ceilings and whirling fans maintained a cooling breeze. The shine of the Formica tabletops reflected the light blue walls. Sliding glass doors opened onto a lawn decorated with potted plants. Tamana chose to eat a packed lunch with the drivers, while the women filed into the restaurant, unsure of how to proceed yet not wanting to seem ignorant. I gestured for them to sit near the window. A waiter came and unceremoniously dropped a stack of menus on the table, which the women picked up and studied, pretending to know how to read.

The team filed in after the women and, before I could object, sat at the opposite end of the restaurant. Maneesh ordered for everybody. So as not to uphold the segregation, Amrit and I sat with the women. Ranavva pointed at different foods and made me repeat the names, making the women reel with laughter. Presuming the women to be low-caste meat-eaters, and the crew high-caste vegetarians, the waiter served both tureens of chicken curry to the women's table. By the time the error was noticed, the women had already helped themselves from both tureens. Although there was plenty left, suddenly none of the crew members were inclined to eat chicken. Maneesh later confided to me that he admired me for having 'taken food' with the women. 'I know it's wrong,' he said, referring to caste restrictions, 'but I can't help myself.' Raising his hands to his face, he cringed and added, 'No, no, I just can't bring myself to do it.'

TWENTY-TWO

Respect, kind treatment and everything else that is agreeable, should all be given unto the maiden whose hand has been taken in marriage. Women should always be worshipped and treated with affection. When women are treated with respect, the deities are filled with joy.[30]

—Bhisma in *Mahabharata*, Section XLVI

THE OUTING TO BADAMI, followed by a ladies' lunch at the guesthouse at which caste rules were ignored, marked a turning point in our relationship to the women. They now informed us of their plans and invited us to film them. We filmed them making rotis, chatting on Ganga's verandah and blessing the sugarcane before the harvest.

Ranavva, my special friend who distinguished herself by her hard work, her discretion and her insight, had warmed up to the film team. She was close to her paramour Sanjay's wife. The two women got along well. We often saw them sitting side-by-side sifting grains. 'She's thrilled to have me around,' laughed Ranavva. 'That way *she* doesn't have to sleep with him.' Ranavva greatly regretted not having children, so Sanjay's wife sent her children over every morning for a visit on their way to school. One day, we stopped by to find Ranavva braiding Sanjay's daughter's hair. Ravi and Dadar followed me inside and we filmed her tying off the braids with shiny blue ribbons. 'This is Anu, Sanjay's youngest daughter,' said Ranavva, without prompting. 'He has five children. Two girls, then two boys and then Anu. The boys come to see me less these days. They're too grown up now, but I still have this one.' Anu smiled sweetly at Ranavva, then ran out the door to school. 'Sanjay has over a hundred labourers working for him during the harvest season,' continued Ranavva. 'He is used to having his orders obeyed. He was very worried when we went to Badami with you. He doesn't like me spending time with you, but what right does he have to tell me what to do? If we were married, it would be different . . . Family women hardly dare talk to men the way we do.'

Although the women were now coming to us with ideas for the film, they remained edgy about certain subjects. For example, Ganga and Ranavva refused to discuss caste discrimination. Aware that that it was illegal and fearing we would confront high-caste villagers or take their complaints to the authorities, they gave us 'politically correct' answers. As for their opposition to the continuation of the devadasi system, however, Ganga and Ranavva were clear. They opposed new dedications in the village. One morning as we sat in Sumithra's jagha room, Ganga said, 'My sister and I have pooled our money to send my niece Lakshmi for sewing lessons. We're saving in order to buy her a sewing machine. The only way to secure Lakshmi's future is to give her the tools to be independent. To rely on a man is a dangerous thing. What if he dies or leaves her? Then what will she do?' In slow and determined speech, she lectured me on the importance of economic independence for women. 'Both of you earn money,' she said to Amrit and me. 'You don't have to depend on men.'

Rukmini and Shanti now joined us. Rukmini began teasing the other women about their lovers. We sat quietly and kept the camera rolling as she raised the stakes. The women were torn between trying to change the subject and laughing at each other's innuendoes. Their witty banter, full of puns and double meanings, became heated.

'Let's ask about the "night of the girl-virgin",' Dilip whispered to Malika.

'When does the first pattam [dedication] take place?' she asked.

'Any age,' said Ganga, 'but it should be before puberty.'

'And the second pattam [defloration]?' asked Malika.

'Once a girl reaches maturity,' said Rukmini. A long silence followed.

'How does it happen? Tell us about your first night,' Malika dared them. The women burst out laughing. An awkward silence followed.

'The first night is terrifying,' said Ranavva. 'We run around, we pray, we fall at their feet and beg them to let us go, but no matter how much we beg them, do you think they'll let us go? When we are in their hands they completely fulfill their desire.'

'They just grab hold of us and satisfy themselves,' said Chandra.

'On the night of the girl-virgin, men are in their festive mood. After eating sweets and drinking, they are bursting with vigour and readiness to do it,' said Rukmini, laughing, 'Do you really think they are going to let us off the hook?'

'When a man says give, it is our duty to serve . . .' said Chandra. 'They just throw the girl on the bed and do it any way they want.'

'No matter how much we kick and scream, they won't let us go,' said Rukmini.

'Even if you kick them where it counts, they receive it gladly,' snorted Chandra.

'And how did you feel then?' asked Malika.

'How do you think I felt? Kicking him and beating him, he took me like that!'

'I didn't have the privilege of a first night,' said Rukmini. 'I was taken in the field by the son of a landlord . . . I was too young to understand what was happening to me. I was ten or eleven, no bigger than Renuka. We went to the field to get the fodder for the buffaloes and he came there with three friends and snatched away our sickles and knives. "Come, let's go," he said. "No," I answered. "Whatever you have to say to me, say it right here," I said.

'He grabbed me and carried me behind the shed. It had rained the night before and the fields were muddy. I was kicking and crying and pleading with him to let me go . . . I kicked him hard and he tripped.' Rukmini laughed. 'He slapped my face and I started screaming and insulting him; I didn't understand what he was doing.

'"What are you going to do, why are you holding me this way?"

'"Let it be, lie still," he said. I kept screaming and

pushing him away and asking him why he was falling over me, and he kept slapping my face . . .

'The children went to get his cousin and told him there was something unusual going on. I was going to tell about his antics, but he made a threatening face and gestured for me not to complain. I lied and said a snake was coming to bite me and that was why I was crying. He told me to go home. I got the fodder and ran home to my mother and told her what had happened. After that, I didn't go back to work at his place. He asked my friends why I wasn't coming. I didn't see his face for two months, and when I saw him I told him, "You are an ass." I would spit whenever I saw him and run away . . .'

At this point the film stock ran out and Ravi lowered the camera. Dilip went outside to get a new magazine of film from Ravi's assistant. Slapping a new magazine onto the camera only took a minute, but we took advantage of the break to get an update from Malika. She was too flustered to be able to relate Rukmini's monologue coherently.

'They were telling us about the night of the girl-virgin, and Rukmini, she, oh, it's terrible . . .' As Dilip plied her with questions, I noticed Ravi was attempting to get a shot of Rukmini and turned to look. No longer the centre of attention, she had allowed her mask of good cheer to melt, her unseeing eyes a window onto pain and sadness.

'She told us about how she was raped,' Malika finally blurted out. Ravi removed his eye from the viewfinder and looked at me. We all exchanged looks and turned our attention to Rukmini, who looked disconsolate.

'Roll camera,' Dilip whispered to Ravi, and then to Rukmini, 'Tell us something good. Tell us about your man; how did you meet him?' he asked, trying to cheer her up. 'Catherine's met him, why haven't I?' In no time Rukmini was laughing again, and talking about her present lover.

TWENTY-THREE

Taking the earth as bowl,
the vast sea as oil,
and the burning sun as lamp,
I laid this garland of verses
at the feet of the lord
who holds a dazzling red wheel
to keep the ocean of sorrows far away.[31]

—Poykay Alvar, seventh-century Bhakti saint

MALIKA AND AMRIT SET to translating the interview as soon as we got back to the lodge. By the time they had finished, night had fallen. The electricity was out, so Dilip brought a table out onto the patio, lit some candles, and sat down to read the text. When he finished, he stood up and offered me his seat. I motioned for Ravi to pull up his chair. Malika and Amrit sat quietly on the stoop of the men's quarters, watching us read. When we finished, there was a long, empty silence. Ravi was the first to speak.

'Rukmini's experience is common. Devadasis have a certain ritual status, but basically they're looked upon as prostitutes and their children as bastards. For the landlord, raping the girl child of a devadasi is not a serious offence . . .

he probably figures she's going to become a prostitute anyway. What shocks me most is not that women—or even sexually immature girls—are raped, but the degree to which it's just an accepted part of society.'

Dilip looked at me. I couldn't bring myself to say anything.

'Rukmini, she's so young, yet she's been through so much,' said Malika. 'All the women, what they have to go through!'

Dilip, having grown up in a rural village, had more exposure to this type of a mentality than Ravi, who had matured in the educated elite circles of Mumbai. 'It's terrible, but that's how every girl in rural India loses her virginity,' he said.

'I beg to differ,' interrupted Malika.

'You grew up in a city,' said Dilip. 'I know what it's like in villages like this. It's terrible, but in this country there are oceans full of pain and sorrow.'

*

Amrit and I knocked on Ranavva's door. Her mother opened it, and I heard Ranavva calling to us from the back room. As I stepped in, it took a moment for my eyes to adjust and realize that she was taking her bath. Squatting in a small slate basin built into the corner of the room with only a petticoat around her midriff, she poured water through her hair. A pot of water heated on a small hearth near the basin; the steam took the chill out of the morning air. Seeing me hesitate, Ranavva insisted,

'Come, sit.' Taking my cue from her, I bowed down before the basin, touching the ground before her as if she were a deity. Ranavva laughed and played the role of a heavenly nymph, allowing the water to run down her neck and shoulders. Amrit looked uncomfortable and sat facing away from Ranavva. Stoking the fire of the hearth, Ranavva chattered away, jokingly suggesting that we send for Ravi to film her.

As Ranavva dressed in a green sari and rubbed oil over her face and arms, Amrit and I sipped the sweet tea her mother had brought. Once her hair was pulled into a bun and she had placed a bindi between her eyes, she sat down between Amrit and me.

'Ranavva, I would like to interview you now,' I said.

'Here? You want to bring the men in here?' she asked.

'Just Ravi. I'll hold the microphone and we'll have Dadar and Dilip wait outside.'

'My mothers are here right now. And I'm already late for the fields . . .'

'Ranavva, it won't take long,' I said.

'I promise I will let you interview me, but not here, not in front of my mothers. Come one day when I'm working in the fields, when no one is around.'

'Okay,' I said. But I was shaken by the previous day's revelations and wanted to further our discussion about the 'night of the girl-virgin'. In an awkward attempt to broach the subject, I explained that in my country if a man forces himself upon a woman, he is sent to jail, which made Ranavva laugh heartily. Annoyed by her mirth, I turned to Amrit and asked, 'How can she take the matter so lightly?'

'You misunderstand,' said Ranavva. 'None of us take the matter lightly. It is a very painful event in a girl's life. For eight days, I cried without stopping. But what can we do? We are powerless. If we are sad or complain no one will come to see us, and then how can we survive? This is the life that God has given us. We must somehow manage and get through it. It is better not to dwell on bad things. It only makes it harder . . . No matter how much a *jogti* [devadasi] suffers inside, you will not hear her complain. That is something we simply cannot do.'

'Does Sanjay hit you often?' I asked. Amrit stared at me, wide-eyed, then remained silent.

'Go ahead, tell me what she asked,' said Ranavva to Amrit.

'Is it acceptable for a man to hit his wife?' she asked, changing the question, I later discovered.

'If she is late with dinner, then yes,' Ranavva said, knitting her brows. Then after a pause, she added, 'But he shouldn't hit her without good reason.' Attitudes such as these were difficult for me to swallow, but I remembered a newspaper article I had read about a failed NGO intervention. Social workers had worked with devadasis for months, trying to get them to renounce the system. They told the women they must speak out about their difficulties in order to convince the government to help them. But by speaking out about their problems, the devadasis alienated themselves from the landlords in their village, and when the NGO's economic package fell through, they were left in the lurch with no means of survival. The devadasis felt betrayed by the social workers whom they had trusted.

'Anger and complaint only bring starvation,' snorted one devadasi. *And what would feminist confrontation bring Ranavva at this point*, I wondered? Probably only harm. Any ideological change would have to be accompanied by an economic one. Ironically, at this point, only the attributes extolled in the Yellamma myth could help the women: restraint, sublimation, resilience and self-sacrifice. This myth—one of many models of devotion and self-sacrifice for women in Hindu mythology—gave them the strength to bear their hardships.

*

The door to Sumithra's house was open. Malika knocked and called inside.

'We're back here; come on in,' said Sumithra.

Malika and I stepped inside. In the front room, Renuka was sweeping ashes over the hearth. In the jagha room, Shanti was sitting against the wall, watching Sumithra put the goddess's paraphernalia back in the trunk. Her eyes were red; she was scowling. Malika sat down beside her and took her hand.

'What's the matter, Shanti?'

'My life is terrible, that's what's the matter,' she said, taking back her hand and wiping her nose with the end of her pallu. I went outside to get Dilip, Ravi and Dadar, who filed into the jagha room discreetly and set up their equipment.

'Malika, ask Sumithra to sit next to Shanti,' said Dilip. 'What have they been talking about?'

'Shanti's been fighting with her father again,' said Sumithra.

'Roll camera,' Dilip whispered to Ravi and Dadar. 'Tell Sumithra to ask why she has been fighting with her father.'

'I'm not fighting with him,' answered Shanti. 'He's fighting with me. He doesn't like me. He doesn't like who I am; he doesn't like what I do, though he's the one who put me into it.'

'So when he speaks to you, just obey him and be quiet, don't say anything,' said Sumithra.

'How can I do that?' asked Shanti. 'He says to me, "Leave my house". He wants me to go back to Mumbai, but how can I do that with this baby in my stomach?'

Rukmini now stepped inside and sat down with Shanti and Sumithra. 'Don't worry, they are your parents. They'll care for you,' said Rukmini.

'No, my father cares only about his drink.'

'Hasn't he quit drinking?' asked Sumithra.

'No. He will never quit. He is destroying himself and our family. I won't be able to get through this without his support, but he doesn't care about me.'

'Yes, he does, you're his daughter.'

'He says "You're not my daughter". He loves all the other children, but not me. He showers his love on my younger sister. He tells me my children are not his responsibility. I can only hope that my children's destiny will be better than mine.'

'Be brave, control yourself. Don't lose heart by listening to your father,' said Rukmini.

'He wants me out of his house, but if I have to live

separately then how will I manage? He blames me for the
death of my brother, but it wasn't my fault—it was his! He
let them into our house . . . they were drunk and they killed
him . . .' Shanti seethed, nostrils flared, chest heaving. She
clenched her teeth in an effort to regain control of herself
and push back the tears.

There was a long silence. Malika leaned over to me.
'Her brother was killed by some villagers—landlords.'

'Why? When? What happened?' I wanted to know, but
Sumithra and Rukmini both looked stunned.

'Nothing, never mind, no one was killed,' Shanti
backpedalled. Sumithra and Rukmini looked relieved. The
momentum of the interview was destroyed. Unable to think
of a way to kick-start it, I ripped the page of questions I
had prepared for Shanti from my notebook and slipped
it to Malika.

'When were you dedicated?' asked Malika.

'When I was very small. I don't remember anything.'

'Who dedicated you?'

'I can't speak about that.'

'Who was your first man?'

'He was from Gulbarga. He took care of me for a few
months, but then he left me for some prostitute, and after
that I went to Mumbai. I've told you about that.'

'How did you meet the father of your daughter?'

'I met him like any other customer, and then he became
my joolwa husband, the one constant person in my life.
For two years we were together, but now he is gone. I just
have to suffer through this life. Sometimes I think I'm
already dead.'

'Did he give you anything? Did his family help you after he died?'

'No, they have not helped me. While he was alive he spent on me extravagantly—clothes, jewellery. After giving birth, I fell sick. He took me to the hospital and stayed with me there, and then when I came home, he nursed me back to life. He cooked for me and fed me with his own hand. He drank from my cup; he paid no heed to caste. We lived life together; we did everything together . . . but he didn't put anything aside for us. Who could have imagined that his life would be cut short so brutally? Who could have dreamed such a thing? And now here I am. I have to return to dhanda and somehow make it through this life. My father wants me to go back to Mumbai, he says he'll take care of my kids, but how can I trust my babies with him? And anyway, I hate Mumbai. I can't bring my children there. And yet, if I stay here—if my parents don't help me—I'll never earn enough to feed them.'

'Don't worry, the goddess will look after you,' said Sumithra.

'No she won't. The gods have forgotten me. My fate is to suffer.'

'With time things will get better,' said Rukmini. 'The children will grow and your life will get better. Looking at your children's faces, you will feel happy.'

'There will be no good times, Rukmini. I have to work, and eat out of what I earn. I have no past, no future. I have nothing to look forward to. Everything is behind me now. All the good times. My man is gone,' said Shanti, tears rolling down her face.

'Wipe away your tears,' said Rukmini. 'You must move forward now. Your daughter is your blessing, and your future. Be thankful for that. Crying and not eating properly will not bring your man back.'

'Tell us about your man. He loved you very much?' asked Dilip in Hindi.

'I don't want to talk about him. Ask whatever you want about my present situation, but not about him.'

'Tell us about your life with him,' asked Dilip.

'Don't be afraid. There is no need to mention your husband by name,' said Rukmini. 'She loved him so much, she couldn't live without him. If he didn't come see her for one day, she wouldn't eat. Until she saw his face again, she couldn't eat. He used to take her to visit temples and to festivals. He took her all over.'

'There is no need to talk about all that. He is gone now. I have no past, and no future. The only desire I have is that my children go to school, so that they will be fit for some job. I hope they will have a better life than I've had.'

'Where did he take you?' asked Dilip.

'If you keep digging me with your questions, how can I control my grief? Please stop,' said Shanti, wiping away tears with her pallu.

'Shanti, I have spoken to you like a sister,' said Dilip. 'I will not lie to you, I will not hurt you. Trust me. Tell us about your man.'

'I cannot speak about him.'

'Only three months and you have forgotten him already?' asked Dilip.

'How dare you say such a thing!' said Shanti, her face

contorting with anger. 'How many times do I have to tell you not to ask such questions? I've done many things in my life, but never anything like this. Why should I speak to you about my man? I told Catherine I would speak about my present situation, but not about my man . . .' Tears streamed down her face. 'I loved him so much—how could I forget him? If they dig into me with their questions like this, I can't control my grief.'

'Wipe your tears,' said Rukmini. 'Nothing will come of your grief.'

'How can he ask if I have forgotten him?' asked Shanti. 'Ask them to turn off the camera . . .'

'Why did you bother to come before the camera?' asked Malika.

Shanti lashed out at her. 'I'm in trouble, that's why!' she screamed. 'If everything were fine, why would I agree to be filmed? Don't I have any rights to own my life? I am crumbling under necessity. I have no choice but to submit and somehow bear the pain.'

*

I didn't grasp the extent of the interview's brutality until after it had been translated. Although interviewers sometimes have to resort to nasty techniques to provoke, this session was cruel by any standards. I was confused by Dilip. Why was he so insistent that Shanti speak about her relationship with her lover? Shanti's case was interesting because it illustrated the precarious situation of even those devadasis who were well taken care of. That she had a loving relationship with her paramour seemed beside the point to me. I confronted Dilip on the patio after dinner that night.

'Ah, Catherine!' said Dilip, exasperated. 'We don't want to depress our viewers with her gloominess. Devadasis' lives are far from *all* pain and suffering. They all have clients that they love—and it's important to show that, too.'

I didn't know what to say. From the start of our project, Dilip and I had differed in our appreciation of the devadasi system. I had assumed, however, that once he was 'in the field', once he met and talked to devadasi women, his views would change. Now I started having doubts.

The next morning, Amrit and I went to see Shanti. She was alone. I slipped her an envelope with three thousand rupees in it.

'For your child,' I said.

'If you're giving me this because you want me to come before the camera, then forget it. I may have to sell my body for money, but no one can make me sell my intimate thoughts,' she said.

TWENTY-FOUR

Creatures exist by food, food grows from rain, rain springs
from sacrifice, sacrifice arises from action. This ritual action,
you must know, originates from the brahman of the Veda,
and this brahman itself issues from the syllable OM. [32]

—Bhagavadgita

'FOLLOW ME IF YOU dare,' shouted Basappa over his
shoulder at the film crew, taking an uphill path from
behind his house. The crew, followed by Sumithra, Ganga,
Ranavva and a few other devadasis, struggled to keep up
with him as he walked briskly along the path between the
forest and the sugarcane fields. The long stalks obscured
the view, but once we reached the top, I could see his three
sugarcane fields sloping gently away from the wood. Ganga
and Ranavva, subdued by Basappa's presence, silently
stretched out a long green sari and threaded it through a
bunch of stalks, pulled it tight, made pleats, and arranged
the pallu. The devadasis then took off their gold necklaces
and draped them over the head of the effigy, some sort of
goddess of fertility.

Sumithra raised the jagha above her head and circled
the effigy with it, but Basappa ordered them to await his

wife's arrival with sweetmeats. The troupe found a log to sit on and settled in. The Sumo soon appeared, tilting sideways along the deeply pitted path, able to inch along at only a few miles an hour. Rukmini jumped out from the back, flashed a bright smile, and ran to join the other devadasis. Dilip looked at me and raised an eyebrow. Over the past week, Dilip, finally acquiesing to take an interest in Rukmini had developed a close, playful relationship with her. Slipping into the driver's seat of the Sumo, he put on a Bollywood soundtrack and beckoned for Rukmini to join him. She climbed into the passenger's seat without further ado. Over the next ten minutes, the crew and the devadasis waited while listening to Rukmini giggle and sing bits of Bollywood songs. Finally, Dilip called out to me, holding the back door open.

'I want you to get this information. We'll speak Hindi and I'll translate for you,' he said. But their conversation was mere chatter about Bollywood movies and stars. I think the true reason he wanted me there was that, for Dilip, it was a delicate dance. He needed to maintain Rukmini's friendship, yet not give her false hopes. In his presence, she was constantly singing, laughing and making jokes. Under his gaze, she opened up like a flower. She was dazzled by his sophistication and culture. Her dream was to dance in Hindi films. Since Dilip had once met Shahrukh Khan, I think she began to see him as an escape route from her current life. She would have been willing to give up anything and everything to get into the film circuit in Mumbai.

When Basappa's wife arrived, Sumithra and the

devadasis began singing devotional songs and circling the makeshift goddess of fertility. Offerings were made, and then Sumithra, late for another appointment, rushed off with her troupe. Rukmini offered to take us to a sinkhole where she and her friends went swimming when it was hot. 'I'm ready to be interviewed now,' she said. She sat against a tree with her feet dangling in the water, lush vegetation all around her.

'Where is your lover now?' asked Dilip. 'He should see you sitting here like an Apsara [a heavenly dancer].'

Rukmini laughed. 'He's afraid of you. He tells me not to talk to you. He scolds me, but I just laugh and ask him, "Who are you, and what right do you have over my life?" And he doesn't like that, but it's okay, I am here with you, is it not?'

'So tell me, Rukmini, when did you meet Naga?' asked Dilip.

'Around three years back at the Dussehra festival. On that day they offer banni, gold leaves and gold candies, so I went with my friends and we came upon these boys and they were plucking leaves, and they were funny because they were twins, so I was looking at them and he said to me, "Why are you looking like that, and why don't you say something?" so I said to my friend, "Who is that bugger?" and the other twin said, "Don't address him like that, he is my brother," and then he winked at me and my friend said, "He's trying to get friendly with you," and I asked, "Is that what getting friendly means?" I was so young—I knew nothing at all. And then I said, "I am going to climb the tree and pluck banni," and he said,

"No, don't climb up there; the ants will bite you. I will do it for you," and then he offered us banni in a gesture of friendliness, and he asked me my name. How many times did he offer banni to me that day? I can't count that high. Everywhere we went, he would follow us and offer banni. "I want to offer you gold," he said, but when his friends tried to give me some he said, "No, don't take it," and then my friends started gossiping. But I resisted him for a long time. A few months later, he stopped me and said, "In whose field you are working? How much are you earning?" and I said "Five rupees." And he said, "You come to my field now and I will give you ten," and I said, "Okay." We saw more of each other after that, and one night there was a performance in the next village, and he came outside my mother's house and signalled to me and we went off together. Then people started complaining to my mother about us, saying we had dirty habits, but we were so young, we were just small children, we told them to shut their mouths . . .'

'Rat-tat-tat-tat-tat,' went the film in the camera. The roll had run out. Rukmini had talked for almost ten minutes without stopping. I looked over at Dilip and asked, 'Did you understand a word of that?'

'She switched into Kannada after the first few sentences . . .' said Dilip, shrugging.

Although we had brought equipment for simultaneous translation, which was supposed to enable us to guide the interviewee and elaborate on points of interest, we had abandoned it early on. Amrit had started out conducting the interviews, but as a social worker she was used to drawing out the women in rapid-fire conversation; this technique was inappropriate for film—cutting the interviews back in the editing room would have been impossible. Attempts to get her to adapt her style failed, and Malika, therefore, took over the questioning, which meant that Amrit was required to translate simultaneously. The pressure, however, was too much, and her English was not up to par; she would freeze as soon as the speaker began. Dilip and I had long ago resorted to making lists of questions, briefing Malika, and hoping for the best.

'Maybe we should try using the simultaneous translation kit again,' I suggested. 'At least we could reorient her.' While Ravi went back to the car to get another magazine, Amrit and I sat next to Rukmini

'I think there are some children in the bushes. Take me away from here where no one can listen. Why don't we go to your place?' Rukmini asked. 'I'll have to pick up my son, though, in the village.' In no time, we had picked up Gajanan and were on our way to the guesthouse. Rukmini rode in the Ambassador with Malika, Amrit and me. She was unusually silent.

'Do you have any questions?' I asked, seeking to put her at ease.

'Where did you say your film will be shown?' she asked, her voice wavering.

'Only in my place,' I reassured her. 'Ruki, I would never do anything to hurt you. I would never let any part of this film be used in a way that could hurt you. You can trust me, Ruki; I think you know that. Besides, we will change your name; we will change the name of your village. You have nothing to fear.' I took Rukmini's hand and she held it tightly all the way to the lodge. We set up the camera in the women's quarters. The soundman clipped a microphone to Rukmini's blouse and left the room. Ravi crouched behind the camera while Malika, Dilip and I sat across from Rukmini and Gajanan. Amrit stood outside with earphones and the microphone, ready to translate. 'Just a general idea is okay; no need for simultaneous translation,' I said, trying to put her at ease.

Once the camera was rolling, Dilip said, 'So tell us, Rukmini, tell us your true love story.'

'True love story?' snorted Rukmini sarcastically. 'What's there to tell?' She looked defiantly at Dilip, then dropped her eyes to the floor. Speaking now with resignation, she said, 'I used to love him very much. For his sake, I was ready to give my life. My family tried to force me to leave him, but I swore I wouldn't. Now he doesn't love me anymore.' There was a long silence; only the hum in the camera could be heard. Then Rukmini looked up suddenly, a spark in her eye, and continued. 'He came to me and said, "Why did you go with them [the film crew] when I told you not to?" and I said, "Who are you to tell me what to do? I'll do whatever I want," and he told me that he could get plenty of tomatoes in the market, and I retaliated by telling him that even I could get plenty of bananas. Then he said he could easily pocket twenty girls like me and I retaliated by saying that if I roamed in the market even I could get twenty men.' Rukmini threw her head back and cackled. 'He said, "Go on roam, let's see you roam," and I laughed at him and said, "Yeah, you can very well see me roaming." He had nothing to say to that. He went quietly after that.' Gajanan, who had been playing quietly on Rukmini's lap, now started crying.

'Are you upset because I criticized your father?' Rukmini asked Gajanan, bouncing him on her leg. 'Don't you think your father deserves criticizing?'

'Rukmini,' said Dilip, 'I heard your man is going to be getting married.'

Rukmini, surprised by the question, stared back at Dilip in silence for what seemed like an eternity. When she finally spoke, it was with resignation. 'The wedding should be some time soon; I don't know when. Just thinking about it, my heart falters. I must learn how to make myself hard and turn my heart into stone. He says that when he's married, he'll spend one night with his wife, and one night with me, but who knows if our love will withstand his marriage. If he gets a beautiful wife and sleeps beside her, then he'll look at me and ask himself, *Who's that beggar-like thing?* One day, sooner or later, he will desert me. That's why I must have the courage to leave him now. If I wait for him to leave me, then I will lose all my senses and roam around like a mad dog. Better I leave him now.' Rukmini busied herself with Gajanan's curls, so that she would not have to look up and reveal her tear-filled eyes to us.

'But he said he'd spend one night with her, and one night with you . . .' said Dilip, trying to cheer her up.

'That's what he says now. . .'

'So, it's not true?'

'Who knows. Once he has a wife, he'll forget about me. Love never lasts.'

'Will you be upset if he gets married?' asked Dilip.

'Upset?' asked Rukmini, incredulous. 'If I stay here, I will surely die, so instead I'll go to Mumbai. How can I see him marry someone else? He says that he won't get married unless I come to the wedding, but how can I see that? All the important people will be there, and they'll sit there drinking soda pop while everyone clicks photos. How can I watch that? I'd rather die. I'd rather kill myself by drinking poison in the marriage hall. That is why I've decided to go away. I'm going to leave so as to forget him. I've decided to return to Mumbai.'

'To Mumbai?' asked Dilip.

'Yes, I've decided to go to Mumbai. My time has come. I'll go after the full-moon festival. I already sent word to my mother. She's going to come down and take me back.'

'But in Mumbai, will you be able to forget him?'

'They say that time heals all wounds, so eventually I suppose I'll get over him. Some days I'll think of him and cry, other days I'll remember all the things we did together and I'll smile. The sorrow will always be there, but no one can take my memories away from me; I'll keep his photo on my breast. What else can I do? We are helpless. Every day I fight with my family because of Nagappa. They beg me to leave him. "We will support you," they say, "Take whatever you want, but leave him." If he doesn't come to see me for a day, I don't eat. Today, men, they run after the young girls promising this and that, lavishing gifts on them, but then another one comes along and they say, "This one is good, but that one is better," saying things like that, they make us go out of our senses. We love them, but they don't really love us, so we should get smart and leave them first.'

'Who dedicated you, and how old were you?'

'I can't talk about that. Please don't ask me such questions. I was very young, I can't remember.'

'How do you feel about your dedication now?'

'Now that the beads are tied, there's nothing I can do. If I had known, I wouldn't have let them do it. I would have met a nice boy and married him.'

'But even now you can get married,' said Dilip.

'No . . . no . . . no one will take me now. I'm too old, and I have a child. Who'll take me now? I'll just spend my days looking at my son's face. I have no need for a man.'

'You are speaking with such sorrow . . .' said Dilip, seeking to cheer her up.

'Yes . . . yes . . . such sorrow. My life is full of sorrow,' said Rukmini, breathing deeply and pressing her lips together.

'Why such sorrow?' asked Dilip.

'What can I do?' asked Rukmini. 'I have a son now. If only I had no child, I would have run away with anyone and gotten married, but with this child, who'll take me? When I found out I was pregnant I prayed to the goddess to give birth to a son, because if I had had a daughter, her life would have become dirty like mine, so I prayed and promised to offer the baby's weight in sugar if it were a boy.'

'What would you have done if it had been a girl?' asked Dilip.

'I would have killed her. Really, I would have strangled her at birth. Nobody criticizes boys. Even if a boy doesn't get married, he can get women in the market and no one says a thing, but for a girl, it is not like that. She would have become a devadasi, like me. Her life would have been full of pain and sorrow like mine . . .' Rukmini stopped speaking and stared at the floor. The hum of the film running through the camera could be heard as we waited to see if she would start speaking again.

The tail end of the film whipped through the magazine. The roll was over.

*

Rukmini's time had come; she could no longer hide in the fantasy that one day her lover would marry her. He was destined to marry a highborn girl, and Rukmini would have to replace her mother in Mumbai. Social workers estimate that fifteen thousand girls are dedicated as devadasis every year. Rukmini was just one of many girls who would end up in brothels in Mumbai and other south Indian cities. By bearing witness, Rukmini gave a human face to this ancient form of sexual slavery, which we needed for our film. However, any relief we might have felt was overshadowed by the revelation of her imminent departure for Mumbai. The news hovered like a poisonous cloud over the crew. After dinner, we sat on the terrace racking our brains to find a way to help her.

'I'd offer her a job caring for my child,' said Ravi, 'but I know it would never work. My mother's impossible and Rukmini hasn't the proper training, much less the discipline to hold her tongue.'

'Giving her money isn't a solution. If her uncle doesn't confiscate it, she'd spend it within a few months,' said Dilip. 'Isn't there some sort of vocational training for women, some sort of course that we could enroll her in?' asked Chandi.

'She'd have to go to Belgaum district for that,' I said. 'There are no NGOs active in this area.'

'Maybe she has relatives she could stay with there,' Malika suggested.

'In the past two years several NGOs working with devadasis in Belgaum were shut down for misappropriation of funds. Besides, they focus on villages, not individuals. And Rukmini's too old for school. There aren't really any programmes that would be appropriate for her,' said Amrit. There was a long silence. The inevitability of Rukmini's situation made it hard to breathe. We all stared at our feet.

'Well, we'll be giving each of the women a few hundred dollars at the end of the shoot. Money might not be the solution, but it's better than nothing,' I said. 'Maybe we can give Rukmini something extra.'

'I know,' said Dilip, 'we'll buy her a buffalo. She'll be able to milk the buffalo and live from the proceeds. We'll give it to her publicly before we leave so that no one can take it away from her. It shouldn't cost too much, and Patel's son-in-law should be able to find one for us. I'll talk to him tomorrow.'

The crew breathed a collective sigh of relief. Thinking of the spirited, sensitive Rukmini in a stinking Mumbai brothel, exposing herself to AIDS—and worse—was too much. At least this way, she would have an alternative.

The next day Mr Patel confirmed that they could find us a good buffalo for a mere three thousand rupees—seventy-five dollars. This solution gave us the impression that we were 'doing something', and it allayed our feelings of guilt.

TWENTY-FIVE

With hands that have fondled the courtesan's breasts,
they offer to the god.
The mantras they recite come flavoured
with the breath of betel chewed in their mouths.
They never hesitate to steal the god's own treasure.
What divinity would reside in images served
by grasping priests like these? [33]

> —Venkatadhvarin, seventeenth-century
> Nayaka court playwright

CHITRAGUDI IS A SMALL hamlet with a large Yellamma temple perched on the banks of a river near ancient ruins. Every year an important new-moon festival takes place there. Although Vani and I had visited during our research trip, we had not planned on filming. An unexpected turn of events, however, brought us to the site. After breakfast, Amrit and I had called the NGO Myrada's headquarters to enquire about Kempavva's theatre troupe of former devadasis. Lathamala, a social worker with the NGO whose economic initiatives enabled hundreds of devadasis to give up the tradition, told us that they had just left for the festival in Chitragudi. Sumithra had invited us to accompany her to this festival, but so much seemed to be happening in the village, we had declined. Realizing that this was an excellent opportunity for Kempavva and Sumithra to meet, we jumped into our cars and rushed after her, arriving by mid-morning.

The wealthy landowner/priest who owned the temple, twirling his handlebar moustache and swatting at the parrot on his shoulder, said he was pleased to see that Vani and I had decided to come, but lamented that we had missed the highlight: he and his sons had demonstrated their devotion by firewalking. Earlier, they had traversed a bed of burning coals. As we spoke to him, a succession of devadasis, of whom he barely took notice, prostrated themselves at his feet.

The tiny hamlet had been transformed into an immense fairground. Village processions, trumpets blaring, swarmed over the surrounding hills and converged upon the temple. Makeshift stalls selling fruit, flowers, calendar art of Yellamma and her acolytes, pastries, cowry shells and bangles, saris, creams and beauty products of all sorts had mushroomed across the fields. A spice vendor sat impassively next to her ancient scale, dwarfed by tall pyramids of colour. The air reeked of tangy spices, incense and hair oil. To improve their karma, pilgrims offered small change to ascetics who had taken eccentric vows such as to stand on one leg for ten years, or never sleep. There were contortionists, fire throwers, men hanging on hooks, and dancers thrusting skewers through various body parts. It was possible to have your hair cut, ears cleaned and shoes shined, all at the same time. A dentist, whose only tool was an oversized pair or iron pliers, invited passersby to sit in his colonial relic of a wooden dentist's chair. Wide berth was given to the still-smouldering 20-foot bed of hot coals which the priest with the pet parrot had earlier traversed. Musical troupes and devadasis, with Medusa-like hair, were in great number.

Myrada had set up a tent, so we found Kempavva easily, but surveying the huge crowd, I despaired of ever finding Sumithra. There were many women carrying jaghas, and most wore the same auspicious green sari.

'Come, I know where to find her,' said Kempavva. Amrit and I left the film team at the tent and followed Kempavva across the river to a hillside where a hundred or so devadasis in green saris were sitting beside their jaghas. Within a few minutes, we had located Sumithra and Renuka. Learning that Sumithra was about to take the jagha to the temple, Amrit went to fetch the crew. I felt slightly anxious about what Kempavva would make of the mother/daughter pair and wondered whether we might get them in trouble. But Kempavva and Sumithra chatted amiably.

When Amrit returned, we made our way to the temple. A door to the inner sanctum opened onto the river. A thick knot of devotees, thigh-deep in the current, waited for the goddess to shine her divine light upon them. As we approached, I caught sight of Ravi with the camera on his shoulder, and retreated to the far bank to stay out of shot. Unable to push her way through the crowd of devotees, Sumithra passed the jagha forward. Yellamma sailed overhead as devotees stretched out their hands to receive her blessing and pass her forward to the inner sanctum where the priests were waiting. Once the jagha was inside, they pulled the curtain closed, and performed a special rite to renew its power.

Devadasis in trance waving horsetail whisks paraded around the temple in muddy saris, occasionally prostrating themselves on the riverbank. On firm ground, a group of men and small boys shrieked and shouted as they threw coloured balls of powder at the temple walls. When the curtains opened again, I caught a glimpse of the jagha beside the glistening black icon of the temple.

In the dark and damp recesses of her cave-like dwelling, Yellamma reigned. Priests in white dhotis received offerings, presented them to Yellamma, and then passed them back. Kempavva nudged me and pointed to a small, scowling girl of around ten. With only a shimmering cloth around her loins and a sprig of neem between her teeth, prepared like a suckling pig for the roast, she was being tugged towards the temple by her guardian. Fighting back tears, she desperately tried to cover her budding breasts. Kempavva looked at me, took a deep breath, and, with a wave of the arm, invited me to survey the crowds. Looking carefully now, I saw more than a few small girls naked or wearing skirts of neem leaves on their way to the temple.

As dedication was illegal we couldn't tell Kempavva about Sumithra's plans for Renuka, but there was no need; she knew. Kempavva intercepted Sumithra as she left the temple and asked her to attend her troupe's performance, which was to be carried out in the mandapa of a medieval temple in ruins, 400 yards from the main temple.

After parading through the crowds pounding large drums to announce their performance, the troupe made its way to the ruins. Sixty or so people were in attendance. The first scene depicted villagers consulting the goddess Yellamma about a terrible drought. 'There are no rains and the fields are not yielding properly. The boys behave badly,' the elders complained. The goddess, speaking through the head devadasi of the village, demands that a child be sacrificed to her, singling out the daughter of a devadasi. The mother begs for her daughter's life: 'Oh, Mother, please don't ask for my daughter. I'll send her to school and get her married. I have no other children. Please, Mother, no! Don't ask her to be a devadasi like me. Don't ask her to live this rotten life. Please, no . . .'

But the goddess doesn't relent. She threatens the devadasi and the whole village with death and disease unless the child is sacrificed. As the head devadasi, pretending to be in trance, pressures the devadasi to dedicate her daughter, a group of Dalit youths steps in to demand that she prove her sanctity by walking through fire. The head devadasi admits to being a fake and begs for mercy, explaining that such shenanigans are her only means of survival.

The head devadasis then tears off her costume and addresses the crowd: 'The devadasi system exploits women in all respects. Young girls who are offered to Yellamma end up as prostitutes in Mumbai, Pune and Sangli. Her children do not have a father and will be looked down upon and humiliated because their mother is a devadasi. A devadasi's life is hell. For these reasons, we ask you not to dedicate . . . we will now sing a song written by a devadasi. It depicts the humiliation and suffering of the woman who has been dedicated.'

Then she sings:

'Oh, Mother, my life has been only pain and sorrow.
Death is far better than this wretched life.
With beads and nose rings and arms full of green bangles,
They make me believe that God is my husband.
Oh, Mother, pain and sorrow burn my life!'

The chorus then joins in:

'Do not tie the beads and dedicate your daughter.
Nowhere is it written in the epics or the scriptures that girls should be dedicated.
Yellamma does not ask for girls to be dedicated.
Believing in superstition, we are deceived by cheats.
The system is only here for economic reasons.
Yellamma does not ask for girls to be dedicated.
To satisfy the hunger of lust, our daughters are sacrificed and exploited.
Do not tie the beads and dedicate your daughter . . .'

Sumithra remained stone-faced as she watched the play, as if the subject didn't concern her. When it was over, actors and chorus mixed with the crowd. Sumithra placed the jagha on top of her head, called to Renuka, and started to walk away. Amrit and I caught up with her to offer her a ride back to Kalyana in the Sumo. She accepted and, returning to the ruins where the cars were coming to fetch us, she sat down to wait.

'We hope that you have not taken offence . . .' said Amrit.

'No, of course not,' Sumithra replied, turning away, but it must have been humiliating for her. Kempavva soon appeared and sat down next to Sumithra. Taking her hand, she asked, 'Did you like the play?'

'Yes,' said Sumithra. 'It was very good.'

'What are your plans for your daughter?' asked Kempavva.

'We are going to get her married. Even I am married. We are looking for a boy for her,' said Sumithra.

'I am glad to hear that,' said Kempavva. 'There is no need to dedicate your daughter. The gods do not demand it. Nowhere is it written in the scripture that girls should be dedicated. It is only superstition that leads women to dedicate. But we must get educated now. There is no reason to fear the goddess. She does not need or want bonded servants. Look at me: four years ago I broke my vows to the goddess, but nothing has happened to me. Shushila also. Many women have shaved off their *jats* [matted hair], and today they all are fine. We must stand up against this system which destroys our lives and the lives of our daughters.' As Kempavva was lecturing Sumithra, Ravi and Dadar arrived.

'Yes, you are right. We must all leave the system,' said Sumithra as Ravi filmed her.

'Why don't you leave the system? Why don't you put the jagha in the river and leave it there?'

'Yes, I will do that,' said Sumithra. Kempavva and Sumithra spoke for several minutes. I could see that

Sumithra was agreeing with everything Kempavva said. When the troupe was leaving and Kempavva was called away, I turned to Sumithra.

'Sumithra,' I said, 'what did you think of what Kempavva had to say?'

'She speaks with a lot of wisdom. She is right; I should go put the jagha in the river.'

'Sumithra,' I said, 'if you did that, how would you survive? I want you to tell me what you really think. Have no fear. Kempavva doesn't know where to find you.'

Sumithra looked at the camera, and then turned to Amrit and said, 'Our village needs the goddess. If we don't go from house to house on Tuesdays and Fridays, she troubles us. Villagers invite the goddess to their farms because she brings good health and fertility, peace and prosperity. When we bring the goddess everything is blessed—the family, the fields, the buffaloes. If we don't fulfill our duties, the landlords will be angry and the goddess will trouble us . . . How can we leave this tradition? It has been practised since time immemorial; we must continue. To leave it is impossible . . .'

TWENTY-SIX

Is there any sacrifice better than
the Rite of Desire,
where lovers' moans are the mantras,
the vessels for the offering are
full breasts with golden beauty-spots,
caressed again and again?[34]

—Sesamu Venkatapati, seventeenth-century
Nayaka court playwright

TEN DAYS BEFORE THE pilgrimage to Muthaidu Hunimae,
at which Jamadagni's resurrection is celebrated, Kalyana
village seemed to shift gears. Migrant labourers and
sex workers began to return home and everyone set to
scrubbing their houses, their animals, their kitchens. Ganga
bought new cooking utensils and decorated them with
haldi, kumkum and garlands of flowers. The next day she
started boiling down the oddest array of ingredients—
jaggery, salt, tamarind, green pepper, neem flower—into
a sticky green mush. Each caste group was responsible
for making ritual offerings that took days—and, in some
cases, weeks—to prepare. A giant black cauldron, worthy
of the Wicked Witch of the West, was set up in the main

square of the holakeri. Vendors from the market town with wares piled high on the backs of their rickety bicycles, teetered around Kalyana's uneven lanes hawking their goods. Sumithra bought a sari for Renuka, and we filmed her showing Renuka how to apply haldi and kumkum powder to the goddess's face for the puja. Renuka told us on camera about the upcoming pilgrimage and festival. The film team had gradually reached a point where we were light and mobile—catching scenes here and there as they happened. Chandra invited us to film her four-year-old daughter's wedding, explaining that she knew it was illegal, but that it was the only way she could protect her child from being 'taken' in the fields by an upper-caste landlord when she was older. Villagers no longer felt threatened by our presence, and were happy to be interviewed.

*

Tamana, the Yellamma temple priest and Ganga's lover, insisted that we film him performing the puja at the Shiva temple in the ooru. White flowering creepers still moist with morning dew clung to the stone walls of the compound. Scattered among the many trees and bushes were stone tablets inscribed with an ancient script. A banyan tree spread its roots in the far corner of the garden, a small tank of holy water stood nearby. In the centre of the compound was an medieval Shiva linga carved in granite. The linga, which represents Shiva's phallus, was about 20 inches tall and 10 inches wide. It rested on a yoni, an oval-shaped womb with a cervix-like spout.

'Before the Yellamma shrine was built, I was in charge of this shrine,' Tamana explained, ringing the bell hanging from the lintel to scare away evil spirits. I examined the scripts on the many ancient stelae leaning against the compound walls, wondering whether they were commemorative tablets, edicts, or temple records. 'Those were found over the years in fields around the village,' Tamana said. 'Kalyanappa has alerted the authorities, but still no one has come. We don't even know what language it's in.'

Tamana rang the meditation bell as he gathered together the tools he needed for the puja: battered tin cups filled with different coloured powders, milk, flowers, a jug of water. Ravi set up the tripod near the Shiva linga. After a brief prayer, Tamana encircled the Shiva linga first with the clapping bell, then with the incense, and then with an oil lamp. Invoking the god with garlands of Sanskrit words, the meanings of which he knew not, he invited Shiva to descend from the heavens and inhabit the linga. After dressing the linga with a red powder and the lips of the yoni with alternating strips of red and white, he rinsed it with three cupfuls of milk, rubbing away the powder with his hand. The milk collected in the yoni and poured out of the cervical spout, falling onto the stone below. He then covered the linga with white powder, which he rinsed off first with milk, then with water. He repeated this process over and over again, alternating red and white powders to dress the linga, chanting all the while. Tamana occasionally looked at the camera and smiled; he seemed to enjoy being filmed. Twice he leaned over to catch the milk as it flowed from the spout of the yoni and drink it or sprinkle it over the crown of his head.

In Hindu creation myth, the gods and demons churn the 'ocean of milk'. Milk is the light of the moon; milk is divine wisdom sucked from the breast of the goddess. Red is blood; red is violence. It has the potential to pollute, but it can also be transformed into a creative force; in men, blood is transformed into semen and, in women, blood is transformed into milk. Red and white; blood and milk. Tamana now covered the linga with white powder and drew three horizontal lines of red across its centre, signalling Shiva's descent into the linga. The last touch, a red dot applied near the top, represented the god's third eye. Blood and milk were now transformed and Shiva conceived anew.

*

As soon as the ceremony was over, Amrit and I scouted the holakeri in search of something to shoot, and ran into a woman we had never seen before. She stopped in her tracks and looked at me searchingly. Jet-black hair offset her fair skin and olive green eyes. A tentative smile spread across her face. In an instant, I knew it was Padmini, Rukmini's mother who had arrived from Mumbai.

'Catrin,' she said, reaching for my hands. She had a heart-shaped face and pouting, sultry lips. She was still beautiful, although dark circles under her eyes made her look older than her thirty or so years. Her gaze was at once open, receptive and weary. Life had taken its toll on her.

'Rukmini amma,' I said, making her laugh ('amma' means mother). We stood smiling at each other, not sure what to do next.

'Come,' said Padmini, pointing up the lane towards Rukmini's house.

Rukmini pulled out some mats for us to sit on, stoked the hearth, and put on a kettle for tea. Once we had settled down, I complimented Padmini on her daughter.

'She has many talents,' Padmini agreed. 'Have you heard her sing?'

'She is always singing and laughing and playing,' I said. 'I never tire of her company.' I had so many questions; I didn't know where to begin. 'Has Rukmini told you about our film?'

'Yes, she told me everything,' said Padmini. 'She said you wanted to interview me.'

'Yes, would that be all right?'

'I don't see why not--I have nothing to hide,' she replied.

'I'll go get Dilip,' said Amrit, rising. I noticed a black duffel bag with the English words 'One Way' written across it in pink fluorescent lettering.

'Kya hey?' I said in Hindi. 'What is that?'

'These are the gifts my mother brought from Mumbai, but she won't allow me to look yet,' said Rukmini, pulling the bag towards her and giving her mother a pleading look.

'Acha, acha,' said her mother. 'Okay.' Taking the bag and opening it, she drew out one sari after another and placed them before Rukmini, laying a few aside for her sister's family.

'Where's the blouse for this one?' asked Rukmini, pouting and dissatisfied. Perhaps the gifts were no substitute for her mother's presence.

By the time the film crew arrived, the floor was strewn with clothes.

'What's this?' asked Dilip in Hindi. 'Are you selling saris?'

Padmini laughed. 'These are gifts for Rukmini and my sister.'

'Look at this beautiful pallu,' said Rukmini. 'Too bad the rest of the sari is not this colour . . . is there a blouse to go with it?'

'No, there isn't; but look, here's the petticoat. This one's a special gift from Ganesh,' said Padmini.

'Ganesh is your man?' asked Dilip.

'Yes, he's a taxi driver.'

'Why have you come back to the village?'

'I have come back for the festival. I vowed to the goddess that without wearing any blouse, that with only a robe of neem leaves, I would climb the hill and walk three times around the temple. I have prayed for the wellbeing of Rukmini and her son. I have prayed that their health should be all right. All I have asked for is good health.'

'So even in Mumbai, you worship the goddess?'

'Yes, we have brought her there from our villages. We worship her just like in the villages.'

'When will you return to Mumbai?' asked Dilip.

'As soon as the festival is over.'

'And you will be taking Rukmini with you?'

'Yes, Ganesh wants me to bring her back so we can

live together. He is a nice man. He has three children, and they all go to school. He has promised to send Gajanan to school too.'

'Rukmini has been in the village all this time. Isn't it hard for you to be so far away from your daughter?'

'Yes, it's very hard. My sister begs me to return, but what can I do? I have no choice. If I don't work, I don't eat, nor does my family. Who do you think pays the bills around here? I try to put money aside, but something always comes up. When Rukmini was taken [raped] in the fields—I heard she told you about that—she suffered from internal bleeding and spent a whole week in the hospital. And then again when she gave birth, she was so young, her bladder tore and she had to have an operation. Both she and Gajanan were very sick.'

'So after the festival you will be taking Rukmini with you to Mumbai?'

'Yes, she wants to come,' said Padmini. Rukmini slipped her arm through her mother's.

'I should be the one there in Mumbai,' Rukmini said. 'I have not been a good daughter. I should have gone long ago. My mother has been working all this time looking after me, but now it is my turn to look after her.'

'Mumbai is no place for my daughter. She's not strong enough; that is why I am still there. If I had known it would be like this, I would have married her off. I pray to God that both of us can be happy. What can I do?' Padmini paused and bit her lip, struggling to keep back the tears. 'She is not happy in this life, and neither am I. You take her away to your country. Really, take her along with you. Tell

Catherine akka to take her to her place. I'll pull through this wretched life alone. If Rukmini meets a nice man, I will marry her off . . .' Padmini buried her face in her hands.

Dilip gave Ravi the signal to stop filming. 'I think that's enough for today,' he said.

'But wait, we should ask her about the reasons for dedication; she's very articulate. We need it for the film,' I insisted.

'We don't have enough film. I've been meaning to talk to you about this—we're getting very low. And who knows what will happen at the festival? Anything could happen, and once we run out of film it's finished. We can't get the same stock in Mumbai. We'd need to go all the way back to Paris, and you know that's impossible. We really need to be careful. I've been thinking about just calling the shoot to a halt until the pilgrimage.'

'Dilip, this is an opportunity we can't miss. We need it.' I was confused.

'Okay, but only a few questions.'

When I turned back to Padmini, she was playing with Gajanan, who was peeping out from behind his mother's shoulders and smiling. 'He is the light of my life,' said Padmini, tweaking his cheek. Malika tried to reach out and tickle him, but he dodged behind his mother.

'Do you mind if I ask a few more questions?' I asked.

'I don't know where your questions will lead us, but I am ready. You have a kind face. Ask whatever you want and I will answer if I can,' said Padmini.

I signalled to Ravi to roll the camera. 'Why were you dedicated?' I asked.

'My sister and I, we lost our parents when we were very young. We had no food to eat, no clothes to wear, and no bed to sleep in. Complete poverty and hardship, do you understand? Only after I was dedicated did I start eating—'

'Didn't you have your uncle?' interrupted Rukmini.

'That uncle,' she said with a snort. 'What did he do for us? As soon as I was old enough, he got me dedicated; that's what he did for us. Once I was tied with the beads, I was given to a landlord in this village. After a few months, I became pregnant with Rukmini and then he stopped coming to see me. After that I went to Mumbai. Only then did my sister and I start to eat. I returned to the village to give birth, but then I had to go back to Mumbai again.

'I went to Mumbai just to earn our food, just to be able to eat, not for anything else! Not for luxury, not for money, just for food, just for the stomach!

'After some time, my sister took over caring for Rukmini. She told me not to go to Mumbai, but I had no choice; I had to go. That's the only way I had to survive.'

Padmini studied me as Malika translated what she had said. I nodded and then asked, 'Why did you dedicate your daughter?'

'I tied the beads because she is my only child. How will we survive when I can no longer work? Rukmini's hospital bills wiped out all my savings. I need someone to look after me in my old age. What else could I have done? If I had given her away in marriage then she would have belonged to her husband's family. They would not have allowed her to support me. What choice did I have?'

'There is one thing I don't understand,' I said to

Padmini. 'You say that you dedicated because of the pain of hunger—but then, why do you worship Yellamma, who is at the root of all your misery?'

'Yellamma demands dedications. Look how miserable we are. If we don't dedicate, she will punish us,' replied Padmini.

'Some women have broken their vows to Yellamma and learned to earn a living by weaving or sewing,' I said. 'Some have even shaved off their jat, their matted hair.'

'Sooner or later,' said Padmini, shaking her head, 'they will be destroyed. Yellamma is all powerful, she is behind everything, she is Shiva, she is Durga, and she is Mother of All Things.'

While Padmini clearly identified the economic basis of the tradition, by giving it up she would have deprived herself not only of her only source of income, but of her pride, dignity and her hope for a higher status in her next life.

TWENTY-SEVEN

The beatitude that is brahman is achieved by the seers whose
evil has been caste off, whose doubts have been resolved, who
have mastered themselves and are dedicated to the wellbeing
of all creatures. [35]

—Bhagavadgita

THE FIRST STARS SHIMMERED overhead as we waited for
the cook to emerge with dinner. Beyond the wall of the
patio, insects flitted nervously above Patel's flowerbeds.
With only two days left before the pilgrimage to Saundatti
Temple, the film team was restless; everyone's thoughts
were turning home. Dilip suddenly burst through the gate
to the guesthouse with startling news: the driver of the
Sumo, a handsome twenty-six-year-old named Ramesh,
had requested his permission to ask for Renuka's hand in
marriage. Dilip's eyes were shining; he could barely contain
his delight. He had found a happy Bollywood ending for
the film.

Before I had time to react, Ravi sat straight up in his
chair. 'Is this a joke?' he asked.

'He wants to marry her!' said Dilip, defensively. 'He

has heard that she was going to be dedicated, so he wants to propose to her.'

'Come on,' said Ravi. 'What do you think his family will say to that? An upper-caste boy—a driver, for God's sake—marrying the daughter of a devadasi? Ramesh!' he bellowed, walking to the gate. 'Ramesh! Come here!' Ramesh appeared at the gate looking sheepish.

'Come inside,' said Ravi. Ramesh came and stood at the edge of the patio. Ravi sat down again, crossed his arms over his chest and tilted back in his chair. 'What is this I hear? You plan on asking for Renuka's hand?'

'Yes, sir,' he said meekly, staring at his feet.

'And your family? They will accept her into your house?'

'Well, no, sir, they won't, but I'm not on good terms with my parents anyway, so let them say what they want.'

'So it's a love marriage?' asked Ravi.

Ramesh turned red and pressed his toes into the edges of his thongs.

'Marriage is for life,' said Ravi. 'Are you really prepared to take on an uneducated village girl as a wife? She doesn't even know how to read!'

Ramesh stared at his feet. Ravi continued, 'By the way, I want you to tell me where and when you got to know Renuka well enough to want to marry her.'

'Don't get the wrong idea, sir. I don't know her well. I've only seen her around with her mother.'

'I've never seen you at Sumithra's house. When were you there?'

'Well, sir, we sit all day outside the village, so we have gotten to know some of the villagers.'

'You mean Renuka comes to sit with you on the road? I haven't seen that.'

'Well, sir, when I take the others, her mother sometimes cooks for me.'

'What others?'

'The other drivers, sir.'

'What do you mean? When do you take the other drivers?'

Ramesh gazed pleadingly at Dilip, then dropped his eyes to the ground again, where they remained. There was an awkward, brooding silence.

'Tell me!' bellowed Ravi.

'Sometimes I take the other drivers in the evenings,' he said quietly. 'They have friends there. Not me, I just sit at Sumithra's.'

'What?' said Ravi, the veins on his temples now throbbing. 'You go there in the evenings? Get those bahen chod in here!' He strode toward the gate calling for the other drivers.

'Wait,' pleaded Dilip. 'You know, maybe it's not such a bad thing. Maybe they're part of the reason that the villagers finally warmed up to us.'

Ravi turned to Dilip, his face contorting with anger. 'You mean the villagers like us because we bring them business? To hell with you! I don't want to have anything to do with this! Not on my time. I don't give a damn whether it's good for your film or not.' Ravi strode down the lane to where the cars were parked, tore open the door of the minivan, grabbed the driver by the shirt, and pulled him out. The third driver stepped out of the passenger seat and cowered behind the car while Ravi screamed, 'If I hear of any of you associating with Kalyana villagers, you will be fired immediately. And you won't be paid your salaries. Now move your cars across the street from the gate where I can keep an eye on them. No cars are to leave the premises without my permission.'

Ravi stormed back into the men's quarters and slammed the door behind him. All of us sat still. Nobody said a word. When dinner finally came, I brought a plate of food inside to him. He sat scowling on his cot with his arms crossed. 'Thanks,' he said, not looking at me. Then he added, apologetically, 'Perhaps I should have expected something like that.'

*

Glass shattered on the concrete patio. I sat up straight in bed, terrified. My covers fell away and the frigid black night wrapped itself around me. A moment passed and I regained my senses.

'What was that?' I asked, fumbling for my clock. It was five in the morning.

'It must have been Dilip,' Malika whispered back. 'Sounds like he knocked something over. He's been pacing up and down outside, coughing.'

As if on cue, Dilip succumbed to a hacking bronchial cough just outside our window. He sounded as if he were drowning. I snuggled back under the covers and, between coughing fits, listened to Amrit's snoring and the crickets' chirping their way through the jet-black night. When I reached for my clock again, it was already five-thirty. *In half an hour we will have to get up anyway,* I thought to myself. I wrapped two woollen shawls around my shoulders and went outside in my pyjamas.

'Do you want medicine?' I asked Dilip.

'No thanks, I've taken something already,' he said, pulling up a garden chair for me to sit in. We were due to leave on the pilgrimage in a day's time, and then we would be on the road for another three days, spending two nights at a government rest house near the temple and another in Belgaum before chartering a bus to Mumbai.

'There's something I wanted to talk to you about. I'm not sure I want to film the sacrifices,' said Dilip.

'Which ones, goat or buffalo?' I asked, thinking that we could probably skip one.

'Both,' said Dilip, glancing over at me.

'What do you mean?—blood sacrifice to the goddess— it's the perfect metaphor!'

'Have you ever seen a buffalo or a goat sacrificed before?'

'No.'

'Believe me, you don't want to. And don't forget, I'm a Brahmin, and a vegetarian. I don't think I can handle it.'

Dilip's Brahminism was not an argument I was sensitive to, especially since his friends in Delhi giggled at those pretensions. Many Indians, they said laughing, change their caste when they travel west. 'If you want, I'll go with Ravi, and you can stay here,' I said. 'Blood sacrifice speaks a world about life here; I don't think we can miss it.'

'There's another thing I wanted to talk to you about . . .

What do you think of Ramesh's proposal? Don't you think it would make a good ending for the film?'

'A good ending for the film? It's a Hollywood ending! I don't know. It seems strange. Is that what he really wants? Ravi seems sceptical.'

'I don't know, but I promised to sound Sumithra out for him. Will you come with me?'

'Do you really need me for that?' I asked.

'Yes.'

*

The cook picked his way around the crew members scattered around the patio and huddled on stoops, filling outstretched cups with steaming hot coffee and collecting finished plates of idli. The sun had risen, and with it, the temperature. Dilip and I had decided to give the crew a rest day before the departure on the pilgrimage. Chandi was bobbing his head to the beat of his iPod as he dusted lenses; Ravi was reading a book. Dilip scribbled in his notebook. Amrit had gone off in search of the dhobi, the washerman, who still had some of her clothes. Malika was preparing to leave for Belgaum for the day.

'Catherine, may I speak to you privately?' Malika said, calling me inside the women's quarters. 'Would you like to come to Belgaum with me for the day? We'll have delicious food and can visit the Belgaum Fort.'

'I promised Dilip I'd go talk to Sumithra today . . .' I had no intention of spending six hours in a car.

'Ah,' she said, looking dismayed and pulling me further

inside. 'Listen, the next bus to Belgaum isn't until midday, so Maneesh has offered to take me in the Sumo. It would mean so much to me to have a full day with my kids, but I don't feel comfortable riding in the car alone with him. He's always putting his hands on me—I'm a married woman! It's not proper! Besides, if my husband found out I was alone with him, he would be angry.'

I felt my face flush with anger. 'Why didn't you tell me before? I'll talk to Dilip immediately and make sure he never touches you again. It's outrageous.'

'Oh, no, don't do that. Promise this will stay between us, please!'

'Why? Let Dilip talk to him; he'll know how to handle it.'

'No, please. I don't want to make a fuss. We're almost at the end of the shoot. Let it be. I don't want anyone to think I'm complaining.'

'But you *should* complain. It's unacceptable. He's so sleazy.'

'I shouldn't have said anything,' said Malika.

'On the contrary, you should have said something much earlier!'

'I guess I'll just take the bus.'

'Take the Ambassador for the day; I don't need it. I'll take the Sumo.'

'Thank you so much, Catherine! Please don't say anything about what I told you. It's not a big deal. I can handle it myself,' she said.

When I told Dilip, he burst out laughing.

'Malika said *that*! What a joker she is! That's too much.

She's the one who has been chasing him. She sees him as the ticket out of her marriage. She hates her husband. She's desperate. She wants Maneesh to take her to Mumbai with him!'

'I don't believe it,' I said, half to myself, wondering how Dilip knew she was unhappy in her marriage. 'No matter how desperate she is, I can't see how she can be attracted to Maneesh.'

'Are you kidding? He's going to be producing a soap opera for the new TV station. He already has her reading scripts! Maneesh has done very well for himself, and he's still a bachelor. He's not as unattractive as you seem to think—at least, not to Indian women.'

I thought about it for a minute, and then shook my head. 'That's Maneesh's version,' I said.

'Oh, no; Maneesh is panicked about it. He doesn't know what to do. She's just covering herself. Keep your eyes open, and you'll see.' Dilip seemed so sincere, I almost believed him, but then he was good at seeming sincere. I didn't know what to think anymore.

*

Sumithra squatted beside the hearth, scraping slivers of browning onion off the bottom of a wok with a metal spatula. She was only half-listening to what Amrit was saying. She flipped over the onions, sprinkled them with water, then sat back as they sizzled angrily. 'What time will we be leaving?' Sumithra repeated the question absentmindedly as she eyed her onions.

'It's hard to say. By late morning we should definitely be underway.'

'Where will you stop for the night?'

'Sometimes we stop in the field on the left after the bridge, but if we leave late, we don't always make it there by sundown. Then we just set up camp wherever we can. There's a lot of cooking to do—we have to prepare food for six days.' Sumithra sprinkled sprouts of green gram into the pan, mixing them briskly while stoking the fire.

'Sumithra,' said Dilip as Amrit translated for him, 'there is also an important matter involving Renuka and Ramesh that I would like to speak to you about.' Hearing Renuka's and Ramesh's names mentioned in the same sentence, she put down her spatula and turned to look at Dilip with renewed concentration. 'Normally it wouldn't be for me to speak to you, but since I am in charge of the film team, I feel that it is my duty,' said Dilip. 'Ramesh, our driver, has told me that he would like to marry Renuka . . .'

Sumithra asked Amrit to repeat the translation. She had heard correctly. Sumithra's brow clouded in confusion and she shook her head. 'Ramesh is a nice boy,' she said, 'but what does he want with my daughter? How can I take such a proposal seriously? His family would never accept her, and as soon as he tires of her he'll leave her without a second thought, saying she should be a devadasi. I would never make such a foolish match for my daughter.' Sumithra turned back to her frying pan, taciturn.

'Are you sure you want to dismiss him so quickly?' asked Dilip. 'I have spoken with him, and he seems willing to take on the responsibility. Villagers, fearing the wrath of Yellamma, won't want to risk marrying their son to a girl who is already carrying the jagha.'

'Villagers are not as ignorant as they used to be,' shot back Sumithra. 'Look at me—I married, and nothing happened. We'll find a boy. It's a question of time.' Sumithra set her jaw and flipped the green gram with determination.

Rukmini now appeared at the door with Mariamma, who smiled bashfully.'

'Dilip, this is Mariamma, the girl I told you about. We should definitely interview her.' I said smiling and embracing her. There was something so sweet, child-like and defenceless about her; she was irresistible.

'We gave everyone a day off,' said Dilip, uninterested. 'Maybe tomorrow . . .'

'We are going to gather firewood,' said Rukmini. 'Would you like to come with us?'

'It's lunchtime,' said Dilip. 'I must be getting back. We have a lot to prepare for tomorrow. We won't be coming back after the festival.'

'All the more reason that you should come.'

'I'm sorry, I can't,' said Dilip. Rukmini's face fell.

'I'd welcome a walk,' I said, knowing that I was no replacement for Dilip.

'Me, too,' said Amrit.

'Okay,' said Rukmini, 'but Dilip, you must return this afternoon, I have a surprise for you. Promise me you will come. Just you and Catherine, no one else.'

'We'll see.'

'No please . . . you must promise me.'

'All right,' said Dilip. 'Maneesh and I have to see Kalyanappa in the afternoon, so I'll come find you after that.'

'Good,' said Rukmini. 'I'll be waiting for you. Oh, just one more thing—I want you to wear black.'

'Why?'

'Just promise.'

✴

It was with much trepidation that Dilip climbed the short staircase to Rukmini's house. Rukmini had changed into a black sari, and seeing that Dilip had worn black too, she clapped her hands with delight.

'What's the significance of black clothing?' I whispered to Dilip as Ruki installed us on mats.

'I have no idea,' he said, rolling his eyes. 'I'm not sure I want to know.'

'Just one moment,' Rukmini said, disappearing into the next room. Several minutes later, she emerged with two cups of steaming hot buffalo milk.

'I'm not a big fan of buffalo milk,' said Dilip.

'I've boiled it and put in a touch of sugar just for you,' said Rukmini.

'No really, I can't,' said Dilip in Hindi.

'Just a small amount . . . please,' said Rukmini, looking hurt.

'What's the big deal, Dilip?' I asked, somehow managing to refrain from asking if he feared polluting himself. Dilip still claimed he was on a religious fast every time he was offered food. Although I didn't always accept food, I did so on a regular basis. 'Garum garum,' I would say, insisting on boiled food so I wouldn't get sick. Surely if I could bear their food, so could he. Although back in Paris I had heard Dilip speak eloquently about his family's progressive attitude towards caste, observing him in Kalyana, it was clear to me that he had not fully overcome his prejudices.

'After all she's done for us, can't you just give her this?' I whispered scathingly, attempting to conceal the rage and disgust surging within me.

Dilip reached out, accepted the cup with a tense smile, and placed it in front of him. Rukmini went back into the next room to serve herself. Taking advantage of her turned back, Dilip picked up his cup and tried to empty its contents into mine, but I whisked my cup away in the nick of time, and glared at him defiantly. I knew his tricks well enough by now.

'Come on,' he said, staring at me through clenched teeth. 'I can't drink it.'

'Why not?' I asked, staring back. 'You drink the local milk-coffee.'

Dilip said nothing, but stared at me with an intensity that made me feel uncomfortable. I had come to despise Dilip's hypocrisy, and it was hurting our friendship, which was not good for the film. Ultimately, although Dilip didn't finish his buffalo milk, he consumed a respectable amount—Rukmini was happy.

'Was it so bad?' I asked Dilip as he trundled down the steps of Rukmini's house, but he didn't look back or reply. As we walked to the road outside the village, a retinue of young boys began trailing us. As I looked back over their heads at the crumbling, sun-baked houses, I was overtaken by a sudden fatigue. There was still so much to understand, and so much left unsaid. The dusty dirt road was empty; the driver had not yet returned from dropping Amrit off. The sugarcane that once grew tall had been cut. The dry, cracked earth lay bare and open, prey to the elements. The wind suddenly began to gust, and whirling towards us from afar came a dusty plastic bag. In the holakeri, plastic bags and empty water bottles are rare and much-coveted items. A battle cry sounded and the boys, in a sudden frenzy, jostled each other in the hope of becoming its owner. I stepped out of the way, but at the last moment the bag veered towards me. Twelve-year-old Bala lunged for it and suddenly we were face-to-face, eye-to-eye, only a few inches apart. In the rainy season, on many occasions, he had offered me his shoulder as I negotiated my way through the treacherous muddy lanes. He was always near when I was in need of a hand, but averted his gaze in deference. Now he found himself looking me in the eye. We were both taken by surprise. I peered back at him, at the sweet tenderness of his youth mixed with fear and wonderment. I don't know what he saw in my eyes, but he was unable to unlock his gaze. Time seemed to come to a halt. Still searching my eyes, Bala hesitantly offered me the plastic bag he had been clutching to his chest. A gift. I took the bag, wrapped it around my water bottle, and pressed it back into his arms. Finally tearing himself away, he turned and went skipping down the lane to bring his newly gained treasures to his mother. I looked at Dilip, hoping he had noticed, but he was lost in his own thoughts.

TWENTY-EIGHT

On your left side is a well
on your right, the lake
ahead of you this forest fire
the fire has spread wild flames in front of you
behind you the tiger comes creeping closer[36]

—Purandara Dasa

WHEN DILIP AND I arrived at the lodge, Maneesh was pacing up and down the patio like a caged animal. Even before the car came to a stop, Maneesh and Dilip were screaming at each other in Hindi. Ravi, Dadar, Chandi and Amrit were sitting on the patio looking anguished. *Something terrible has happened,* I thought. Maneesh and Dilip locked themselves into the men's quarters, and I drew Ravi into to the relative privacy of the women's quarters.

'Half of the production kitty was stolen,' he said, whispering.

'Oh,' I said, relieved that no one was hurt.

'A lot of money,' added Ravi, seeing that I was unimpressed. 'Four hundred thousand rupees—ten thousand dollars!'

'What were we doing with so much cash?' I wondered.

'In these parts, that's all that works.' Ravi had a point. In Belgaum, even banks refused traveller's cheques, and hotels didn't take credit cards. Maneesh had left the bag unlocked; the thief had removed only half of the bundled bills so that the robbery would not be detected immediately.

After half an hour of muffled, violent argument, Maneesh walked out through the gate and down the road to town. Dilip, forgetting he was angry with me, came and sat down on the stoop beside me. 'That sisterfucker,' he said. 'He left the suitcase with the cash in it *unlocked*. He isn't even capable of telling me *when* the money went missing! "Some time in the last three days," is all he has to say.'

'But isn't the door to the men's room always locked because of the equipment?' I asked.

'Yes, supposedly it's always locked. He said he trusts everyone on the team a hundred per cent.'

'Understandable. But who else could have taken it? Who has another key to your room?'

'He refuses to investigate! He says only the chowkidar has a key, and he says he'd rather give up his salary than point fingers . . . look, I don't think it was anyone on the film team either, but I wonder about that chowkidar. I'm going to go talk to Patel. I want you to come with me.' Although not so much as one rupee had gone missing from my bag, I had noticed sticky fingerprints on my stacks of photos; someone had rifled through my things. I didn't know what to think. I was upset and confused.

We found Mr Patel sitting by his red telephone under the central dome of his house. 'So glad you have come to see me,' he said, puffing out his chest. 'I understand you're off the day after tomorrow?'

'Yes. We want to thank you again for all you have done for us,' said Dilip, leaning forward and pressing his fingertips together, not quite sure how to broach the subject.

'Think nothing of it; you are welcome any time,' he said. Then, noticing Dilip's pained look, he asked, 'Is there something troubling you?'

'It seems, it seems . . .' said Dilip, stumbling, 'something has gone missing from our rooms . . .'

'Something's gone missing?' repeated Patel doubtfully.

'Yes. We were carrying cash with us . . . four hundred thousand rupees.'

Mr Patel raised an eyebrow then bit his lip and stared at the ground for several minutes, looking peeved or angry, I couldn't tell which. Then he shook his head. 'I'm sorry to tell you this, but it could only have been someone on your own team,' he said, turning to bark orders at the servant in the next room. 'The only person to have keys to your room is my chowkidar. He personally sweeps your rooms out every day. You know whom I mean, Shivaputra. He is a loyal and trustworthy servant.'

'Are you sure about him?' asked Dilip.

Patel sat back in his seat, pressed his lips together and then looked up again. 'He was born in that house by the gate. So were his father, and his father's father before him. His family has been in service to mine for so many generations, we have lost count. When his daughter gets married, I myself will pay her dowry. Her wedding party will leave from this house only! He has no need for even so much as one rupee, for I take care of his family's every need. When his wife was sick, she had the best medical care this town has to offer. Why would he risk his family's security for even twice that amount of money? What would he do with it, anyway? Where would he go? He can't read or write—he has no bank account!'

A silhouette appeared in the doorway. The light was beginning to fall, but I recognized the chowkidar. He was a tiny man with dark skin and a bowl cut. His eyes and his shoulders were round with fear. I thought I perceived trembling in his knees.

'Shivaputra, come here!' bellowed Mr Patel. The chowkidar advanced a few inches, bobbing his head, but didn't dare cross the threshold. His bare feet were grey with dust, and his hands were clasped in terror. Speaking in Kannada, Patel addressed a few questions to Shivaputra, and provided us with a translation.

'Who sweeps the rooms in the guest house?'

'I do, sir,' said the chowkidar in a barely audible whisper. I heard him swallow.

'Does anybody help you?'

'Sometimes my daughter.'

'How old is she?'

'Eight years old, sir.'

'Where do you keep the keys to the guest house?'

'Here, sir,' he said, fumbling in his pocket and stretching out his hand to show them. The keys fell on the floor. The chowkidar dropped to his knees to scrape them up, and stretched out his hand again, not daring to step forward.

'Who else has a set of keys?' asked Patel.

'Your guests, sir,' mumbled the chowkidar, hand still outstretched.

'Anyone else have keys?'

'No, sir.'

'Did anyone ask you for the keys?'

'No, sir.'

'Do you have any questions you would like to ask, Mr Patil?' Mr Patel asked, turning to Dilip with a cold stare.

In my peripheral vision, I saw Dilip shake his head no. I couldn't bring myself to look up. My stomach knotted. Outside, the fluorescent garden lights snapped on, casting a sickly green glow over the scene. My head felt light and a foul taste filled my mouth. Had I really witnessed—had I really participated in—such a scene? Patel probably now felt proud of himself—he had protected his untouchable slave. But what of his dignity? Why, such lesser beings have no dignity, of course. I rose, made the sign of 'namaskar' to Patel and stumbled out into the night. I heard Dilip spewing polite phrases, attempting to plaster over the ugliness of it all.

Lifting my eyes from the garden path, I was momentarily blinded by the fluorescent beams streaming out from the guest house's orifices. I stopped in my tracks. My breathing was laboured. I could not bring myself to move forward. I made my way to the edge of the driveway and sat on a stone. Wrapping my arms around my shins, I rested my chin on my knees. A cricket chirped behind me. Another answered and then another. A dragonfly with an eight-inch wingspan flew past me. I turned sideways and looked over the garden. Bees and insects hovered and darted over the flowers, bright against the ink blue wash of sky. In the distance, by the pond, I heard something screeching. Was it a bird or a monkey?

'May I join you?' asked Dilip, startling me. He sat down next to me. The roar of crickets and buzzing insects filled my ears. 'I'm not so sure about that chowkidar. Did you see how terrified he was? He must have something to hide.' I glanced sideways at Dilip, but couldn't find the strength to speak. Wave after wave of disgust broke over me—disgust for Dilip, disgust for filmmaking, disgust for India and disgust for all things uncertain and dishonest. I noticed that the skin on Dilip's face was dry and tight. He looked anxious, unsure of himself, and much older than thirty-four. I remembered noticing on the plane on the way over that the birth date in his passport made him five years older than he claimed to be. He somehow explained the discrepancy away, but now I knew he had lied. He had lied about his age, his caste, his background, his work experience. He had lied about everything. He had come to Paris and simply reinvented himself. So many things that had perplexed me—that I had put off to cultural difference or lack of language skills—suddenly made sense: Dilip was a compulsive liar, a trickster, a confidence man. I thought about the stories he collected about heists and tricksters, his heroes, and the delight with which he recounted them. I detected flashes of glee in his eyes when telling the most improbable tales. Now I realized—that's 'duper's delight'.

Now that I had the proper interpretive grille in place, I

was certain that Dilip had taken the money from Maneesh's bag, probably to teach him a lesson for leaving it unlocked. Maneesh knew it, and, furious with Dilip, refused to investigate. How could he expose his own paymaster? Perhaps Dilip had intended it as a joke but had not counted on Maneesh's fury—a practical joke gone awry. Rather than lose face, Dilip had turned upon the nearest scapegoat, the nearest untouchable, the chowkidar.

My stomach churned; I went cold. Sweat beaded my forehead. I wanted to scream, but clenched my jaws instead. I rose, made my way to my room, and crawled under the many layers of blankets. My head swirled. *No open confrontation; think of what's best for the film,* I reminded myself before falling into a deep sleep.

*

When I awoke, the Milky Way and pinprick stars had exploded across the night sky. Dinner plates had already been cleared away. Ravi and Dilip were huddled in conversation on the patio, and I could hear Chandi and Dadar packing and stacking equipment inside the men's quarters. I sat down on the stoop of the ladies' quarters, out of sight, and looked out over the silhouettes of the flowers in Patel's garden. I was deeply shaken by Dilip's accusation. If he was capable of pointing a finger at an innocent, defenceless man in order to save face, what else was he capable of? I felt like an insect caught in a spider web, certain in the knowledge of my impending doom. I tried to run all the possible scenarios through my head, but my thoughts were racing so fast I could not keep up with them. Direct confrontation, my usual method, was surely not the way to go. I had to grin and bear it, and keep my priorities straight. Patel had not believed Dilip's story, so the chowkidar was okay. *All that matters is the film,* I reminded myself. In less than a week, we'd be back in Paris, and once we were in there, everything would be okay. I knew the editing process wasn't going to be easy, but we would be on my home territory. I would have the advantage. We were making a documentary; we had ethical constraints.

Ravi walked to the edge of the patio, lit a cigarette, and then noticed me. 'Hey, how are you doing?' he asked, walking over and sitting down.

'Okay,' I said, despondent. I trusted Ravi and wanted to confide in him, but when I opened my mouth words would not come out.

He pulled out his pack of cigarettes and offered one to me. 'It's so weird and upsetting. I can hardly believe it. I don't understand why Maneesh refuses to do anything about it,' said Ravi. 'Dilip thinks the chowkidar is in cahoots with someone else, but I don't believe that for a minute. I've chatted with the chowkidar quite a bit over the past weeks. He worships Patel, and his great ambition is for his son to inherit his job! He's a very simple man . . . Dilip and I have gone over every movement of every crew member for the past three days. Except for Malika's going to Belgaum this morning, nobody went anywhere. And of course, it couldn't have been Malika, because none of you has access to our room.'

'I just remembered, Chandi went to the post office this morning,' said Dilip, walking up behind Ravi. 'Catherine and I dropped him off on the way to town. Maybe he sent it to himself!'

'How could he have carried it? He didn't have a bag. You'll have to find something better than that, Dilip,' I said through clenched teeth, and then bit my tongue for speaking so harshly. *Not good for the film,* I said to myself.

'She has a point,' said Ravi. 'Four hundred thousand rupees in one-hundred-rupee notes—you definitely need a bag, a big bag . . . So what did Maneesh say?'

'He won't speak to me. He says I can take it out of his salary,' said Dilip, rolling his eyes and smiling at me. I clenched my teeth and smiled back.

'Look, Catherine, I can tell this has been really upsetting for you . . .' I looked up at Dilip. He sensed something was wrong and was trying to be nice to me.

'She has the blues,' said Ravi.

'I'm fine,' I said, bristling.

'What's that?' asked Dilip, crouching down and lifting my forearm to the light. The inside of my elbow was covered in hives. 'Do you have allergies?'

'No,' I said, surprised. 'Poison ivy, maybe. Do you have that in India?'

'Maybe you should go to a doctor.'

'I'll put some calamine lotion on it; it'll be okay.' I went back inside to get some medicine and then lay down again on my bed. I needed to be alone. After some time, I heard the sputtering of an engine and gravel crunching under wheels. Malika had returned from Belgaum. Wrapped in a blanket, I went out to the patio where Amrit, Ravi and Dilip were sitting. Malika, re-energized by the afternoon with her children, emerged smiling from the darkness into the light of the patio. No one smiled back.

'Catherine, you look terrible. Why are your eyes so red?' she asked, touching my forehead. 'You have a fever!'

'Maybe,' I said, 'but we have other worries.'

'What happened?' she asked. No one said a thing.

'You tell her, Catherine,' said Dilip.

'I think this is something for you to explain, Dilip,' I said pointedly.

'The production money was stolen from Maneesh's suitcase. He left it open,' said Dilip. Switching to Hindi, Dilip and Ravi filled her in on the details. Malika searched their faces, trying to come to terms with the news. She finally dropped herself into a plastic garden chair and shook her head in disbelief. When she opened her mouth to speak, I interjected, 'English, please.'

'With the driver as my witness, I only took one small handbag with me to Belgaum today.'

'Nobody thinks *you* stole it,' said Ravi.

'But just to clear the air, I want you to check my bag.'

'Yes, mine, too,' I said, rising and calling to Chandi and Dadar, who were playing cards. Within a few minutes, everyone's bags, except Dilip's, were on the terrace.

'Maneesh, get out here,' yelled Ravi. Maneesh appeared in the doorway and looked at the pile of bags. 'We want you to check our bags.'

'Yes, check our bags . . . just to clear the air,' everyone chimed in.

'I know none of you did it,' said Maneesh. 'I trust all of you completely, and I won't stoop so low as to rifle through your things. I already told Dilip that I will pay him back in Mumbai. I don't want to hear another word about this matter.'

'Please, at least to clear the air,' begged Chandi.

Maneesh stared at the floor, his jaw set in anger, and shook his head no.

'Dilip, tell him to check our bags!' insisted Ravi.

'I can't force him,' said Dilip.

'Then you do it,' said Ravi.

Dilip turned away and dropped himself into a plastic deck chair at the edge of the patio with his back to the rest of us. Putting his feet up and lacing his fingers behind his head, he shrugged. 'It's Maneesh's job,' he said.

I walked over to Dilip, but his face was closed. He didn't look at me. 'Dilip, why don't you bring out your bags, and *I'll* do the checking,' I said.

Dilip turned his head slowly in my direction and stared at me with cold, beady eyes that sent a chill down my spine. 'Don't be stupid,' he hissed and looked away again.

'Bring out your bag,' I said calmly, challenging him. 'Why are you the only one who hasn't?' I stood over him, waiting. I looked back over my shoulder and caught Maneesh's eye. He was petrified. My suspicions were confirmed. When I turned back, Dilip was glaring at me again, a murderous look in his eye.

'Thought so,' I murmured under my breath, turning away and walking back to my room. Sensing something had happened, Ravi searched my face as I walked by, but I kept my eyes glued to the ground. And then I thought of Rukmini.

'Maneesh,' I said, stopping. 'What's happening with Rukmini's buffalo?'

Maneesh flushed and stuttered. 'Well, I don't know what to say . . . that plan was called off.'

I spun around on my heel and confronted him. 'What do you mean, "called off"? Why was it called off? Who called it off?' I heard my voice becoming shrill. I was sweating and felt my arm tremble as I gestured in impatience. *How can things have gone so wrong?* I wondered.

'What's Rukmini going to do with a buffalo in Mumbai?' Dilip sneered, his eyes filled with cold cruelty.

'At least she would have had a choice about going,' I replied.

'She wants to go—she told us so,' he said.

'She hates Mumbai. She's going because she has no choice. It's her turn to support the family. Her mother is at the end of her run . . . A buffalo is the only way to give her a bit of security,' I replied, becoming angry all over again. 'Maneesh, tomorrow I want you to find a good, healthy buffalo.'

'You don't understand,' Dilip told me. 'She doesn't want a buffalo. She is not interested in village life. Besides, we're giving her money,' said Dilip.

'She'll spend it. She can't spend a buffalo,' I snapped. 'Maneesh, I want you to find a buffalo, I'll pay for it out of my own pocket if I have to.'

'Me, too. I'll contribute,' said Ravi.

'But it takes time to find, the market was yesterday . . . I'll see what I can do,' said Maneesh, glancing at Dilip.

TWENTY-NINE

I have lighted a lamp inside my body,
and pushed the wick up to make it burn bright.
Grasping a means to release, I try to rise,
but the five [senses] whom you have placed within me
to bar the way,
have proved stronger by far.
Lord of Holy Pukalur [Shiva], what shall I do? [37]

—Appar

'CATHERINE, CATHERINE?' MALIKA WAS peering over me. I turned over in my bed. I heard the cases of film equipment scraping and banging on the patio. The cars were being packed. 'You have a fever. You were talking in your sleep last night. Come, Mr Patel has given me the address of his doctor. He's just by the STD booth at the end of the road. Get yourself dressed; we're going.'

I sat up in bed. Sliding up the sleeve of my pyjamas, I saw that my arm was covered with marble-sized hives from my wrist all the way up to my armpit. I reached for the mirror on the windowsill. The side of my neck was red. Although I had suffered many a blistering rash from poison ivy, I had never seen anything like this before. I was alarmed.

'That's something,' Amrit said, sitting down beside me. 'I saw you touch that fern yesterday, the one growing over the stone slab in the wood. It was too late to warn you, so I didn't say anything, but a lot of people are allergic. My sister's allergic . . . but I've never seen that before. Does it itch?' No sooner had she uttered the words than the skin on the inside of my arm began to boil. A million tickling and biting ants seemed to be devouring the flesh, which I began to rub vigorously with the palm of my hand.

'Disgusting,' said Malika, recoiling. Amrit helped me dress, and five minutes later we were outside a peeling pastel three-storey house with wooden lattice balconies. 'DR S.S. SHETTY,' announced a carefully polished metal plaque. I rang the bell. An old woman cracked the door, then swung it open and beckoned us inside. I cringed as we crossed the dark and dingy waiting room, but when she threw open the door to the doctor's office, sunlight poured through the many windows. A young doctor, writing out a prescription, sat at a large wooden desk across from a patient. His office was sparse and neat. There was an examination table partially concealed by a metal frame with a sheet stretched across it. 'Good morning, ladies. What can I do for you?' he asked in perfect English, glancing up. In his late thirties, he had an open face and a ready smile. 'Please have a seat.' The man sitting across from the doctor stood up.

'It's nothing urgent,' I said. 'We can wait.'

'Please, please,' the doctor said, gesturing for us to sit down. 'We were just finishing up.' He handed the prescription to the patient and accompanied him to the door. Returning to the window behind his desk, he sat down on the sill and crossed his feet. 'What brings you here?'

I unfolded my arm for him to see. He gestured for me to go to the examination table. Taking my arm, he turned it in the light. Peering at the welts, he asked, 'Have you been walking in the woods?'

'Yes,' I said.

'There's a fern in these woods; a lot of people are allergic to it,' he said.

'I saw her touch it,' said Amrit.

The doctor moved back to his desk and wrote out a prescription. 'Take two this morning and then one three times a day for three days, or until the rash is gone. I'm giving you antihistamines; they may make you a little drowsy. Should be completely gone in three days.'

'Three days, that's all?'

'Three or four days,' said the doctor, returning to the examination table and peering into my eyes 'But tell me, you seem to be running a fever. Let me take your temperature. Maybe there's something else.' The doctor stuck an electronic thermometer in my ear. Pressing the button, he removed it, looked at the reading, and started over. After the third reading he looked at me and asked, 'How are you feeling?'

'Not very well, I have to admit,' I said.

'You're not sweating . . . have you been shivering?'

'No,' I said.

'Are you taking a prophylactic?'

'A prophylactic?' I repeated, not understanding.

'A course of malaria prevention.'

'Oh, no,' I said. 'I was told there was no malaria at this time of year.'

'Who told you that? I think you may have contracted malaria. You have temperature of 104. As soon as you leave this office, I want you to take a thousand milligrams of paracetamol and drink two litres of water,' he said, pulling a needle out of its sterile wrapping. 'I'm going to take a blood sample and send it over to the lab. I'll have the results in an hour.'

'But there's no malaria here,' I said. The doctor did a double take.

'Who told you that?' he asked. I had asked the executive producer to pay for the cost of a two-month course of expensive malaria prevention medication, but claiming to have contacted the centre for tropical diseases, she refused on the grounds that there was no malaria in Karnataka.

'Well, I haven't been bitten,' I said, disbelieving.

'The bites can be very small. They're not always noticeable,' he replied.

'But there's no malaria here,' I protested, in denial.

The doctor, befuddled, searched for a response. 'What can I say? In the dry season, I see several cases a month, and in the wet season, I see several cases a week. There's a malarial pond hardly 300 feet from this house,' he said, pointing in the direction of Patel's.

Inwardly, I kicked myself for having left such an important question in the producer's hands. 'Couldn't it be the allergy?' I asked.

'I doubt it,' he said. 'Come back in an hour and we'll see.

In any case, we only very rarely have cases of falciparum—cerebral malaria—so I doubt there's any grave danger.'

I thought for a moment, and wondered if the tea I had gulped down before coming might have caused a false temperature reading. Except for what seemed to me like a slight fever, I had none of the symptoms of malaria. 'How much do I owe you?' I asked.

'Nothing at all. Any friend of Mr Patel's is a friend of mine,' he replied.

'How did you know we were staying at Mr Patel's?'

'An educated guess. The malarial pond I mentioned is adjacent to his estate.'

'I insist . . .' I said, pulling out my wallet.

'I'll see you in an hour,' he replied, showing us out.

※

In the Ambassador on the way to the village, I fished some paracetamol out of my bag. On the outskirts of the village, two boys, holding a long stick between them with a cloth bundle hanging in the middle, darted out in front of the car. We screeched to a halt, covering the villagers in a cloud of dust. From the bundle dripped a dark, viscous liquid. 'Blood,' said Amrit. 'They're going to bury their share of meat in their field. It's a fertility thing. We missed the buffalo sacrifice.'

The Sumo now pulled up alongside our car. 'We've been told to wait by the sugar factory at the end of the road,' said the driver. Amrit and I got out and walked towards the village. Landlords, followed by scampering children, many carrying viscous bundles of bloody meat, were running in all directions. As we entered, I noticed the village boundary post was wrapped in a yellow cloth. *Is it a sari?* I wondered, leaning towards it. When I looked up, I saw a man stumbling towards me. On his head teetered a platter with a leering buffalo head on it, a hoof stuffed in its mouth. *Thwack,* a lump of bloody rice hit the post a few feet away from me. Amrit and I fled to the holakeri. In the pit before the two Yellamma pots in the central square lay the flayed remains of the buffalo. Bloody rice was scattered over the ground. The demon had been defeated; the vindictive goddess propitiated.

In the distance, we heard trumpets screeching like wild elephants, and the thunder of drums: Yellamma was on her ritual rounds of the ooru. Amrit and I pressed through the crowd in the direction of the noise. Men in white or yellow turbans and women in brightly coloured saris crisscrossed our path, foreheads plastered with horizontal lines of yellow haldi. The musicians stopped as suddenly as they had started. Yellamma had disappeared into the home of a village elder. The musicians, leaning on their instruments and drinking from flasks, waited for her to re-emerge. The elder appeared in his doorway, followed by Sumithra with the jagha on her head. Again, the discordant instruments screeched, the procession pressed on. Closest to Sumithra were ten devadasis, and as many musicians, stumbling drunk or in a trance, I could not tell which. Behind them thirty men seethed forward, pushing the crowd, stopping, turning, twisting, screaming out, 'Tai Yellamma udho, udho.'

A devadasi in a green sari, her hair a tangled mess, peeled herself away from Sumithra's side and, spinning like a top, wheeled back through the men, spitting on them and bumping her bottom into them. Sumithra moved forward again.

As we approached the main temple, I spotted Ravi and the film team on the roof, the camera aimed at the crowds below. Villagers poured into the temple compound. Kalyana's devadasis were arrayed on the right, in a place of honour. Ranavva, Ganga, Chandra, Shoba, Mahadevi and many other women, surrounded by their children, stood proudly on an elevated platform, looking on, as the crowd passed before them, pushing, pulling, pulsing and somehow circumambulating the temple. Sumithra handed the jagha to the priests inside the temple for the puja. Then suddenly to the left of the temple a blue sheet was spread 3 feet above the ground. On the roof of the temple, a priest holding a bundled infant, perhaps four months old, appeared. Villagers held tightly onto the edges of the sheet. The crowd paused and fell silent: the infant was dropped from the roof of the temple onto the drawn sheet. Landing on its back, it bounced back up and the crowd cheered. The baby, seemingly undaunted, was placed back in its anguished, but smiling mother's arms. What more precious offering, what greater proof of their devotion, could the villagers give than this rite, surely a vestige of an ancient form of human sacrifice? The village chiefs made their offerings, and then threw many handfuls of the sugar-candy prasad over the crowd. Frenzied children scrambled to gather up the sacred leavings.

By publicly making offerings and receiving honours,

the elite display their power and affirm their place in the hierarchy. The order in which offerings are made as well as the type of honours received speak the world about a community. All members of society, from village chief to lowly untouchable, have an essential role to play in the temple festival's reconstituted ideal vision of the world. Devadasis have a place of honour and the procession moves forward to the beat of the untouchable's drum; until he has touched the god's palanquin, it cannot not move forward. Having a role in this collective, ideal representation of society is a source of great pride, even for the most exploited members of society.

The priests returned the jagha to Sumithra and she left the temple grounds, making her way past the waiting bullock carts. Devadasis and villagers spilled out of the temple, following behind her, forming a new procession. Amrit and I waited for the film crew outside. Cart drivers poured homemade brew down the gullets of their beasts of burden to prepare them for the long haul. Horns painted green and red, and carts festooned with palm fronds, they stamped their feet in anticipation. Climbing into their seats, drivers now urged their beasts forward with whips. With a creak and a groan, the carts, bedecked with foliage, began their journey to the Yellamma temple.

'Tai Yellamma udho, udho,' the villagers sang out.

Amrit and I watched as a few hundred villagers passed through the palm-frond archway that had been erected at the edge of the ooru. At least one member from every household in the village was present. Half an hour later, as tardy villagers scrambled to catch up, we came to the conclusion that the film crew had taken another route out of the village. Hoping to catch up with Sumithra and the crew, we joined the procession and, walking quickly, began passing the villagers. Pleased to see us among their ranks, they smiled.

'Namaskar,' they called out, saluting us, and inviting us to climb aboard their carts. As we turned onto the dirt track outside the village, an ice-cold shiver went down my back. I realized my body was cold, damp and heavy. My skin beaded with sweat. Putting one foot in front of the other required all my concentration. The din of the procession seemed to evaporate and I felt I was walking on cushions, or was I stumbling? A fireball seemed to have hit my thigh and was moving up my throbbing spine. I noticed I was sitting down; Amrit was peering over me. I watched the villagers striding by; seconds stretched into minutes. I lost track of time. I wanted to ask Amrit how long we had been there, but couldn't open my mouth to speak.

I could no longer hear anything. I sat in a noiseless bubble where time did not exist. When sounds finally began to reach me again, the high-pitched whine of a scooter filled my ears. Sanjay, Ranavva's joolwa husband, jumped off and leaned over me. The sun glinted off his white teeth and black, oiled hair. 'I am Sanjay, Ranavva's humble servant. I have been dispatched to fetch you.' He smiled warmly. Amrit translated. Her words were out of synch with the movement of her mouth. *This is malaria,* I thought to myself. Sanjay looked at me searchingly and then smiled. He was a tall, handsome man with a broad chest and shoulders. Cleanly shaven and in a crisp white shirt and pleated pants, he looked more like an urban businessman than a farmer.

'We're getting on the scooter,' said Amrit.

I shook my head. I wanted to stand, but couldn't move. My eyes met Sanjay's; his face was a mask of concern. He squatted down beside me. 'Please, you must come. The doctor will give you medicines, and soon you'll be better. Why, if anything happened to you, Ranavva would eat me alive. You're her little sister, after all. I'll go slowly, I promise.' I felt hot tears rolling down my cheeks. Amrit and Sanjay looked at each other, puzzled. Then, each taking hold of an arm, they hoisted me up.

Once on my feet, I felt better. 'Will you be going on the pilgrimage, Sanjay?' I managed to squeak out as we walked to the scooter, hoping to seem as normal as possible.

'I regret that this year, I have too much work on the farm. I suppose I'll have to entrust Ranavva to you after all,' he said with a laugh. After he coaxed me onto the scooter and placed my fingers around straps on the seat, I found myself sandwiched between Amrit and Sanjay. We took off at breakneck speed, and a rush of adrenalin revived me. The villagers called out to us as we passed, smiling and waving, and I smiled back. The thrill of the speed, the wind in my hair—the strangeness of it all—the sacrifice, the procession, finding myself on Ranavva's lover's scooter—all of these reminded me of my days in boarding school when friends, pretending to be my mother, would call and get me released for the weekend. In a convoy of station wagons led by a VW bus, we would travel to some absurdly distant place for a concert or a party that would last all night . . . the joy and jubilation . . . being part of the group, giving oneself over to it. Just for that moment, I tapped into the excitement and energy of the pilgrimage.

As Sanjay sped past the head of the procession, I spotted the film crew walking alongside Sumithra and Renuka. We stopped near the sugar refinery, where our vehicles were waiting. I peeled myself off the scooter, made the sign of 'namaskar' to Sanjay, and collapsed in the back of the Ambassador. Throbbing pains moved up and down my body; I felt as if someone were beating me with a crowbar. Before long, Dilip was peering down at me. He found a nice soft duffle bag for me to put under my head and sat beside me.

'Catherine, I thought you were taking malaria pills,' he scolded me, his eyes full of gentle concern. I felt so appreciative of his show of sympathy, I closed my eyes and willed myself to believe that our friendship could be restored to its former state of warmth and respect. Perhaps the nightmare of the missing money and Rukmini's buffalo—all of it—was just a fever-induced hallucination.

'We're going to drop by the doctor's office, but after that, maybe you should go back to Belgaum and wait for us at the Sanman.'

I found my voice. 'Once the drugs kick in I'll feel better . . . don't leave me alone,' I pleaded.

'You'll be much more comfortable at the Sanman. Bed rest will be good for you. You can order up tea and buttered toast whenever you want . . . for the next two days, we're going to be in constant motion,' he said.

I shook my head: 'No.'

'Okay, but don't say I didn't warn you,' he said. The Ambassador started moving.

In Halamid, Dilip accompanied me to the doctor's office. 'Malaria,' the doctor announced, eyeing me obliquely, as if expecting me to get anger. '*Plasmodium vivax*: the predominant strain here in Karnataka.' The doctor paused.

'What is malaria, anyway?' I asked.

'Parasites that penetrate your red blood cells and multiply, causing the blood cells to rupture. They lie dormant in the liver, and come out whenever they see fit.'

'Which strain did you say I have? Will it come back again?' I asked.

'*Plasmodium vivax*. I'll write it down for you. It can come back again even if you finish the treatment. When you get home you can talk to your doctor about a preventive treatment—in the meantime, get lots of rest, drink lots of water, and take your medicine. Good health will help you keep it at bay. It's true what they say about an apple a day,' he said, scribbling out my prescription. 'There's a good pharmacy in the next block. Make sure you check the expiration date.' He tore the leaf off the pad and handed it to Dilip. I didn't have the strength to ask more questions.

For the next two nights, Maneesh had reserved rooms at an inspection bungalow near Saundatti Temple. At Patel's, while the crew finished loading the last of our belongings and equipment into the minivan, I lay in bed, resting. Dilip filled my prescription, brought me water, and stacked duffle bags in the foot-wells of the Ambassador so that I could lie down and sleep without slipping off the seat. After lunch, we left.

THIRTY

For a wedding of dwarfs
rascals beat the drums
and whores carry on their heads
holy pitchers;
with hey-ho's and loud hurrahs
they crowd the wedding party
and quarrel over flowers and betelnuts;
all three worlds are at the party
what a rumpus this is
without the Lord of Caves [Shiva]. [38]

—Allama-Prabhu

OUR CONVOY RUMBLED ALONG the potholed ribbon of
tarmac towards Saundatti Temple under the now blazing
sun. My fever eased, and I sat up. The frequency of village
processions increased as we neared the temple, slowing us
to a snail's pace and giving me time to study the angular,
turbaned heads of villagers. Girls slated for dedication,
surrounded by clusters of devadasis, led processions of
mostly men. This was an opportunity for virgins to be
seen; offers from neighbouring landlords would soon be
rolling in.

'Few family women are in attendance,' I remarked to Dilip, who was riding shotgun.

He slung his left arm over the back of his seat and turned to look at me.

'Feeling better?' he asked.

'Yes,' I said.

'I'm sorry this had to happen,' he said.

'You have nothing to apologize for,' I replied.

'I feel like I do.'

'Nonsense,' I said, smiling, but Dilip gazed at me wistfully and didn't smile back. There was a sadness, a heaviness in his demeanour that led me to suspect he had something on his mind. I recalled our silent confrontation the previous evening. Dilip and I studied each other. My illness had made me dependent on him and had momentarily brought us together again. *Maybe I'm being paranoid,* I thought to myself. *Could the Dilip I have known and liked so much have been willing to throw an innocent man—the father of two lovely children—to the dogs just to save face for his practical joke gone awry? Did he consider the chowkidar disposable because he was untouchable? How can this be?* I wondered. But he had cancelled the plan to buy Rukmini a buffalo and this was an incontrovertible fact. Why had he seemed so resistant to allowing the women to bear witness? *He lied about his age and his caste. What else did he lie about?* I wondered. I had always admired Dilip's ambition, but now it scared me. How ruthless could he be? How far was he prepared to go?

Dilip and I contemplated each other in silence. I forced

a smile in an attempt to conceal my thoughts, but Dilip
did not smile back.

'Dilip, are you okay?' I asked. 'Do you have something
on your mind?'

He stared at me intently, and then spoke.

'The material we have is contentious. I think the BBC
might find it objectionable.'

'Objectionable? I'm not sure I understand,' I replied.
'Remember that film about homosexual rituals in New
Guinea? That was made for the same series . . . it has
about the same shock value.'

'Yes, but there's a big difference. There's a sizable South
Asian community in England, and they're sensitive to the
way that India is portrayed in the media,' said Dilip.

'I don't know what to say,' I replied. 'They knew what
they were getting into. We didn't discover anything we
weren't expecting. Besides, given the material we have,
our portrayal of the women will be *positive*. The women
are going to come off like heroes for emerging from such
a brutal system with such wisdom and grace! This is an
opportunity to *humanize* the untouchable women of India.
The women are so moving, so articulate, viewers will
empathize with them; they will feel for the women—and
it's precisely that connection that has the potential to make
this a great film. Any mother, any woman—and most men
in the world, I would say—will be moved to see Shanti
and Ruki talking about their lives . . . how can one listen
to them and remain indifferent?'

Dilip looked at me blankly, and then glanced away.
'There's another thing we need to think about. We came

into the country on a false pretext. Many foreigners have been banned from India for making films that displease: Louis Malle, Yolande Zauberman, Mike York . . . we have to be careful, or you'll become persona non grata. They can't ban me, but they can refuse me shooting permits in the future.'

'Of course I don't want to be banned from India,' I said. 'And of course, not being able to obtain shooting permits would be a big problem for you, but we could always have our names removed from the broadcast version of the film. I'm sure if we think creatively, there's a solution to that problem, don't you think?'

'Maybe you're right,' he said, sighing and looking at me wistfully. I felt confused, as if I were missing something. I ran over the conversation we had just had in my head.

'You've been a really good friend to me,' said Dilip, interrupting my thoughts. 'I want you to know that I appreciate all that you've done for me, introducing me to producers and everything. If it weren't for you this project would never have seen the light of day.'

'You have no reason to thank me,' I said, even more puzzled. 'I'm the one who should be thanking you for bringing me on board . . .' Dilip turned around in his seat and stared ahead. I tried to concentrate my thoughts on the significance of our puzzling exchange, but fell into a deep sleep.

Several hours later, I awoke to throbbing flashes of pain moving through my limbs. I felt like my skin was on fire, burning and dripping off my body. I was tumbling through a dark void, a mere bundle of muscle, sinew and vein.

We must have been in an accident, I thought to myself, terrified. I forced myself to focus and open my eyes. The falling sensation stopped. I discovered that I was alone in the car. The car was parked. Somebody had covered me with a blanket. The pain became a tight ball of fire whizzing around my body, stopping to pound my knee, my shoulder, my thigh. The crowbar was thwacking me again. My thoughts galloped wildly behind the pain. I looked out the window and tried to concentrate on something else. By the angle of the sun, I saw it was late afternoon, time to take my medicine. I closed my eyes and waited for some respite to haul myself into an upright position so I could find my bag and my medicines, but none came. Seconds stretched into minutes and I drifted into a morass of suspended time. When my senses returned, I tried to channel my energy once again. It took all my mental strength to sit up, but once I was up, it was easy to reach for my bag. I popped the pills, drank half a litre of water, and then fell back down and slept.

The next time, I woke to the sharp cries of little boys playing. The paracetamol had brought my fever down. I sat up easily and looked around. The light was fading fast. The Sumo was parked directly behind me. In the distance, I could hear many voices, and just near the front wheel of the Ambassador, there were a few boys huddled together. I wanted to find Dilip, and wondered if I could muster enough strength to get out of the car. I watched the boys playing. They were taking turns throwing something at the chain-link fence in front of the car. The intensity and urgency of their play piqued my curiosity, and I leaned over to see if I could catch a glimpse of what they were throwing. Tennis balls, old dirty tennis balls. *Do they have tennis balls in India?* I wondered, looking closer. No, they were little balls of fur. Did I see a teeny triangle of an ear, a short, stout tail? Newborn puppies! I gasped in horror and sat up, electrified. Boys swinging cats by their tails and throwing them into garbage bins—I had heard of that sort of thing. I reminded myself that in India, dogs didn't have the privileged status they did in the West. *Perhaps their mothers had asked them to kill the dogs*, I rationalized. Thump! The puppy slammed once again into the chain-link fence. Thump! I steeled myself, trying to remain calm. Thump! The puppy hit the fence again.

'Stop!' I screamed at the top of my lungs, throwing open the car door. 'Stop it! How can you be so cruel? How can you be so cruel?' With clenched fists, I glared hatefully at the boys, who dropped the puppies and fled. The puppy that had just been thrown took a few tentative steps and bobbed its head up and down. I gathered it in my hand and held it next to my stomach. Tears were streaming down my face; I was sobbing uncontrollably. I noticed our drivers standing a few feet away, looking on, aghast. I sat back down on the seat and sobbed some more. Seeing the puppies' mother hovering around me, I put the puppy back near the fence.

Suddenly, Dilip emerged, out of breath from having sprinted to the car. 'What happened?' he asked, but I couldn't speak. The driver, clearly bewildered by my outburst, recounted the scene. Dilip rolled his eyes.

'Come, wash your face,' he said, reaching for a bottle

of water, and helping me up. He poured the water into my hands, and I splashed it over my face. 'There's some hot tea and biscuits over by the camera. Kalyana villagers are camping in the courtyard of that farm over there. The devadasis are dancing in a circle, and Ravi is filming from the rooftop. The full moon is rising. It's a beautiful scene. Do you want to see?'

I shook my head no and slumped back down into the seat.

'We'll only be twenty minutes or so, then we'll head over to the inspection bungalow for dinner. You didn't have any lunch today. You need to eat something.'

*

The next morning I woke to the sound of twittering birds. The sun was already high. I had managed to keep the fever at bay through the night with steady doses of drugs. I was feeling better and the hives on my arm had almost all completely disappeared. I joined Dilip and Ravi on the patio as they surveyed the scene. The inspection bungalow, located atop a hillock, overlooked the Malaprabha Dam, and beyond it, a mountain, on whose long, flat plateau the Saundatti Temple was located. Its barren, rocky flanks were covered with close to a hundred thousand pilgrims. Although the mountain was seemingly packed to capacity, village processions along the roads on either side continued to converge upon it in creaking, overloaded bullock carts. Directly across the reservoir, whose waters spread from the dyke like a crescent moon, was the jogula-bhavi, a bathing ghat shaped like an enormous inverted pyramid with steps leading down to the water where pilgrims performed their ablutions before climbing the switchback road up to the temple.

When the chowkidar brought tea, Dilip charmed him into digging up some long-forgotten lawn chairs. For over an hour we watched, mesmerized, as thousands of villagers in turbans and brightly coloured saris filed past in the distance. Coming not only from Karnataka, but also from Maharashtra, Andhra Pradesh and Goa, many had walked for hundreds of miles. The single-minded determination, the devotion of hundreds of thousands of people—the temple was expecting three hundred thousand—was difficult to fathom. In the afternoon, Dilip and the interpreters drove up and down the road, searching for Kalyana villagers and panicking when they couldn't find them. When night fell, the villagers covered their carts with white tarps and hung oil lamps beneath them to light the way, forming one long, glowing snake, undulating through the landscape. The mountain twinkled with lights from the encampments.

Village processions continued their march on the temple through the night, and in the morning, the impossibly steep mountainside was covered with an enormous, restless camp of white-clad pilgrims and covered wagons. Clusters of women and elaborately caparisoned bullocks provided a few flashes of colour. A haze of dust hung in the air. What few scraggly bushes had managed to survive the previous festival were now mercilessly trampled underfoot. Our drivers had located the villagers and the crew was preparing to meet them at the jogula-bhavi. My first reaction was panic. 'We'll never be able to make it through the narrow pass above the Malaprabha Dam, much less find Kalyana villagers,' I said to Dilip, who had appeared next to me. He laughed.

'This is nothing; you should see a Kumbh Mela! But you know, if you're still feeling weak, maybe you should stay here. We're only going to be taking the Sumo, and I don't know how we'll all fit.'

'We'll have to find a way,' I replied. Chandi and Dadar crammed into the back of the Sumo; Dilip, the interpreters and I rode in the backseat, while Ravi took the camera on his lap in the passenger seat. Beeping continuously, and travelling at only a few miles an hour, the Sumo pushed its way past the bullock carts, over the dike to the jogula-bhavi.

The four sides of the sacred ghat were terraced with steps where pilgrims could make themselves comfortable. The steps led down to a large, square pool of thick, grey water, 40 feet long on each side, where the pilgrims 'purified' themselves. A crowd of thirty sloshed about in the water while those who had already performed their ablutions ate or chatted with friends as they waited for their clothes to dry. Saris stretched over the stone steps had transformed the well into a multicoloured chequerboard. Ritual servants picked their way through the crowds offering haircuts, shaves and earwax removal. Devadasis that had made special vows and girls preparing for dedication stood bare-breasted, with only a small skirt around their loins, while neem vendors wrapped them in robes of leaves. Above the well, a dedication party, led by a girl covered in neem, eschewed the switchback road and struggled up the seemingly vertical boulder field that led to the temple as the crow flies.

Dilip located the Kalyana villagers on the steps of the well. Sumithra, Renuka, Ranavva, Ganga and Kassi proudly donned the brand-new traditional embroidered saris that I had given them. When Ravi finished filming the women, I sat beside them and rested my head on Ranavva's shoulder.

'Poor thing,' said Ranavva, putting her arm around me.

'I can't walk up,' I said gesturing to Ranavva, breaking my longstanding promise to climb the hill with her. I had been looking forward to the pilgrimage for months, but now I couldn't muster my enthusiasm. My only desire was to get back to Paris as quickly as possible. I climbed into the Sumo with the crew, and we began our ascent to the temple. On either side of the road, an assortment of yogis and fakirs displayed their astonishing skills: hanging from hooks stuck deep in their flesh; standing on one leg for days at a time; piercing their limbs and their cheeks with long metal spikes. There were numerous snake-charmers and fire-throwers; there were also sculptural installations depicting the various stages of Yellamma's life; Yellamma's dismemberment was a favourite theme. A constant stream of pilgrims passed through this show, occasionally donating a few small coins. What could the authorities do in the face of the implacable devotion of three hundred thousand pilgrims determined to worship the goddess? A few years back, four police officers, two women among them, attempting to stop nude worship, were surrounded by a throng of devotees, forced to strip naked and marched up to the temple in an act of forced devotion. What could Kempavva and her troupe accomplish? They were just another sideshow. I sank down in my seat, plagued by reservations about our role in making the film. Perhaps we were just exploiting the women all over again?

The Sumo, its motor straining to capacity, rounded one hairpin bend after another, and we finally arrived on the plateau, cramped and anxious. Vendors had set up makeshift stalls and were hawking every imaginable kind of souvenir, offering and edible: incense, haldi, kum-kum, myrrh, wreaths of carnations, lotuses, jungle-fire blossoms, bananas, coconuts, cowry shells, bangles, tea, soda, pakoras, silver anklets, beads, bangles, nose rings, posters of the bejewelled Yellamma, cassettes, saris, perfumes. As we made our way through the crowds, we were engulfed by clouds of smoke wafting from cooking pots, sometimes so pungent with spice they made my eyes water. A drop of hot oil landed on the nape of my neck as we passed one stall. Startled, I looked back. The vendor fixed me with a manic gaze and waggled his head. 'Bhang,' he said, pointing to a pitcher of what looked like lassi, a yogurt milkshake. Bhang is a drink traditionally laced with hashish. A troupe of startlingly tall jogappas with a boom box blaring Michael Jackson danced their way past us.

*

'Amr*iiiit*, Catr*iiiin*,' screeched someone from afar. I finally spotted Kalyana's devadasis in the long, dense line wrapping itself around the temple compound. I joined them, dragging along the film crew. Devotees would have to wait for hours before being allowed a small glimpse of the goddess.

'There's got to be another way to do this.' Ravi rolled his eyes, shifting the camera on his shoulder. Dilip picked Sumithra, Renuka, Ranavva, Ganga and Rukmini from the line. 'Come with us,' he ordered them, leading us around the temple to the main gate. As soon as we had stepped inside the compound, a policeman approached us. I winced, prepared for the worst, but then realized that he was leading us over to Yellamma's pavilion. He gestured for us to enter the pavilion, but hesitated for a moment when it came to the Kalyana villagers, who were not normally allowed in this area, but Dilip quickly explained that they were with us. We were led to an inner sanctum near the goddess. On the other side of the metal gates were throngs of villagers, rapt with devotion, shouting, singing, and swaying their way past the goddess. Policemen with their lathis herded villagers through the gates, shouting, pushing and poking at those who dallied.

A throng of priests busied themselves performing the puja.

'What is your name?' a sweaty, fat priest asked a terrified Renuka.

'Renuka,' her mother replied. A puja was performed in her name and the baskets of offerings were blessed. Ravi and Dadar recorded the sequence. Moments later we found ourselves standing outside Yellamma's pavilion. This was it; we had what we needed. It was time to say goodbye. Dilip went in search of Maneesh to get the cash envelopes he had prepared as a way of thanking the women for their cooperation, while Malika and I stayed behind with the women. As the crowds were channelled through the pavilion, the temple compound itself became relatively quiet.

Ganga, Ranavva, Sumithra, Rukmini and Renuka, deep in discussion amongst themselves, drew us to the temple water tank.

'We have something important to say,' said Ranavva, gesturing for everyone to sit. 'Malika, Catherine, you are very special to us and we want you to know that. We talk about you all the time and all the things you did with us.'

'Yes,' interrupted Sumithra, 'it was very special for us to be inside the temple today. We got a very good darshan. The goddess's power was strong; I could feel it. This will bring prosperity to our village.'

'Six months ago, when you and Vani came to our village for the first time, we thought surely we would never see you again,' said Ranavva, 'but you came back and then Malika, Amrit, Dilip and the rest followed. We want you to know that the only reason we have worked with you is because of the kindness and respect you showed to us. We didn't think that people like you had time for us. For this reason only, we have worked with you. We want you to know this.' Ranavva spoke slowly, allowing for Malika to translate sentence by sentence.

'You showed us love and affection,' said Rukmini, 'and we have taken you into our homes and our hearts. Some people say we have done this in the hopes of receiving money, but it is not true. We have worked with you because

of the love and affection that you showed us. How will
we manage after you leave? Every day we will be thinking
about you and missing you.'

'You have treated us with kindness. That means a lot
to us,' said Sumithra. 'You have grown dear to our hearts.
We will miss you when you are gone.' Rukmini and then
Ranavva started to cry. I turned to ask Malika to reassure
the women that we would come back soon, and noticed
tears rolling down her face.

Ganga gathered my hand in hers and looked me in the
eye. She spoke slowly and deliberately. 'One of the women
in our community—Chandra, you know her, the one who
has taught herself to read and write—is going to help us
write down in a book everything you did with us: how
you and Vani came, how you took us to Badami, and how
you invited us into your house and fed us. How you came
into our houses and, refusing to sit on mats, ate our food.
You have come from so far away and you are important
people, yet you listen to what we have to say. This we will
not forget. Everything you did with us, we are going to
write it down so that from generation to generation it will
be remembered and not get lost with the passage of time.'

Chandi came to tell us that Dilip was waiting for us at
the Sumo, and the women rose to accompany us back to
the car. We said our final goodbyes, and I watched Maneesh
press envelopes into the women's hands.

'How much are we giving them?' I asked.

'None of your business,' replied Dilip.

'How much?' I pressed him.

'A small fortune, don't worry.'

We travelled to Belgaum, where a retired school bus was waiting to take us to Mumbai. In no time, I was on a plane to Paris. When I reached there I promptly had another malaria attack and this time my platelets dropped to dangerously low levels, which kept me in the hospital for over a week. But my friends filed in one after the other, bringing sweets, and the nurses were so kind, and there was a magnificent greenhouse where I could go for walks once I felt strong enough. I had a spotlessly clean, private room with my own bathroom—it was heaven. I felt profoundly grateful to be home and vowed never to complain about anything ever again.

PART THREE

THIRTY-ONE

The moon that day stood in the sign of Magha, and in the heavens the seven great planets converged in a blaze of light. When the sun rose, it seemed as though it had split in two, and when it had finally risen in the sky it was burning with a crest of flames. [39]

—Bhagavadgita

IN FEBRUARY, ONE MONTH after my return to Paris, the film was digitized and Dilip and I started to edit. The producer reserved an editing suite for us in a no-frills facility on the outskirts of Paris. As I waited for the bus on our first day, unrelenting, ominous clouds hung over the rooftops and the humid cold bit into my skin. Dilip and I had hardly spoken since our return to Paris, and it came as no surprise that, when we sat down to edit, he refused to look me in the eye.

What happened in the editing room over the next month had been determined long before Dilip and I had ever met. Dilip was raised in an impoverished, uneducated family in the remote provinces of India. By wile and by wit, he had gained acceptance into India's best schools and clawed his way out of his rural province. However, unable to completely assimilate into the ranks of India's educated elite, he moved to the West. While many men are able to see beyond the perspectives of their own caste and gender, Dilip never quite made this step. He was too consumed by ambition. For Dilip, devadasis were dispensable cogs in the machinations that he hoped would bring him fame and fortune.

As for myself, I was a privileged, upper-middle-class New Yorker with a liberal arts education who believed it was possible to improve societies and keep governments honest by exposing injustices. Except in the matter of the circumstances of my birth, I saw no great difference between any other human being and myself, and therefore, had no trouble empathizing with people from radically different backgrounds. I had been deeply moved by the devadasi women of Kalyana and the stories they had to tell. They were my sisters. I felt an obligation to make their voices heard. But to do so would reflect badly on the conservative ranks of the upper castes, to which Dilip pretended to belong.

I hoped that our film would spark concern for Karnataka's untouchable women, resulting in literacy programmes, vocational training, and micro-credit loans— the stepping-stones of social change. But these issues simply did not interest Dilip. Dilip and I found ourselves on opposite ends of a debate that was by no means new. The devadasi system had always been a sensitive subject in India. While some denounced it as an oppressive structure of Brahminical patriarchy, others celebrated it as a Great Hindu Tradition. And the devadasi question was inscribed in wider, highly politicized debates concerning colonialism, nationalism and an emerging Hindu identity. Some historians and anthropologists, eager to carve out a place in Indian history where women were powerful and independent, pass over the details and glorify the tradition. They focus only on a few, exceptional devadasis and claim that devadasis' lives were all right. They point out that some accumulated wealth and were lovers of kings and generals—Muddupalani of Thanjavur, for example, who wrote the *The Appeasement of Radhika*. They forget about the vast majority of nameless devadasis who were forced to render sexual services for a pittance (in medieval times, client's fees were collected by temple priests).

During the first few days of cutting, Dilip and I fought over almost every edit. In the war that was to follow, both of us made serious strategic errors. Dilip's first was to hire a young American from Connecticut to edit the film. His name was Dougie Taylor. When I walked into the editing room and saw Doug, I had to suppress a smile. The tails of his pinstriped Brooks Brothers shirt hung loosely over a pair of faded Levi's. His flaxen wool ski socks stuffed into his topsiders made his feet look like sausages. Under an untidy mop of blond hair, which in places stood on end, were pale blue eyes that never looked at anything too directly. At twenty-eight, Doug was a few years younger than me.

When Dilip went to get some coffee, Doug turned to me and asked, 'Did you go to boarding school at Saint Paul's? I've seen you before.' In Dilip's presence, Doug retained a professional distance, but at the end of the day, Dougie and I would loiter about the editing room, and then, after

Dilip left, go out for a drink and plot how to thwart Dilip's increasingly evident intention to censor the material.

The gulf that separated Doug and me from Dilip was at its greatest when it came to editing what we called 'The night of the girl-virgin' sequence, in which the women discussed the 'second pattam', their defloration ceremony. I arrived late to find that Dilip had intercut the women talking about how they were raped with close-ups of them laughing. The close-ups had been taken from a conversation filmed half an hour earlier, in which the women were mimicking their neighbours. Rukmini's description of how she was raped in the field was spliced back to back with another part of the interview when she was talking about how much she loved her man.

I was dumbfounded; I sat back in my chair, stupefied. I had already called the producer to discuss my unease with Dilip, but she put me off. *I'll have to insist,* I thought.

When Dilip rose to take a break, I lashed out at Doug. 'How could you make those edits?' I demanded.

'I had no idea what they were saying,' said Doug.

'But I gave you a set of transcripts specifically so you could follow along!'

'He came in this morning with the sentences marked off and numbered. I couldn't push the buttons and follow along with the text at the same time . . . he just told me where to drop in those cutaways. He didn't ask my opinion.'

When Dilip returned from his break, I was reading a section of the transcript to Doug. After describing how she was raped, Rukmini said, 'After that I didn't go work at his place. He asked my friends why I wasn't coming. I didn't see his face for two months, and when I saw him I told him, "You are an ass." I would spit whenever I saw him and run away . . .' But Dilip had cut this part away and replaced it with a snippet taken from when she was talking about her lover. 'I didn't see him for two whole days,' Rukmini giggled, 'I missed him so much, I could hardly eat. After that, we were inseparable.' He was trying to make it seem like Rukmini had suddenly fallen in love with the man who raped her.

'You know,' Doug said to Dilip, 'Catherine and I were just looking at this edit, and I don't think it makes sense.'

'What do you mean? It makes perfect sense.'

'Dilip,' I said, 'Rukmini is talking about two different people. In the first part she's talking about the landlord who raped her, and in the second, she's talking about her lover.'

'What do you mean? They're the same person!'

'Dilip, you know very well it wasn't Nagappa who raped her!' I said.

'There you go using that word again. Rukmini doesn't use the word "rape"; how can you? That's just your cultural bias,' Dilip shouted.

I was disconcerted. I had never heard Dilip raise his voice in anger before.

'She describes getting taken in the field kicking and screaming. That's generally what we call rape, even if she doesn't use the word,' I said flatly, glancing out of the corner of my eye at Doug, who looked petrified.

'She doesn't use the word "rape", so how can you? That's just *your* cultural bias. You're being ethnocentric,' said Dilip.

'Let's look again,' said Doug, rolling back over the edit. We all watched Rukmini onscreen. 'See how the light changes? The splicing together from two different scenes is too obvious. Doug swivelled around in his chair and started pushing buttons. 'This edit just doesn't work,' he said, undoing it. 'Nobody's going to understand.'

'Okay,' said Dilip. 'Let's just get rid of the whole thing.'

'Okay,' said Doug, and in a flash, Rukmini's tale of rape was gone.

'Dilip,' I said, 'I think that sequence needs to be in. It's one of the few instances in which we see the violence that is part and parcel of the women's lives . . .'

Dilip did not respond; he just stared tight-lipped at the ground.

'Catherine, the women talk about ritual rape already; we can do without Rukmini,' Doug intervened.

'Why are the two of you calling it rape?' Dilip snapped. 'They don't call it that; why should you? I've got to get out of here.' Dilip gathered his things and left.

Doug and I stared at each other. The tension was palpable. After a few minutes, Doug rose to open the door, and then collapsed back into his swivel chair. 'We have to do something,' he said. 'Having both of you in the editing room is unbearable. We're never going to get anywhere.'

I reached for the phone and called Estelle, the executive producer. Failing to persuade her to come down to the editing room and look for herself, I begged her to receive me in her office so we could go over some of the transcripts together.

'I'm too busy, Catherine,' she replied. 'I just don't have

the time. Let's do this: you let Dilip do his edit—that's what you agreed to before the shoot—and if you're not comfortable with it, then we'll look at it together and, if need be, go back to the editing room.'

Both Doug and I were befuddled by Estelle's refusal to come to the editing room. 'She calls herself a producer?' asked Doug. 'She hasn't even been here once.' Later that evening, Doug called me at home. 'Estelle just called me,' he said. 'I think Dilip must have gone to see her. She threatened to fire me. She said I should be supporting Dilip's vision. She insinuated that editors who are not "*solidaire*" get bad reputations, and then never get hired again. I have a wife and daughter to feed. I don't want to get blackballed.'

From that point onwards, I went to the editing room every day but only intervened when it came to editing the interviews. Dilip pretended to go along with my suggestions, but when I absented myself for two days to do research for another film, Dilip re-edited the interviews. Out of a desire to validate the existence of some impossible male fantasy, he represented the devadasis of Kalyana as willing participants in the system as a result of their religious devotion. For him, the devadasi cult was a divine realm where both spiritual and sexual needs could be gratified. Interviews that revealed the dire economic straits of Karnataka's landless labourers, and the violence to which the women were subjected, were dropped. There was no mention of the trafficking, or of the sexual enslavement of women and children to feed the brothels of Goa, Pune and Mumbai. Both Rukmini and her mother were dropped from the film, and other interviews were compromised with tricky editing. Shanti was only shown speaking about how much she loved her keeper.

This ludicrous representation of the system was Dilip's second major strategic error: Who would believe it? Any experienced filmmaker would be able to detect the contrived editing in the interviews. With only a few days of editing left, I called Estelle and asked her to come see the film, but she refused again.

'Estelle, Dilip intercut a scene where the women talk about how they were raped with close-ups of the women laughing. Why not just let the scene roll? There's no need to make any cuts at all. Let's just let the women speak for themselves!'

'Dilip has been up here and has explained everything to me—'

'You mean you had time to receive Dilip, but not me?' I interrupted.

'You don't understand,' she said, 'those women don't *feel* the same way we do.'

'*Those* women don't *feel* the same way we do?' I repeated, incredulous. 'Is that because they're devadasis or because they're untouchables?' I seethed.

'I don't have time for this. Militant feminism just isn't interesting,' Estelle spat back.

Regaining my composure, I checked myself. 'Estelle, please just come down and see the film for yourself.'

'Catherine, you are not listening to me. I have neither the time nor the money for a few extra days of editing. If you are going to be so difficult, I don't know how I can work with you on your Raves film (she had just obtained financing from Arte, a French-German broadcaster, for a film I had proposed).' I refused to capitulate and so, dismissing me as an 'ethnocentric, militant feminist,' she stopped taking my calls. At first I couldn't understand why she refused to hear me out or view the material, but I later found out that she was planning to shoot another film in India and needed approval from the Embassy and the Ministry of External Affairs, whose wrath Dilip would not have hesitated to exaggerate. His persuasive powers were formidable. She had been conned.

※

Devastated by the travesty of a film we had made—a film which purported to be a documentary, but in fact distorted the women's words and wilfully misrepresented the devadasi system as it existed in northern Karnataka—I hired a lawyer and threatened to oppose the film on ethical grounds, which by French law was my right as a co-director. While I managed to get the most offensive edits corrected, the film remained a sham. It was discredited among documentary film circles in Paris and none of the many festivals to which it was submitted would touch it. While a private French broadcaster agreed to air it, the BBC, for whom it had been made, refused to do so.

For years I remained disconsolate, ranting about what had happened to anyone who would listen, to the point where Estelle's lawyer—much to my delight—sent me a letter threatening to sue me for damages for ruining the reputation of her film company. While I didn't regret opposing the film on ethical grounds, I detested myself for having been so naïve and failing the women.

THIRTY-TWO

Season, day and hour went out of kilter,
so did earth, water, the planets and the skies,
fire, wind, the mountains and the stars:
O what a roaring meal of chaos
our lord made of the seven worlds![40]

—Nammalvar

THREE YEARS LATER, IN 2005, I returned to India to make
a film about the Kondh tribe in the highlands of Orissa.
I carved out two weeks for myself to visit Mumbai and
Kalyana. Rukmini had given me her mother's address in
Kamathipura, the red-light district in the heart of the city.
I hired an interpreter, Mona, to take me there; we arrived
in the late afternoon. The peeling, pastel houses with
wooden shutters and balconies, three and four storeys
high, opened onto the lanes. Bored, defiant-looking girls
draped themselves in doorways or over balconies of the
grid-like streets along which men strolled, arm in arm. Fat
old gharwalis languished on settees outside their houses
while their minions prepared meals over gas-burners on
the sidewalk, filling the lane with the pungent aromas of
spices. The absence of cars gave the area a distinctive village

feel. Peddlers pulling wooden carts hawked their goods, while half-naked children played happily on large cotton durries next to open sewers where rats scurried observed yet untroubled by alley cats.

Confused by the address, we started asking around. 'Padmini, Rukmini! There are five Padminis in this building alone,' said a Madam on her settee, laughing at us. And as it turned out there were more than a few Kalyanas in Karnataka. Padmini had said she lived on the fourth floor of the fourth house in Fourth Lane, but there was only a Fourth Street or a Fourth Avenue. However, most buildings had only three storeys. On Fourth Street we entered the narrow door of a building with four storeys, and climbed a few flights of rotten, rickety stairs, through which daylight shone since the rear wall of the house had collapsed. Upstairs, we came nose-to-nose with a door blocking access to the fourth floor. It was bolted shut from the outside with iron bars and heavy metal locks. In the hallway, many of the doors consisted merely of drapes. Ripe young girls poked out their heads to scrutinize us as we strolled by. Inside the rooms, girls lounged on beds, chatting and brushing each other's hair as if they were at a sleepover party. Some girls had rooms of their own, while others shared. The relationship of a Madam to her girls is said to be that of a mother to daughter, but also master to slave. Madams know how to be warm and affectionate and provide needed emotional support, but they can also be brutal and violent.

Mona questioned the girls, but they shook their heads. As she tried to explain our purpose, the mysterious bolted door drew me back to it. Could it be the door to Padmini's room? Why was it bolted on the outside? None of the other rooms had such elaborate security.

'Who lives here?' I asked through Mona.

'A family,' said the young girls gathered around me, eyes solemn and wide.

'A family? How many children?'

'We think there are four or five. We never see them, but we hear them crying sometimes,' replied a bold, pleasantly plump girl with green eye shadow and oversized gold hoops.

'They don't go to school?' I asked.

The women shook their heads solemnly, eyes wide. *How could they never see the children?* I wondered. Two young men suddenly came bounding up the stairs, the first almost knocking me over as he reached the top. The women backed away. The man hovered above me, glaring at me with bulging beady eyes.

'We're looking for Padmini and Rukmini,' said Mona. The man's shoulders relaxed; the tension dissipated.

'You mean the Rukmini who had the abortion?' he asked.

'I don't know,' I said. 'Her mother was Padmini.'

'Yes, Padmini. And Rukmini had a little boy of around five or six.'

'That would be Gajanan,' I said.

'They left months ago. I think they went back to their village, but I'm not sure,' said the man. His companion peered over his shoulder, eyeing me suspiciously.

'*Shukria*, thank you,' I said, deciding it was time to leave.

✳

That night I woke up in a cold sweat. I sat up in bed with the certainty that the 'family', the girls had told me about was not a family at all, but a child prostitution ring. The girls never saw the children because they never went out. They were prisoners, they were sex slaves. Children. My limbs went numb, a bitter metallic taste filled my mouth. I went to the bathroom, kneeled down on the cement floor and retched.

In the morning, I called Mona.

'Are you sure?' she asked, as she tried to comfort the baby in her arms.

'Yes,' I said. 'Positive.'

'I have a friend who works for an NGO in the area. She'll know whom to contact. There must be some child protection agency.'

'Yes,' I said, but we both suspected it was futile. Even if Mona located the proper authority, the pimp's contacts in the police department would warn him long before any raid took place.

✳

That night I boarded the sleeper train to Belgaum. Vani was waiting for me. She threw her arms around me. 'I'm so glad to be back here with you, you have no idea. I think so often of our trip together and the women we met. They're such an inspiration to me. Did you bring the film?' she asked.

'I did, but Vani, we need to talk. Let's have breakfast,' I said, steering her to the restaurant. Slumping into the red vinyl seat, I remembered sitting there with Vani for the first time, so full of hopes and dreams for the film we were about to make. I stared at the reflection of the whirring overhead fan in the Formica tabletop and felt my throat tightening.

'Milk-coffee,' I managed to squeak out to the smiling waiter whom I vaguely recognized. Vani studied me with large saucer eyes, waiting for me to speak, but words would not come.

'What happened?' she finally asked.

'It's the film. I did everything I could. I hired a lawyer, I fought with everything I had, but Dilip won. He outmanoeuvred me.'

'I don't understand,' said Vani.

'Dilip censored the film. He cut everything related to the economics and the violence of the system. He twisted the women's words around to make it seem like they upheld the tradition out of religious devotion.'

Vani stared at me, uncomprehending. 'But who would believe such a thing?'

'No one, I don't think. Not really. The producer submitted the film to every film festival she could think of, but it was rejected everywhere. The film is more a puerile male fantasy than a documentary, any professional filmmaker can see that.'

'I thought the executive producer was a woman?' said Vani.

'She is, but she was taken in by him. He told her a pack of lies, and she believed them. She's not an intelligent woman. And she had another film to shoot in India; she didn't want to jeopardize getting a shooting permit.'

Vani sat back in her seat, shaking her head in disbelief.

When she looked up, I saw anger and disappointment in her eyes. I was not surprised; I felt the same way. Three years had done nothing to attenuate my feelings of failure and guilt.

'I did everything I could,' I said, staring back. 'I spent every penny I ever made on lawyers' fees. I got some changes made, but it wasn't enough . . . I don't know what to say. The women trusted me, and I betrayed them. I allowed them to be exploited all over again.' I felt all my old wounds reopening. 'I haven't given up hope, though. I'll do something for them yet.'

Vani stiffened. She didn't want to hear my apologies; I couldn't blame her. 'I took the liberty of asking the concierge to arrange a car,' said Vani. 'We should probably get on the road.'

THIRTY-THREE

You don't grant grace to your devotees
who dance, and sing songs to the proper beat . . .
Though I am weary, wandering about, looking for you,
you never think of me. [41]

—Cuntarar (or Sundarar), eighth-century Bhakti saint

IT WAS MONSOON SEASON, and as we turned down the path to Kalyana, the clouds parted and the drenched earth glistened in the sun. Silver droplets hung off tender stalks of sugarcane and maize. White flowers grew tall in puddles and tapering palm trees reached for the skies. During the drive, I was swamped by feelings of shame and humiliation; I also felt apprehensive about what I would find in Kalyana. HIV rates in India had risen exponentially over the past few years. The infection rate among Mumbai prostitutes was almost seventy per cent.

Vani directed the driver into the village and had him park near the Yellamma temple. The children, hopping with excitement, scampered in all directions to spread the news of our return. Vani and I made our way to Ganga's hut. Villagers crowded around us, beaming with delight, holding our arms, and calling us by name. Ganga intercepted us and brought us to Ranavva's, across the street.

We all sat on the charpai while Ranavva's mother prepared tea.

'Not a day goes by that we don't think about you and talk about you,' said Ranavva, shaking her head, smiling and wiping a tear away.

'The same is true for us,' I said.

Sumithra appeared and squeezed in next to us. We all held hands and beamed at each other, drinking in this special moment.

'And Rukmini, and Shanti . . .' I had hardly uttered their names, and already I was being reassured. I breathed a sigh of relief.

Villagers started filing through the house to greet us, and children, pushing and shoving each other, packed in to stare at me. Soon there was so much of a racket that we couldn't hear ourselves think, and there was no air left in the room. Vani and I began to wilt.

'The Durga festival starts tomorrow. Many people have gone for provisions,' shouted Ranavva.

'We have to find rooms in town,' said Vani, 'but we'll be back tonight at six. Have everyone meet us at the Yellamma temple.'

Standing up, I found myself face-to-face with Padmini, Rukmini's mother. She took hold of my forearms and bore her olive eyes into mine. 'I have been waiting for you,' she said. She put one arm around Vani and waited for her to translate. 'Come with me,' she said.

✳

Padmini drew a folded blanket from the cupboard for Vani and me to sit on, and put a kettle on the hearth. 'Rukmini has not been well,' she said. 'After you left last time, she went to Mumbai with me, but fell into a severe depression. Her body became limp and she had pain all down her left side. One morning she woke up, and the left side of her face was completely paralysed. She couldn't get out of bed. For weeks on end, she lay in bed; I couldn't even get her back to the village. Nothing I said or promised her had any effect. Ganesh, my joolwa husband, started getting impatient with her. Finally, I called a specialist to her bedside. I told the doctor: "I have only one daughter, whatever it may cost, please find out what is ailing her." He gave her an injection and she felt better. For a while, she had regular injections, but now she only takes tablets and tonics.'

Injections, tablets and tonics. Padmini's words echoed in my ears. I asked her for the names of the medicines, but she didn't know. All she knew was that they made her daughter feel better. Vani and I looked at each other, remembering Lathamala's words: depression, alcoholism and suicide were common among devadasis.

'After the injections started she got out of bed, but she was not the same Rukmini as before. I was scared. Then one day, she went shopping, and when she came back she was with her friend Rupa, and Rupa told me that she thought Rukmini was going to take her own life. The injections gave her strength, strength enough to try to kill herself. I rifled through her things and I found a cache of blades and poison. After that I did not let her out of my sight, not for one minute. I was at my wit's end. Finally,

I took her back to the village and called a priest to the house. He did a puja and got in touch with the spirits. Do you see that piece of wood over there?' she asked, pointing to a slab of driftwood in the corner of the room. It was decorated with kumkum and flowers. An oil lamp burned in front of it. 'Many years ago my grandfather found it in the fields. For a long time, it remained under the cot, but then the priest said it was a divinity and was troubling Rukmini because it was not being worshipped, so we set up this shrine and began to make offerings. She was able to get out of bed after that, but remained lacklustre.

'Rukmini was never a very religious person. She did not show the proper respect to the goddess, but now she prays and makes offerings. Since then the pains have gone away, but life has no flavour for her. She is without her former energy and strength . . . she used to be always singing, dancing and laughing, but since you left she stopped smiling.'

Vani and I stared in silence at the ground, letting Padmini's words sink in. The kettle top began to rattle and Padmini rose to get the tea.

'Where is Rukmini now?' asked Vani.

'She's living with a university student in Sangli,' said Padmini.

'She's not in the village?' I asked.

'She comes and goes. She's not far,' said Padmini, pouring tea into small earthenware cups.

'We're only here a week, and I must see her. Can I go pick her up in our car?'

'It's better if I fetch her . . .' said Padmini, knitting her brow.

'Please, I've come all this way. I even went looking for you in Kamathipura,' I pleaded.

Padmini studied me thoughtfully. 'I'll take a bus tomorrow morning, and we should be back in the village by afternoon,' she said.

'Here's for the bus fare,' I said, peeling four hundred rupees, about twenty times the cost of the bus, from a wad of bills. She tucked them into her sari blouse.

I remembered the stack of photos in my bag and fished out a snapshot I had taken of Rukmini and Mariamma at the hanging bridge in Gokak Falls. Padmini caught her breath when she saw it, and stared at it for a long moment. Tucking it into a suitcase under the charpai, she said, 'I'll give this to Rukmini when the time is right. Mariamma died last year of AIDS—or hepatitis B.'

'Where is her son?' asked Vani.

'Her uncle and aunt have adopted him.'

'And what about you?' asked Vani. 'Why are you in the village? Are you no longer living in Mumbai?'

'I live here now. I'm through with Ganesh; I'm through with Mumbai. I live as a jogti, devoting myself only to Yellamma. In Mumbai I used to sing bhajans, hymns to the gods, not only to Yellamma, but to all the gods. Now I sing only for Yellamma. Sometimes I go with Sumithra on Tuesdays and Fridays to perform worship in the upper-caste homes and sometimes I go with a group from a hamlet nearby. The head devadasi there, Giddavva, worships with a group of five devotees, but one of the ladies is now old and sick and cannot walk far. They are a traditional group and know many of the songs that have been forgotten by others. They are called far and wide in the district, not just by local villagers, so when it's too far for the old lady, they send for me. I've never walked so much in my life. My whole body aches, but we earn good money. Enough for me to eat.'

'So you have become a very religious person?' asked Vani.

'I was always a religious person. We worshipped Yellamma there in Mumbai, but when you are doing dhanda, how do you have the time and energy for all the rituals, to do the puja twice a day, to seek alms twice a week from upper-caste houses? Dhanda itself is worship, so that is enough. Now I am through with dhanda.'

'Looking back over your life, how does it make you feel? If you could change something, what would it be?' I asked

'Change something? What could I possibly have changed? What choice did I have? How could I have done anything differently? I was sent to sell my body in Mumbai even before my period started, I was only eleven years old! My life has been so full of suffering—I can't think about it. I keep my eyes only on Yellamma and don't think about the past, I want to worship her as best I can and somehow make it through my final days. I pray for the health of my daughter and my grandson, that is my only concern in this world!' Padmini paused, struggling. Vani and I remained silent. 'Perhaps, there is one thing that I regret, there is one thing I could have changed . . . I wish I had not dedicated my daughter. I thought it would be okay, I thought I could protect her, but instead, I ruined her life.' Closing her eyes tight, she hung her head; tears fell upon the hand clenched in her lap.

THIRTY-FOUR

In the crown adorning your head are Dhruva loka and
other worlds.
On your forehead bejewelled by nine gems there is the
entire Veda
In your mouth shruti revelation exists, the Maruts are in
your breath,
in your eyes are sun and moon, the stars have their existence.[42]

—Kanaka Dasa, sixteenth-century Bhakti saint

Leaving Padmini's house and turning right into the sodden
grey lanes of the holakeri, I despaired that, in three years,
nothing had changed. The maze of crumbling mud houses
with their leaky tile-and-thatch roofs, and the community
they housed, were exactly the same. Perhaps a few homes
had been built, but only to see others slump into the bog
during the monsoon, leaving behind only a few rough-
hewn bricks and stones. I wondered how many girls had
been dedicated since we left.

'Ruki's in a good place now, don't look so sad,' said
Ranavva, joining Vani and me as we left. 'She's with a
young man, a student. She's away from Mumbai now and

she'll never go there again. Her mother has come back to look after her now.'

I forced a smile and Ranavva slipped between Vani and me, interlocking arms with us.

'We are going to Halamid to find lodging,' said Vani.

'Good, then you can drop me at Sanjay's on the way,' said Ranavva.

As we walked through the stout brick boundary posts of the holakeri, I remembered the terrifying handful of bloody rice that had flown past me. Our creamy bowler hat of a car was waiting for us on the road. The driver jumped out to open the door. Once we were moving, Ranavva announced, 'Sanjay has been sick.'

'Very sick?' Vani asked. I remembered how kind he had been when I was delirious with malarial fever.

'Why don't you come in for a moment and say hello. He'll be happy to see you.'

Still under construction when I was last in the village, Sanjay's house was huge by village standards. Cinder blocks allowed for proportions that traditional construction materials did not. The simple white façade, broken by only a few small windows soared high above anything the village had ever seen. Inside, the traditional threshing floor and verandah had been preserved.

Sanjay's daughters invited Vani and me onto the verandah and served us tea and biscuits while we waited for Sanjay. Ranavva, in accordance with caste rules, remained on the threshing floor but dominated the conversation, pacing up and down. 'Pritya, don't be shy . . . this is Sanjay's oldest daughter.' Ranavva introduced each of his daughters, detailing their marital status and the names of their children.

Soon a bent and withered man with a crutch hobbled in, dragging his left leg behind him. Had his daughter not announced him, I never would have recognized Sanjay. I stifled a gasp. He had lost over fifty pounds and his hair had gone grey. Just three years ago he was a tall, strong man in his prime. It was devastating to see him so diminished. His daughters looked on in silence as Ranavva helped him up the stairs to the verandah. When he reached the top, unable to accompany him further because of caste restrictions, Ranavva let go; Sanjay lost his balance and almost fell. Stretching up, he looked at me for the first time. Perhaps remembering our last meeting, he let out a tormented sob and burst into tears. Mortified, my eyes welled up with tears. Vani shot me an angry look. Sanjay's daughter brought him a chair and helped him sit down. He crumpled and continued to sob loudly.

Ranavva, presiding from the threshing floor, interrupted, 'What is this? What are all these tears for? Sanjay, what do you have to complain about? You are a very lucky man: no more working in the fields! All you have to do is eat and sleep . . . and look at all these beautiful girls who have nothing to do but wait on you day in day out. What I wouldn't do for a life like this?' Sanjay wiped his tears away and laughed.

Sanjay, who could hardly have been forty-five, had had a stroke several months earlier. The left side of his body had become paralysed. 'At first he was unable to walk or speak, but he has gradually been getting better. He is taking medication and the doctor makes him do physical therapy,' said Ranavva.

'My grandmother had a stroke,' I said, 'and with physical therapy, she recuperated completely.'

Sanjay made an effort to speak. The words bubbled in his mouth, then came out long and flat. A long silence ensued, and then he began again. 'Only Ranavva can understand him,' his daughter whispered to Vani.

'He wants to know if Catherine akka remembers how afraid she was to ride on the back of his scooter,' said Ranavva.

'Of course I remember,' I said, trying to sound cheery. 'How could I forget? Had it not been for you, I would have had to walk all the way to Yellamma Gudda.'

Sanjay chuckled, but Ranavva cut in before he could say anything. 'You laugh because she was afraid of you, but really it was *you* who were afraid of *her*. A big strong man like you! Afraid! You begged me, "Ranavva, don't go with them; they'll take you away!" she said, mimicking him. 'A big man like that, you can't imagine how scared he was. He pleaded with me not to go near you!' Ranavva chattered away, making Vani, Sanjay and his daughters reel with laughter.

When Ranavva finished, Sanjay banged his crutch on the ground three times. Silence fell over the room. He raised his crutch and pointed it at Ranavva.

'Ranavva is my true wife,' he proclaimed.

But Sanjay no longer gave Ranavva as much support as he used to before his stroke.

'I wouldn't feel right accepting anything anyway,' she

said later. 'You saw his condition. It's a big blow to the family. His wife calls me to the house frequently. They feed me and give me food to take home to my mothers. I still have the small patch of land he gave me, and I work in the fields. My brother also helps me, and he has two boys, so I don't have to worry. I'm not as comfortable as before, but I have enough to make do. I don't need anything more.'

'Is the land in your name?' asked Vani.

'No,' said Ranavva.

*

In Halamid, the market town, both the IB lodge and Patel's guest house were full. Patel's nephew sent us to the Gandhi Ashram just outside the town. As we inched our way down the tree-lined drive, bushes scraped and slapped against both sides of the car. A traditional two-storey house with whitewashed walls, blue trim, and a large verandah overlooked impeccable gardens and two acres of fields. The four-member ashram had been founded by a swami fifteen years earlier. Originally from Kerala, the founder was a Sanskrit scholar to whom talented students from the local college were sent for private lessons. In a simple white dhoti, his long, pale, arms resting in his lap, he explained in partially comprehensible English that the ashram was a self-sufficient organic farm. It was obvious to me that he was a Brahmin. Favourably impressed by Dilip and Maneesh when they were looking for housing three years earlier, he offered us a room on the second floor accessed by an exterior staircase. With stone floors, white walls and windows that overlooked fields in three directions, it was ideal.

Pressed for time, Vani and I rushed to Halamid to buy ten large boxes of sweets for the evening ceremony and a sari to offer Yellamma. By the time we reached the temple, over a hundred people had gathered. Ganga and Ranavva helped us push our way through the crowd, up the temple steps to the inner sanctum, where Sumithra and a heavily pregnant Renuka were installed next to the jagha. Women Vani and I knew well gathered around us, gently pinching our cheeks and clucking their tongues—giving us symbolic kisses. We made our way over to Sumithra and sat down on either side of Renuka, beaming at her belly.

'You didn't mention the news to us earlier,' said Vani. 'Did you find a boy for Renuka?'

'We couldn't find a boy. Our community believes that if a girl promised to Yellamma marries, her husband will die. Although Basappa and I are living proof to the contrary, nobody would agree to take her,' snorted Sumithra. 'Renuka took matters into her own hands by running off with the son of a high-caste landlord. After that we had her tied.' Renuka stared at the ground, abashed.

'Is he a nice man, does he take good care of her?' I asked.

'Yes, yes,' said Sumithra, glancing sideways at Renuka, who flushed and bit her lower lip.

The new priest, a small, dour, grey-haired man with a severe limp, violently clanged the meditation bell. Ganga lit the wicks on the trellis surrounding the inner sanctum, illuminating the goddess. The powerful first notes of a hymn rang forth, filling the temple and hushing the crowd. The deep sonorous chords were followed by a chilling lament. Padmini, Ruki's mother, picked her way toward the inner sanctum, her sad song recounting, no doubt, Yellamma's fate, commanding everyone's attention. Nothing in her small, compact frame had prepared me for such an intoxicating voice. After the first verse, Ganga, Kassi and the other women joined in with their instruments, the relentless twang of the chodiki like the beat of a resilient heart.

THIRTY-FIVE

There are two unborn males—the one knows and the other
is ignorant; the one is the lord and the other is not the lord.
There is just one unborn female, who is joined to the enjoyer
and the objects of enjoyment.[43]

—*Svetasvatara Upanishad*

VANI AND I ARRIVED at the ashram late that evening. Inside,
the swami was reading aloud from a Sanskrit text. We
tiptoed past the windows and up the steps to our room.
We had brought our own sheets, but had forgotten to
buy mats in town. Spreading the contents of our suitcases
beneath us, we slept on the slate floor, and woke up
shivering at daybreak. Downstairs, Akka, the only female
in the four-member ashram, gave us each a small bucket
of hot water for our bath. As soon as we had dressed, we
went to Halamid to have breakfast and make phone calls.

At the top of my list was Malika. I had phoned her house
numerous times since arriving in India, but was invariably
told she was 'out of station'. I sensed that something was
not right. This time a young woman answered and gave
me a number where I could reach her.

Malika answered the phone and, upon hearing my

voice, burst into tears. She had never received my messages and was surprised that her in-laws had given me her new number. Sobbing, she explained that she had split up with her husband. 'You can't imagine what I've been through,' she said. Her voice was strained and anxious. She had always complained about how conservative her husband was, but now she revealed to me that he had a terrible temper and had been in the habit of beating her. As his drinking problem worsened, the beatings became more frequent and severe. Unable to take it any longer, she returned to her father's house. The separation was extremely painful for her. For four months, she had been barred from seeing her children. Now she was allowed to see them every other weekend. She considered herself lucky because her parents were willing to take her back home. Many women don't have the resources to leave their husbands or a family to turn to. Malika planned to start an NGO dedicated to providing divorced women with legal assistance and jobs.

When Vani and I returned to the ashram, it became clear that we had somehow caused a diplomatic incident. The swami received us cross-legged on his cot; Akka sat on a stool at his feet. He said that he had explained to Dilip that, as residents, we were expected to participate in the ashram's schedule, which included working in the fields for an hour every morning and returning home by six for prayers, dinner and meditation. He did not think it unreasonable to have expected us to know these rules.

I apologized for the misunderstanding and explained that Dilip hadn't briefed me. Truth be told, he had never even mentioned the visit to the ashram. Vani asked if we could make a financial contribution, but the swami explained that they had no use for money. They didn't buy anything from the outside world; they were independent of the cash economy. Nevertheless, they were in need of help with the harvest. Seeing me look over her patched sari, Akka warned me against buying her a new one: 'Many people offer me new saris, but I only wear these old, torn ones; we live in self-imposed poverty.'

As we left, Vani looked at me, befuddled. 'Self-imposed poverty. Does she think poverty is about wearing torn saris?' she asked. We were sceptical about participating in the ashram's schedule, but for the moment, had no other option.

∗

After wasting a good part of the morning harvesting beans, Vani and I hurried to the Durga festival. Amidst thundering drums and blaring trumpets, a throng of devotees carried Durga, the fierce virgin goddess, slayer of buffalo demons, to the temple. The priest invoked the gods with a mantra. A dense crowd formed a semicircle before the pavilion. I spotted Shanti and sidled up next to her. She flashed a brief smile at me, then turned her attention to the invocation of the goddess. The crowd parted and a tall young man in a simple white dhoti stepped forward. The priest presented him with a wooden rod attached by a chain to a sterling silver ball with inch-long spikes. Trembling and glistening with sweat, he paced wildly up and down in front of the goddess. His eyes rolled into his head and his muscular back rippled in anticipation. Shanti gasped, covering her eyes with her hands, and peeped through her fingers. Planting his feet, he whipped the ball over his shoulder and into his back where it crashed with a thud. Over and over again, the man whipped the spiked ball into his back. His face contorted with pain, and blood flowed. Between blows the priest and his assistant stepped gingerly into the arena to flick turmeric powder mixed with lemon-water at the wounds. With each blow the smell of blood and sweat seemed to increase. The young man finally cried out and stopped. I wondered if he had succeeded in cleansing himself of his sins.

The next penitent stepped forward: a little, frail old woman, a devadasi, as worn and faded as her sari. Shanti, now pressed up against me by the crowd, groaned and shivered. Hiding her hands in her face, she turned away, unable to continue watching. *Did she know this woman*, I wondered? The old lady's skin was as dry and cracked as the land before the rains; she seemed to stoop under the weight of the bun tied carelessly atop her head. Either too old to care or unable to afford a sari blouse, her flat, empty breasts dangled over her washboard ribs. With an impassive face she took her place in the centre of the arena and brought the spiked ball crashing into her back. It seemed that the weight of the blows would knock her off her feet, but she stood her ground firmly. She did not pace, she did not tremble, she did not cry out. Her face was empty, expressionless, as if she felt nothing at all, as if she were beyond pain. It seemed like she would never stop. The crowd cringed, wringing their hands, but she continued, impassive. Finally the priest stepped forward and shouted for her to stop. She handed over the weapon and turned away. Another old devadasi stepped forward. Shanti watched the scene transfixed with awe. The penitents seemed to be slaying their own private buffalo demons, sacrificing them on the altar of the goddess. I wondered what demons were haunting the old devadasis and if Sumithra or Ganga might one day be among them.

*

When the last penitent stepped away, Shanti grabbed Vani and me by the arms and led us excitedly to her house. 'You have returned; I knew you would. I never lost faith in you. I knew you would not forget us.' Shanti was more beautiful than ever. Her wavy hair was pulled tightly back, accentuating her almond eyes and high cheekbones. Her golden-brown skin gave her round face a moon-like quality. Her small two-room house had not changed. She heated tea over the hearth and in her whispery baritone told us that after giving birth to her second child, she started working in a brothel in Halamid. She was lucky; within only a few months she met a man willing to provide for her. He gives her a hundred rupees a month and buys her presents from time to time. The small, fair-skinned baby in her arms was his. Her other children were now three and four.

'I've not forgotten their father; I still love him,' she said.

'Anwar, my new joolwa husband, is a nice man, but for me it is a purely economic thing.'

Over the next ten days, we met Anwar on several occasions. At twenty-three, he was handsome, affable and curious. He was attentive to Shanti and enamoured of his child. He worked as an assistant to the owner of the nearby sugar factory. The ninth child in a family of eleven, he had to wait his turn to marry; in the meantime, he kept Shanti. He told us openly that he loved Shanti, but that marrying her was out of the question. It would mean excommunication from his family and his community, the loss of his job, and ousting from his native village. Nevertheless, he was pushing Shanti to have another child. He wanted a daughter. Although Shanti didn't openly refuse him, privately, she scoffed at the idea, confiding to us that she was secretly taking the pill. 'How can I possibly manage with another child? I'm having enough difficulty as it is. And who can guarantee that he will provide for his kids after he marries? Men are full of promises, but they rarely follow through . . . I have to get as much as I can from him now while he still loves me, because one day I will have nothing. You can't imagine how much I spend on the children's doctors' bills.'

Vani noticed the shadow of a bruise on her left cheek. 'He hit me; I wasn't happy about that,' said Shanti.

'What happened?' asked Vani.

Shanti shook her head and laughed. 'The thing is this: we've got to get them for what they're worth before they drop us. I arranged to have a shopkeeper come to my house when I knew Anwar would be there, and threaten to beat me up unless I settled my bill. I'm not the only one to use this kind of trick—God knows—but someone tipped him off. If I ever find out who, I'll string them up . . .'

Vani, laughing in disbelief, interrupted her. 'Are there a lot of tricks like that around?'

'Yes, there are stories about things women do to extract money or to get revenge. I don't know if they're all true, but they're funny. If a man cheats a prostitute she can sometimes find ways to publicly humiliate him, or spread lies about him or his family—and of course, the *jogamma's* curse is a dangerous affair.'

'Who tells you these stories?' I asked.

'My gharwali in Mumbai was a specialist. She relished telling those stories. I learned a lot from her about men, and their weaknesses.'

'Tell us!' said Vani.

'She used to say that if you have a joolwa husband, the most important thing is to behave like a wife, and make the man think that you are hopelessly in love with him—but don't let yourself fall for him. She said: "You praise your man incessantly, laugh when he laughs, be sad when he is sad, and pretend to be jealous." If Anwar so much as glances at another woman, I fly into a rage and threaten to commit suicide. This way they fall in love with us, and then spend without counting . . . it's not so easy, though. One day, Anwar will leave me. And who knows if I'll be able to get another man after that. I have to learn to make my mind hard like a stone and not become attached. I must learn to show affection to men only according to how deep their pockets are and then dust them off . . . I must depend on Anwar only for economic support and not get emotionally involved.'

*

While some elements of the ancient and medieval courtesan's alternative moral order can be detected in the attitudes of Kalyana's devadasis, their subsistence-level poverty kept them down. They turned to the Yellamma myth for inspiration. As for Shanti, her troubles were not limited to her man. She had a difficult relationship with almost everyone around her. She was volatile and angry at the world. She resented her parents for having dedicated her and complained that they didn't treat her well. 'I ask them, "Why did you leave me to become a prostitute? Why didn't you get me married?" If only I had been married, I'd be happy. Even if my husband were blind or lame, as long as we would have had enough to eat, I'd have stayed until the end. They want me to give money for my youngest brother's wedding, but I can hardly afford to feed my children. My future is insecure. For how much longer will I be able to earn? For four years I earned in Mumbai, but no matter how much I gave, it wasn't sufficient. My earnings dwarfed those of my brothers working in the fields, so they stopped working and became lazy good-for-nothings. This is the problem in the holakeri. Brothers make merry on their sisters' earnings. I left Mumbai with not ten paisa for myself. Between my gharwali and my family everything disappeared. I only kept a few nice clothes. And now, because I am not contributing to their household, they refuse to help me . . . When I gave birth to my third child, I had to manage my two other kids, wash and cook. I couldn't move, but my own sister refused to help me. My very own sister! My older brothers look down on me because I was a prostitute in Mumbai, but how do you think my father paid for their brides! And today they won't talk to me!' Shanti simmered with indignation. She was like a caged tiger. 'God has been unfair to me,' she said.

*

In the meantime, in the jagha room at Sumithra's house, Renuka sat crying, her face swollen and wet with tears. She was in her seventh or eighth month of pregnancy. 'Two years ago, they ran away together without our permission—it's a "love match",' said Sumithra. 'But last week he told her that his parents have found a girl for him. All along I've been warning her that this is going to happen, trying to prepare her, but it did no good. He comes to visit her every day and has promised to visit even after the marriage, but Renuka won't stop crying. I tell her that her tears are not good for the baby, but she doesn't care . . . they seem very attached and well-suited. I think they will stay together, but if they don't,' Sumithra said, shrugging her shoulders, 'she'll find another man, a man from our own community—they're more reliable. Now that she's already had a man, finding a husband will be easy.' In any case, Renuka did not risk having to resort to prostitution; one day she would inherit the jagha and be the head devadasi of Kalyana.

*

Ganga flashed a nervous smile when she saw us approaching her house and pulled her front door shut. She led us across to Ranavva's, though she wasn't there. 'Tamana left me two years ago,' she said. 'He didn't say anything; he just stopped coming. His brothers forced him to go back to work in the fields, but I never imagined it would end like that. For fifteen years we were together and now he walks by my house without so much as a glance in my direction. I never expected this. I cried for a whole year . . .'

'How are you making do?' Vani asked.

'I don't like to have to tell you this, but I know you won't get me in trouble. I had no choice,' said Ganga, studying Vani out of the corner of her eye.

'What happened?' asked Vani, warily.

'I panicked. There was nothing else I could do . . . of my brothers and sisters, only three of us were left. After ten years of marriage, my brother was still childless, and my sister had only Lakshmi. If we married her, she would have gone out of the family and we would have no one to take care of us in our old age. My sister was against dedicating her so during the pilgrimage to the Yellamma temple, I had her tied. When my sister found out, she slapped me so hard my nose ring tore my nostril open. She died of cancer only three months later.'

Lakshmi was given to a high-caste landlord for a thousand rupees and a gold ring. He came for a year, but stopped visiting when she got pregnant. Ganga now took us back to her house. Lakshmi was sitting on the bed with a baby girl in her arms.

'The forty day lying-in period is almost over,' Ganga explained.

Lakshmi had grown into a beauty. Her large black eyes, set in a pale, heart-shaped face, shone from underneath thick eyebrows. Vani and I took turns holding and cooing at the baby.

'How do you feel about your dedication?' Vani asked.

She grimaced and shook her head. 'I don't want to think about it,' she said.

Ganga cut in, 'Lakshmi says to me, "You spoiled my life; I'll never forgive you."'

'Is that how you feel?' Vani asked.

'What's done is done. I don't want to fight with my family,' she said.

While her brother, Ganga and his wife worked in the fields, Lakshmi did the cooking and cleaning. Now that her keeper had dropped her, Ganga planned to marry Lakshmi to her brother, Lakshmi's uncle, so that Lakshmi's future sons would be obligated to take care of the older generation later on.

'What do you think of all this?' I asked Lakshmi.

'What choice do I have?' Lakshmi asked, cradling her baby in her arms.

'And how does the first wife feel about it?' asked Vani.

Ganga laughed and said, 'If anyone is going to make

trouble it'll be the little one . . . this is a good solution. We are all still working; Lakshmi won't be forced into relationships she doesn't want—and her children will have a father.'

Vani and I knew, however, that if the family's fortunes turned, she would be at risk. I sat there in Ganga's house looking at the baby. It was a difficult piece of news to digest. Ganga, who had no children of her own, had always doted on her niece. Three years ago she had proudly showed us the sewing machine she had bought for Lakshmi so she could learn to sew and be 'economically independent'. Looking around, I didn't see it. Ganga had sold the machine and her dreams for a better future for her niece along with it. The warm, loving relationship that Ganga and Lakshmi shared seemed incongruous with her dedication, but these were ways of a community subjected to subsistence-level poverty.

THIRTY-SIX

The possessed shaman with the spear
wears wreaths of green leaves
his jungle tribes have chests bright with sandal
they dance rough dances hand in hand
to the beat of small hillside drums;
the women wear wreaths of buds
fingered and forced to blossom,
cannabis leaves in their dark hair . . .
leaf skirts shaking on their jewelled mounds of Venus,
their gait sways with the innocence of peacocks.[44]

—Nammalvar

VANI AND I ARRIVED at the ashram just before the light began
to fall. The garden was bathed in the golden light of magic
hour. The swami lit clumps of incense in front of Shiva's
shrine, which was built into an alcove in the exterior wall
of the house, while Akka and the other residents stood
in prayer. Vani and I fell into line, as the swami rang the
meditation bell and recited a hymn. The main ceremony
was reserved for Vishnu whose shrine was a gazebo covered
in flowering vines. Abu, the youngest resident, sang a
cappella hymn. His ardent, powerful voice was a contrast

to the withering tranquillity of the ashram. The clear notes rolled through his generous mouth, fusing with the scent of sandalwood. Sheaths of smoke billowed around the god. The tension accumulated throughout the day seemed to dissipate as the burnt orange skies gave way to inky blues.

This all-too-brief reprieve ended abruptly with the hymn. The swami moved forward, bowed down, swept his hand over the pedestal of the shrine and then touched his forehead, symbolically placing the feet of the god on his head. The other residents stepped forward and repeated this gesture in the order of their rank, which purportedly did not exist.

After an agonizingly silent meal on the kitchen floor, the residents of the ashram gathered in the central room for an hour of meditation, but during this hour we were assigned tasks. Vani and I 'meditated' by cutting old postcards into thin strips to be used to light fires, and when we finished, we peeled a mountain of little red onions. The mosquitoes came out in full force and paid no heed to my repellent.

After work/meditation, we shifted our positions to form a semicircle around the swami. Arranging his long, pale limbs into the lotus position, he turned to Vani. 'Each night I read a few verses of the Bhagavad Gita. Tonight I have selected the last eighteen verses of Book Two, the "Song of the Lord".' Several Indian friends had described the Gita to me as the subcontinent's most sacred text; I had read several translations of it and knew the passage well. It described the wise man, the true yogi. Untroubled in the midst of sorrows and free from desires, passion, fear and anger, the wise man is without attachment of any kind. He neither rejoices in good nor is dejected by evil, but draws his senses away from the material world 'as a tortoise draws its limbs under its shell'. Freed from cravings, possessiveness and self-centredness, the wise man is serene and attains the nirvana that brings supreme happiness.

It seemed to me that the core of traditional Hindu religion and philosophy teaches that the material world is the veil of Maya, a meaningless illusion. What is called 'life experience' is merely a mental play of forms without value. According to this philosophy we must detach ourselves from that which we cherish most: children, lovers, food, music, art—all of these are traps. By withdrawing our senses and suppressing our emotions, we can allow our attention to be flooded with a consuming vision of 'Brahman', the undivided whole, the ultimate 'Ground of Being'. It suddenly occurred to me that perhaps it was precisely this belief that has led to a de-valuation of the material world and of empirical knowledge, the bedrock of Western science. If the real world is a meaningless illusion, then true knowledge lies beyond material facts. I thought of Dilip's disregard for the material conditions of the devadasi's lives. Perhaps he justified what he did by aiming to reach a 'greater truth', which lay beyond the harsh realities of the physical world. Or perhaps he was just unscrupulous.

Looking at the swami with his long, aristocratic, pale limbs, his distinguished white hair, and the pretension of his simple white dhoti, it seemed to me that the ashram residents lived in a rarified world, oblivious to and uninterested in what was going on in just the next village. Each time Vani had tried to discuss the benefits that literacy could bring to landless labourers, the swami turned away. In reply to the complaint that they were short of labour, Vani suggested that they barter labour for shares of produce, but this was rejected for it ran counter to their ideal of self-sufficiency. I wondered if India's many miseries were not caused by the world-hatred that the dominant religious philosophy instilled in many of its people. I wondered if such cruel neglect of one's fellow creatures could lead to a truly spiritual life.

The irony of our situation was too much. During the day we were thrust into intensely emotional situations and confronted with the suffering of people we cared about; in the evenings we were lectured on the value of detachment. While in other circumstances, Vani and I might have appreciated the lessons of the swami, as far as the devadasis were concerned, we were not interested in detachment. We were interested in social change and saw plenty of opportunity for it.

✳

The next morning Vani and I spent an hour in the fields picking beans. We had come a long way to see the Kalyana villagers and wanted to spend as much time with them as possible, so we decided to look for another place to stay. The inspection bungalow was still occupied, so we returned to Mr Patel to see if his guest house was free. We found him bidding farewell to some visitors on his patio. 'Don't worry,' he assured them, as he struggled to stuff something in the back pocket of his pants. 'You will get permission for your factory.' When he turned around, Vani drew my attention to the thick wad of rupee notes hanging out of his pocket. Mr Patel had probably been bribed. With a sigh, he drew up his chair, plopped himself into it, and gestured for Vani and me to sit beside him; tea and biscuits were served and his wife came out to greet us.

'So tell me, why have you come?' asked Patel, marking the end of small talk. I explained that I was interested in recording more of the myths and songs of the Yellamma cult, and also in exploring the reasons surrounding dedication. 'Well, the reasons for dedication are very clear. So much has been written about it already. They do it for easy money. What more is there to add? The proof is that there are a lot of poor women in India, but not all of them prostitute themselves.'

Jumping out of his chair and pacing up and down the patio, Mr Patel embarked upon a long speech about 'tourism', which I found out later was an euphemism for prostitution.

'There is a lot of tourism in France,' he said.

'Yes,' I replied, 'France receives over one million visitors every summer.' As he was lecturing Vani and me about 'tourism', a group of petitioners arrived and were silently ushered to the foldout chairs across from us. Mr Patel concluded his speech with the following statement: 'Exploitation only exists because people agree to be exploited. If they joined together and marshalled their forces, who would be able to oppose them?' He turned to his audience for support. I peeked over at Vani and could see her struggling to maintain her composure; now she spoke out. The discussion turned to local politics; I was able to understand only fragments.

'Since the introduction of GATT [free-trade agreements], the cost of medicines has increased tenfold,' said Vani. 'Don't you agree that this is a severe blow to the poor, who hardly have enough to pay for food, much less medicines?'

'This is only a temporary phenomenon; it will change. India's future is bright. Within the next ten to fifteen years, fifty per cent of the population will die of AIDS or hepatitis B. Only then will the economy improve; only then will we be able to compete in the global marketplace,' asserted Mr Patel. I could hardly believe my ears.

Vani stood up. Raising her voice, she said, 'How dare you call yourself a representative of the people!' A few petitioners nodded in agreement with Vani behind Patel's back.

'I don't call myself a representative of the people. How can I? I lost the elections. We didn't have enough alcohol for everyone,' Mr Patel said with a smirk, dismissing us with a wave of his hands.

Vani narrowed her eyes. 'I can see why you're obliged to buy people's votes with alcohol,' she huffed, turning on her heel and leaving. Patel turned to his petitioners, shrugged his shoulders and with a hearty laugh, sat back in his seat and stretched out his legs.

I caught up with Vani outside the gate; she was trembling with rage. 'It's sickening. Can you believe he's a member of the Congress Party?' Shocked and dismayed by the absurdity of the scene we had just witnessed, I could not suppress my laughter, but Vani failed to see the humour in it.

'He must have been drunk,' I said, trying to calm the situation.

'No,' said Vani. 'Those are really his views.' She was disconsolate. After lunch we booked a room at the new hotel near the diner. We filled two boxes with spices, chutneys, a blanket and other odds and ends, and thanked the ashram members for their hospitality. It had been a thoroughly depressing morning. Considering the attitudes of the political and spiritual leaders of the community, it was not difficult to see why change was so slow in coming.

THIRTY-SEVEN

The chariot of Dionysus is bedecked with flowers and garlands; panthers and tigers stride beneath his yoke ... Man now expresses himself through song and dance as a member of a higher community; he has forgotten how to walk, how to speak, and is on the brink of taking wing as he dances . . . Now the slave emerges as a freeman; all the rigid, hostile walls which either necessity or despotism has erected between men are shattered. Now that the gospel of universal harmony is sounded, each individual becomes not only reconciled to his fellow but actually at one with him—as though the veil of Maya had been torn apart and there remained only shreds floating before the vision of mystical Oneness.

—Friedrich Nietzsche, *The Birth of Tragedy,* 1872

RUKMINI GAVE VANI AND me a wan smile as we climbed the stairs to her house. Adjusting the pallu of her cobalt blue sari, she placed a kettle on the hearth. I sensed immediately that she had changed. She no longer wore her hair down. It was neatly combed and pulled into a bun; she was a woman now. 'I'm glad you came,' she said. 'I have to go back tomorrow morning.' She told us that she was living with a university student in Sangli, a small town. She didn't know what he was studying and had little hope that the relationship would last for more than a few years. He came from a wealthy Muslim family. She asked after Dilip and made me promise to send her regards. She hardly smiled, and didn't look me in the eye.

I sensed something was amiss. 'Ruki, please don't leave tomorrow,' I begged her.

'I'll think about it,' she said, and then she asked, 'How much money did you make with the film?'

'We were paid salaries,' I explained. 'Enough to pay for rent and food for a few months. How much were you given?'

'You gave me four thousand [$100] for my son, and Ravi gave me two thousand [$50], but Dilip only gave two hundred [$5]. The other women only received two hundred [$5], but so much money was stolen from Dilip at the guest house, I guess that's why,' she added by way of understanding. I was mortified. Our 'generous' contribution to the schoolhouse, which Dilip had boasted was so extravagant that we deserved to have a commemoration plaque, I soon discovered, was a mere $125— we had budgeted well over two thousand dollars, and had not spent a penny on the flights we had budgeted for the crew. I had no doubt that the money went straight into Dilip's pocket. My cheeks burned with anger and humiliation. I had done the budgeting, but Dilip refused to let me have anything to do with negotiations or payments. How could I have been so stupid?

I scooted over to Rukmini and took her hands in mine. 'Please, you must promise to put off your departure—at least a few days. I've thought about you every day these past three years. I even went to your old house in Mumbai. I've come all the way here to see you.' Rukmini squirmed and refused to look me in the eye. 'Tell me, whatever you ask for, I'll give it to you, but please stay.'

Rukmini finally looked up and held my gaze. 'Okay,' she said.

Over the next few days, we spent much of our time with Rukmini and recorded many conversations. Rukmini vacillated between anger and love for Nagappa, her former lover. 'For years we were together, and he never gave me anything—not for my upkeep, not for his son. Not even for hospital expenses. Nothing! Oh, yes, I forgot: once he gave his son a shirt. How generous! My parents [mother, aunt and uncle] have looked after us like gods. When I see the way they struggle, and when I think about how much trouble and worry I have given them, I feel like crying. I shouldn't have trusted that man. I was warned but didn't listen. I have no faith in anyone anymore. Men make lots of promises, but now I know not to believe them. If God himself came and poured gold at my feet, I wouldn't trust him . . . I bang my head before God and beg him to either kill me or make me forget all this misery. My stomach burns when I think of it all. Because of my son I have not taken my life. If it were not for my son, I would not be living.'

'When did the relationship come to an end?' I asked.

'When I first came back from Mumbai. I was so sick, I couldn't get out of bed. His friends told him I had AIDS so he dropped me like a hot potato. My heart was broken into little pieces.'

Rukmini paused to fight back the tears, and Vani put an arm around her. I checked that the recorder was working, but refrained from interrupting. 'I have accepted my fate now,' said Rukmini. 'I worship Yellamma now and she has brought me solace. My family put up with me for a long time, and now it is my turn to give something to them. My son is everything to me . . .

'Three months ago, Nagappa fell ill. He has a problem with his stomach and is unable to keep down food. I saw his brother earlier today and he said he is thin and weak and that during the past month he has been in the hospital, kept alive through intravenous feeding. The rumour is that the doctors can't figure out what's wrong and he is dying. His mother thinks I cursed him. Not long ago, she heard I was in the village and called me to her house, saying, "I want to see her face." She asked me to let her son be all right. "If he gets better, let him have a wife and keep you also, but please let him be cured . . ." We devadasis, if our hearts are broken, no good will ever come of it. Whoever hurts us, whoever gives us sorrow will go to the dark world of pain and suffering. But no matter how much we devadasis suffer, we never complain. We keep it inside us and grow thin, but we won't open our mouths. Whoever makes us suffer will be touched by the jogamma's curse. Look at what has happened to Nagappa . . . I hope he will be okay.' Tears streamed down Rukmini's cheeks.

'Where is Nagappa?' I asked.

'In a hospital in Belgaum,' said Rukmini. Vani and I looked at each other.

'What hospital . . . do you want to go there?' asked Vani.

'Oh yes, take me there in your car,' Rukmini pleaded, pressing her head on my knee and sobbing. 'Please, I must see him one last time.'

Gajanan, now a handsome boy of five, made his way up the stairs. Seeing his mother prostrate, he stomped up, hand on his hips, and tapped her on the shoulder. Then he put his face up to hers, and smiled as sweetly as he could. 'I love you, Amma,' he said. Rukmini smiled and pulled herself together, wiping her tears with her pallu.

'Do you want me to show your friends how I can dance?' asked Gajanan, pulling away. Gajanan was clearly used to cheering up his mother. Rukmini slipped a cassette into the tape player. Gajanan gyrated his hips to the beat and turned, stamping his foot into the ground, sticking his tongue out with the effort. Rukmini clapped her hands and prompted him to remember the proper facial expressions. He twisted his face into a smile, winked and blew kisses at Vani and me. I recognized the postures from when Rukmini had danced for us on that fateful August afternoon three years ago. 'One day,' said Rukmini, glancing over at Vani and me, 'he'll be a film star.'

*

Torrents of rain pelted the Ambassador's windshield as the single semi-functional wiper smeared water across the window, shifting the slant of the distorted scenery with each pass. Diminished visibility reduced our speed to a crawl. Vani rode shotgun to avoid the sheaths of water that poured in each time the driver cracked the window to reduce the fog creeping up the windows. Rukmini, Vani and I were on our way to see Nagappa in the hospital. It was seven in the morning and the dim early-morning light was further obscured by the endless shrouds of black clouds racing each other across the landscape. The mood was as sombre as the weather; nobody uttered a word. *Am I doing the right thing*, I agonized, *bringing Rukmini to see her bedridden tormentor, the man who used and abused her and whose family is now accusing her of killing him? Am I giving her an opportunity for closure or reopening a painful wound? Not so long ago she was suicidal . . .*

Rukmini sat quietly with her face turned towards the window, her gaze fixed in the middle distance, her unseeing eyes reviewing some interior landscape. Her forehead creased in angst, she kneaded one hand with the other, digging her nails into the palm of her hand. *She begged us to take her*, I reassured myself. I caught and held Vani's gaze as she glanced back to check on our charge. *Are we overstepping our boundaries?* we asked each other silently.

By the time we reached the outskirts of Belgaum, the rain had stopped. Turning off a banyan-lined avenue, we drove into the hospital compound which consisted of a hodgepodge of low-lying colonial-style buildings, shaded by an assortment of magnificent old trees: neem, tamarind, pipal, ficus, rubber, among others. At the reception Vani and I were directed down a footpath through gardens flowering under the protection of the trees, to the last building on the left. Off each side of the long corridor were large, dusty, pale-blue rooms with four beds. Patients' families camped beside them to do the nursing. Bedrolls and butane gas burners poked out from under sick beds. We found Nagappa attended to by his brother and sister. They acknowledged us with a nod, paused for a moment, and then left the room. Nagappa lay on the bed, his skeleton-like figure discernible through the thin grey blanket. A clear drip hanging on a nail in the wall behind the bed seemed to be his only lifeline. His grey paper-like skin clung to his bones. His intense, feverish, black eyes stayed glued to Rukmini as she crossed the room, flickering to Vani and me only for an instant.

Rukmini pulled up a trunk and sat at his bedside. Vani and I made the sign of namaskar, and turned to leave.

'Forgive me,' Vani heard him say to Rukmini as we exited.

Outside, we found Nagappa's twin-brother sucking hard on a cigarette.

'He has stomach cancer. The doctors told us that there is nothing they can do for him. They told us to take him home.' His sentences were punctuated by teeth grinding. Vani and I stood with him outside the door, staring at the ground. Minutes plodded slowly by. Vani felt cold and we went off in search of a teastall. We returned twenty minutes later and peeked inside the room to see Rukmini sitting silently by Nagappa's bedside, her hand lying over his. He was sleeping. Vani tapped gently on the door. Glancing in our direction, Rukmini laid her cheek on Nagappa's hand for a moment then rose and glided towards us, her upper body still and tall, the movement of her feet invisible under the sweep of her sari. Floating past Vani and me and Nagappa's brother, she sailed straight down the middle of the hall towards the double doors. Vani and I nodded farewell to Nagappa's brother and hastened after her. We found her outside, collapsed on a bench, sobbing.

Vani lifted Rukmini's shoulders onto her lap. 'He begged me to let him touch my feet in forgiveness for everything he had done,' she wept. '"I will prostrate myself before you and your jogamma's curse, just once I will touch your feet and I will get better," he pleaded. But how could I allow him to touch my feet? He is the son of a rich landlord. I told him he would be okay, that he would get better, and to try to forget everything that happened. "You get married," I told him, and he said, "I will marry you. If I get better, I will marry you." Yes, he said that, and I know he means it. If he gets better, he will, he will marry me, sometimes these things do happen,' sobbed Rukmini, lifting herself into a sitting position only to collapse back down again into Vani's lap. 'If he gets better he will marry me. I know he will.'

Vani and I delivered Rukmini to her mother in Kalyana, and made arrangements to meet her at nine at our breakfast place. Rukmini would be taking the bus back to Sangli at ten. Vani and I returned to our hotel and collapsed on our beds in exhaustion.

*

'Do you remember that rash you had?' Rukmini asked, rubbing the inside of my elbow and looking for scars. I smiled. We were sitting in a booth in Halamid's diner. Waiters in faded red uniforms yelled orders across the room. The din of plates crashing to the tables and boisterous men surrounded us. Rukmini only picked at her food. 'You have travelled from far away and spent so much money to come see us, but I have not been much fun to be with. From which country have you come, from which direction, I do not know. But you understand our sorrows and you are kind to us. "Why are you looking so sad?" you ask me, and your face becomes sad along with mine. This is what I call human. What is there to life? We just peck and scratch this dry earth, trying to get by, and then we die.'

Rukmini and I stared at our plates. Her bus was leaving soon. A contingent from the village was waiting along with her mother at the bus stop to see her off. A six-year-old kitchen boy scattered a pungent disinfectant on the floor; our eyes and nostrils began to burn. Rukmini placed her pallu over her nose. She was a woman now, elegant and poised. Her hair was neatly combed and oiled and her savings, in the form of gold jewellery, were draped around her neck. This was goodbye. When would we see each other next? Every time she raised her eyes to mine they brimmed with tears and she looked away. Perhaps my presence reminded her of all her youthful dreams that would never come to be.

'Come,' said Vani. 'Let's go.'

The bus stop was concealed by the confusion of a row of merchant stalls. A bevy of girls from the village with colourful umbrellas were waiting for Rukmini. I spotted a pastry shop and went to buy a box of sweets. I had hardly taken a few steps when a young man planted his feet in front of me, blocking my passage. I looked up at the tall, slender young man before me. A smile flickered across his lips. 'Catherinebhai?' he said. My mind raced. *Who could this possibly be?* I wondered. And then the caramel skin and the pale green eyes began to ring a bell.

'Bala,' he said, bringing his hands to his chest, 'and my sister Lalita,' gesturing to the giggling adolescent behind him.

'Bala!' I beamed, hardly believing my eyes. I stepped back and pulled Vani away from the girls at the bus stop. 'Vani, do you recognize Bala, who always helped us across the mud? How could you? He's grown so tall.'

'I'm living in Halamid now. We have moved here with my mother so that we can attend a better school,' said Bala.

'You are both studying, very good,' said Vani, looking over Bala and his sister and adding, for my benefit, 'Few Dalit families can afford to keep their children out of the fields.'

'Yes, I am a good student, and so is my sister. Our father says if we gain admittance to college, he will pay for it,' said Bala. His father was a wealthy upper-caste farmer. But it was unheard of for such men to educate their unofficial offspring.

'That's extraordinary,' said Vani.

'He's an extraordinary man,' said Bala.

'He must be,' said Vani.

'How is your mother, Mahadevi?' I asked.

'She is fine. She misses living in the village, but she goes there during the day when we are in school,' said Bala.

'Next time I return, I will seek you both out,' I said,

looking from Bala to Lalita, 'And I hope to learn that you are both in college . . . promise me you will study hard.'

Bala smiled and nodded to his sister, who stepped past the bus stop. Acknowledging Rukmini and her friends with a nod, they went their way.

Padmini arrived with Gajanan, and within a few moments the bus arrived. Gajanan, angry with his mother for leaving, refused to embrace her. Her friends reached out to pinch her cheeks and straighten her sari. I pressed a box of sweets and an envelope into her hands. She climbed up the steps of the bus and, without glancing back, made her way to the rear.

NOTES

1 Abbé J.A. Dubois, *Hindu Manners, Customs and Ceremonies, Third Edition* (Oxford: Clarendon Press, 1906), 584–85.

2 Wendy Doniger, trans., *The Rig Veda* (London: Penguin Books, 1981), 191.

3 Patrick Olivelle, trans., *Upanishads; Brhadaranyaka Upanishad* (Oxford, New York: Oxford University Press, 1996), 88.

4 Olivelle, *Brhadaranyaka Upanishad*, 61.

5 Indira Viswanathan Peterson, trans., *Poems to Shiva: The Hymns of the Tamil Saints* (Delhi: Motilal Banarsidass, 1988: 1991), 265.

6 A.K. Ramanujan, trans., *Hymns for the Drowning* (London: Penguin Books, 1981: 1993), 73.

7 Velcheru Narayana Rao, David Shulman, Sanjay Subrahmanyam, trans., *Symbols of Substance: Court and State in Nayaka Period Tamilnadu* (Delhi: Oxford University Press, 1992), 158–59.

8 William J. Jackson, *Songs of Three Great South Indian Saints* (New Delhi: Oxford University Press, 1998), 123.

9 A.K. Ramanujan, Velcheru Narayana Rao and David Shulman, Trans., *When God is Customer: Telugu Courtesan Songs* (Berkeley: University of California Press, 1994), 11.

10 Saskia Kersenboom-Story, *Nityasumangali: the Devadasi Tradition in South India* (New Delhi: Motilal Banarsidass,

1987), 173 footnote 162.

11   A. K. Ramanujan, *Speaking of Shiva* (Baltimore: Penguin Books, 1973), 88.

12   Dubois, *Hindu Manners*, 344.

13   Henry Miers Elliot, trans. *The History of India, as Told by Its Own Historians* (London: Trübner & Company, 1872), 106–11.

14   Robert Sewell: A Forgotten Empire: Vijayanagar (London: Swan Sonnenschein, 1900), 255–57.

15   L.N. Rangarajan, trans., *Arthashastra* (New Delhi: Penguin Books, 1992). 351–54.

16   Elliot, *History of India*, 106–11.

17   Rangarajan, *Arthashastra*, 354.

18   Dubois, *Hindu Manners*, 585.

19   In Hindu mythology, the snake is often a protective figure.

20   Ramanujan, *Speaking of Siva*, 83.

21   Jackson, *Songs*, 185.

22   Ramanujan, *Speaking of Siva*, 84.

23   Rao, Shulman & Subrahmanyam, *Symbols*, 120.

24   Rao, Shulman & Subrahmanyam, *Symbols*, 120.

25   H.S. Shiva Prakash, trans., *Medieval Indian Literature: An Anthology* (New Delhi: Sahitya Akademi, 1997) 179–80.

26   Peterson, *Poems to Shiva*, 295.

27   Peterson, *Poems to Shiva*, 259.

28   J.A.B. van Buitenen, trans., *The Bhagavadgita* (Chicago: University of Chicago Press, 1981), 93.

29   Edward Sachau, trans., *Alberuni's India* (London: Kegan Paul, Trench, Trunber & Co, 1910), 157.

30   Trans., anonymous, www.hinduism.co.za/women.htm

31   Norman Cutler, *Songs of Experience: the Poetics of Tamil Devotion* (Bloomington: Indiana University Press, 1987), 125.

32 Buitenen, *The Bhagavadgita*, 82.
33 Rao, Shulman & Subrahmanyam, *Symbols*, 3.
34 Rao, Shulman & Subrahmanyam, *Symbols*, 162.
35 Buitenen, *The Bhagavadgita*, 93.
36 Jackson, *Songs*, 155.
37 Peterson, *Poems to Shiva*, 254.
38 Ramanujan, *Speaking of Shiva*, 159.
39 Buitenen, *The Bhagavadgita*, 51.
40 Ramanujan, *Hymns*, 7.
41 Peterson, *Poems to Shiva*, 234.
42 Jackson, *Songs*, 211.
43 Olivelle, *Upanishads*, 254.
44 Ramanujan, *Hymns*, 112–13.

ACKNOWLEDGEMENTS

I WOULD LIKE TO thank, in more or less chronological order, the following friends and institutions: Gilles Tarabout and the CEIAS Library in Paris for help with the early stages of my research; Amardeep Behl, Vikram Sardesi, Milind Naftde for their friendship and support; the inhabitants of Kalyana for their generosity; Shantha Mohan, Asha Ramesh, Daud Ali and Sanjay Subrahmanyam, for their invaluable insights; the New York Public Library, the British Library and the India Office Library; Pankaj Mishra, Katharine Weber, Krista Ingbertson and Juliette Mitchell for suffering through early versions of this manuscript and for their encouragement; Dominique Delany, Jean-Luc Olivier and Marc Parent for their help; Marie-Christine and Pierre Duranel for their unfailing support; Meru Gokhale, Fazal Rashid at Random House, and last but not least, Mathilde, Eva and Zoé, my prana.

www.servantsofthegoddess.com

A NOTE ON THE AUTHOR

BORN IN FRANCE AND raised in New York, Catherine Rubin Kermorgant studied Classics at Brown University and Anthropology at the London School of Economics. After working in film and television for a number of years, she began to research and write her own documentary films. One of her films, funded by the BBC and Canal Plus, led her to south India, where she spent several months learning about devadasis.

Catherine Rubin Kermorgant lives in Paris with her family.